PUBLIC POLICYMAKING

IN A DEMOCRATIC SOCIETY

The first edition of this book was produced in collaboration with the Center for Civic Education with funding support from the U.S. Department of Education.

PUBLIC POLICYMAKING
IN A DEMOCRATIC SOCIETY
A GUIDE TO CIVIC ENGAGEMENT

SECOND EDITION

LARRY N. GERSTON
FOREWORD BY THOMAS EHRLICH

M.E.Sharpe
Armonk, New York
London, England

Copyright © 2008 by by M.E. Sharpe, Inc.

Library of Congress Cataloging-in-Publication Data

Gerston, Larry N.
  Public policymaking in a democratic society : a guide to civic engagement /
by Larry N. Gerston. — 2nd ed.
    p. cm.
Includes bibliographical references and index.
ISBN 978-0-7656-2240-2 (cloth : alk. paper) — ISBN 978-0-7656-2241-9 (paper : alk. paper)
1. Policy sciences. 2. Political planning—Citizen participation. I. Title.

H97.G475 2008
320.6—dc22   2008007914

Printed in the United States of America

The paper used in this publication meets the minimum requirements of
American National Standard for Information Sciences
Permanence of Paper for Printed Library Materials,
ANSI Z 39.48-1984.

BM (c)   10   9   8   7   6   5   4   3   2   1
BM (p)   10   9   8   7   6   5   4   3   2

To today's students and tomorrow's leaders:
May your accumulation of knowledge and wisdom
help you become active stewards for the public good.

TABLE OF CONTENTS

FOREWORD

This book fills a troubling gap in the materials available to help students become responsible and engaged citizens of their communities. The text adopts the sound precept that we learn best by doing. To that end, Professor Gerston provides deep-textured and thoughtful ways for us to learn politics and governance by doing them. No set of tasks is more important for America and its future.

Educational attainment has long been viewed as a powerful predictor of civic engagement, yet studies have shown a disturbing lack of linkage between education and participation. In their *Voice and Equality: Civic Voluntarism in American Politics,* political scientists Sidney Verba, Kay Lehman Schlozman, and Henry E. Brady surveyed some 15,000 individuals on issues related to civic engagement. They quantified what many of us intuitively already knew—that political participation among young people, particularly educated people, was declining in America.

In an article that attracted considerable attention, "Bowling Alone," published in the *Journal of Democracy,* Robert Putnam of Harvard chronicled the declining pattern of civic participation in America. Across twelve activity areas, Putnam found huge declines between 1973 and 1993. More sobering, the share of the American public totally uninvolved in any of the civic activities rose by nearly one-third over those twenty years. In absolute terms, Putnam found that the declines were greatest among the better educated.

On college campuses, political discussion had declined sharply. Data from annual freshman surveys indicated that the percentage of college freshmen who reported frequently discussing politics dropped from a high of 30 percent in 1968 to 15 percent in 1995. Similar decreases were revealed in the percentages of those who believed it was important to keep up-to-date with political affairs or who had worked on a political campaign.

All this was bad news. But the most disturbing trend of all was that each succeeding generation showed less interest and involvement in political activities. Political disaffection was especially pronounced among youth. Americans growing up in more recent decades voted less often than their elders and showed lower levels of social trust and knowledge of politics.

Disdain for politics does not mean lack of civic concern, however. A study by the Panetta Institute at California State University at Monterey Bay, for example, found that nearly three-fourths of college students (73 percent) had done volunteer work in the past two years, and most (62 percent) more than once. Those students understood that their communities faced real needs and that they could help meet those needs, but they did not see politics as an effective means for change. In other words, they did not see a connection between assisting at a community kitchen and dealing with the reasons why there was a need for that kitchen. Politics—in one form or another—is the primary vehicle we have in American democracy for making such public policy changes.

Surveys conducted soon after September 11, 2001, began to pick up on some positive shifts in the civic attitudes of college students. The mission of this volume is to respond to and encourage that revival of interest. By focusing on civic participation in the political realm, Professor Gerston provides the knowledge and skills for students to serve their communities by doing politics. Such experiences become important vehicles to promote a democratic tradition for today's students and tomorrow's leaders.

Service learning is a particularly important pedagogy to promote civic responsibility, and its use is integral to this book. By using structured reflection as a means of tying academic study to community service, service learning creates a context in which students can explore how they feel about what they are thinking and what they think about how they feel.

The adage that democracy should not be a spectator sport has long been a cliché, but too many people today are not even giving politics the attention of spectators. Our citizenry must be educated to choose political leaders responsibly and to hold those leaders accountable. Much more significant, our democratic society is one in which citizens should interact with each other, learn from each other, grow with each other, and together make their communities more than the sum of their parts. This book is an important contribution to those ends.

Thomas Ehrlich
Senior Scholar, The Carnegie Foundation for the Advancement of Teaching
President Emeritus, Indiana University

PREFACE TO THE SECOND EDITION

"Public policymaking." It sounds so vast and complex amidst the many terms that describe how governments work—or don't. But if the term is expansive, it is also extremely useful in explaining the processes of governmental activities, whatever their levels and wherever they may be. All governments—whether large or small, democratic or dictatorial, national, state or local—enact public policies, which are commitments to extract resources from and/or provide services and programs to societies. These public decisions extend from the national government collecting income taxes to school districts distributing nutrition menus, and a lot in between.

Governments are doing things all the time. We are affected by those undertakings in various ways—sometimes positively, sometimes negatively; sometimes directly, sometimes indirectly. The point is that governments do not operate in a vacuum; rather, they are instruments of and for people. The never-ending flow of government activities allows us to appreciate public policymaking from a variety of perspectives ranging from objective academic assessments to direct political participation. Still, many of us just don't know how to get close to the process.

In *Public Policymaking in a Democratic Society: A Guide to Civic Engagement,* I attempt to reduce some of the distance between political theory and citizen involvement, the latter of which is essential to the well-being of a democracy. I believe that a good many people refrain from participating in the political process because they don't understand how it works. But description alone is not enough; along with knowledge, people need the tools to be shown why their involvement is crucial to their own well-being as well as the well-being of society. All of which takes this discussion to you.

The second edition of *Public Policymaking in a Democratic Society: A Guide to Civic Engagement* represents a continuation of my endeavor to make the policymaking process manageable for the average person. The book contains a comprehensive description of the policymaking process and players at all levels of government, as well as those who seek to influence government. Just as important, the book shows students how they can define and recognize public policy issues. The second edition also includes prominent public policy issues that have emerged over the past few years as well as others that have reemerged. At the national level, public education has been addressed through No Child Left Behind, while stem cell research, immigration, and health care have received spirited debate but no resolution. Other issues still, such as abortion and desegregation, have been revisited by the courts, leading to new policies. Meanwhile, the response to Hurricane Katrina has exposed a national government with poor capabilities of dealing with a major crisis. States have also tackled new questions such as eminent domain, health insurance, and "the right to die." And the immigration dilemma, while stymieing substantive policymaking at the national level, has spawned hundreds of conflicting policies at the state and local levels. Perhaps no other domestic issue has left the nation and its policymakers so divided.

Along with the discussion of current issues, the second edition of *Public Policymaking in a Democratic Society: A Guide to Civic Engagement* contains a special appendix that gives you the tools to move forward with "hands-on" policy analysis, one step at a time. Project Citizen is a guide to policymaking participation that has been developed by the Center for Civic Education, a nonprofit organization dedicated to fostering democracy through thoughtful involvement. Although Project Citizen was originally designed for K–12 use, the appendix has been adapted for use in the college classroom. It's an approach that shows individuals and groups how to define public issues, research how they may be resolved, consider various alternatives, prepare policy proposals, and determine the appropriate government authorities who might consider such proposals. This participatory tool complements the academic information provided in *Public Policymaking in a Democratic Society: A Guide to Civic Engagement.*

Civic engagement has become a mantra of sorts for people who worry that political participation is disappearing from American society. But engagement won't occur unless people have the knowledge and the means to become engaged. Moreover, without an issue or cause to bring about engagement, the concept seems rather academic and one-dimensional. In recent years, scholars and practitioners have tied together these three strands through a fourth concept, service learning, which offers a way to operationalize knowledge about the process by being *part* of the process. Thus, if you are assigned a service learning project, *Public Policymaking in a Democratic Society: A Guide to Civic Engagement* can serve as a manual of sorts, in part, to help you work your way through various challenges.

Some who read this book will say that I have approached the topic with rose-colored glasses. They will point to political corruption, elitism, corporate domination, unresponsive elected officials, and other negatives as evidence that democracy doesn't work—if it ever did. To those people, let me be the first to say that I know the system is far from perfect; every day we witness examples of inequities and injustice at all levels of government. But what people sometimes fail to take into account is the extent to which these problems are routinely exposed and, with enough support, may even be resolved. Here is where citizen engagement is so important. Ours is a porous political system—one in which you can get involved and influence public policy decisions if you just know how.

That said, it is just as important to realize that because we discover an issue in need of redress, it may not be managed the way we want. Not all people see problems the same way, nor do all people have equal amounts of power or opportunities to solve problems in ways that make everyone happy. Every day political realities produce an array of winners and losers. Simply said, there is no guarantee that participation in the process will lead to the outcomes we fight to achieve. But with a better understanding of the public policymaking process, today's "losers" may well be able to join with others to become "winners" tomorrow. The key is to find ways to become engaged as stakeholders in the system.

This book represents not only my description of the public policymaking process but also my invitation to you, the student, to embrace the "system" not only for what it is, but for what you want it to be. The old saying goes, "you can't tell the players without a scorecard." In the world of public policymaking, you can't make change without knowing how the system operates and who to influence to get the right outcome. Seize the tools and you will be surprised at how far they can take you. At a minimum, you will increase your understanding of the political system and the opportunities you have to mold it. In itself, that can be a pretty exciting adventure.

ACKNOWLEDGMENTS

This book is the result of the vision of Herbert Atherton, formerly of the Center for Civic Education. He saw the value of the interplay between public policymaking and service learning in the context of the American constitutional framework. Integrating these ideas into a coherent framework was anything but easy. But like the ringmaster of a three-ring circus, Herb managed to keep the acts in balance and in concert with one another.

Along the way, several scholars provided helpful advice and criticism. At the Center for Civic Education, board member and Campus Compact founder Thomas Ehrlich was an early advocate of the effort. Margaret S. Branson and R. Freeman Butts nurtured the development of the manuscript as a work reflective of the center's mandate. Center Director Charles Quigley gave his blessing to the project, and Michael Fischer ushered the manuscript to its conclusion.

Among those political science scholars in the public policymaking field, William E. Hudson, Cristy A. Jensen, Bernie O'Connor, and Stephen Schechter read the manuscript and offered counsel. Their advice helped me remain true to the necessity of describing core public policy elements.

Several service-learning experts were particularly helpful in overseeing the connection between the discipline of public policymaking and the practice of service learning. I am particularly grateful to Sally Broughton, Michelle Herezog, Maria L. Keenan, Susan Meyers, Terry Pickeral, and Seth L. Pollack.

On the home front, once again I express my gratitude to Elisa, my wife, for putting up with the eccentricities of her "absent-minded professor" husband; I learn from her every day. And I also learned from Adam, Lee, and Rachel, my three children who, with their ascendance from adolescence to adulthood, have taught me much about their own public policy issues.

At M.E. Sharpe, my thanks go to Patricia Kolb, Editorial Director, and Makiko Parsons, editorial assistant.

There is no doubt that contributions of the reviewers led to the development of a much better work than I would have written on my own. Of course, I alone accept responsibility for application of their advice.

PUBLIC POLICYMAKING
IN A DEMOCRATIC SOCIETY

1 THE PUBLIC POLICYMAKING PROCESS AND HOW IT RELATES TO OUR LIVES

Public policymaking has many definitions. At one end of the continuum, some people view public policymaking as simply whatever governments decide to do. At the opposite end, others think of public policymaking as intertwined relationships of offices, public leaders, and issues, all of which constantly change in a kaleidoscope-like fashion.[1] Given such disagreement, it is easy for someone to scratch his or her head and wonder, just what is public policymaking?

At a minimum, *public policymaking* is the combination of basic decisions, commitments, and actions made by those who hold or affect government positions. Typically, such initiatives direct the flow of resources that impact the public. These resources may be defined in terms of economic advantages, individual rights, or shifts in political power.

Public policies often change the status quo by giving benefits to some or taking away benefits from others. But not all policy decisions result in change. Sometimes, public policies may be intentional decisions to do nothing, to reaffirm the status quo. Either way, public policymaking reflects the commitments of public assets.

But who makes these decisions, and under what conditions? Equally important, by what authority do those "in charge" have the right to do these things? The answers to these questions can tell you quite a bit about public policymaking. In a constitutional democracy, public *policy* commitments are made and carried out by people who have been authorized to act by popular consent and in accordance with established norms and procedures.[2] In a democracy most public policymakers are elected officials. Legislative bodies and executives play a major role in the policymaking process. Other policymakers, however, such as federal and state judges, are appointed. Nonelected bureaucrats or civil servants may also have limited policymaking authority. Whether elected or not, however, public policymakers are managers of the public trust who are either directly or indirectly accountable to the public. As such, their actions are subject to public scrutiny and judgment, which, in the cases of elected officials, sometimes lead to their replacement by the voters.

The Public Policymaking Framework

Public policymakers have anything but an easy road to travel. Most of the time they are the recipients of conflicting pressures from people who differ about what should or should not be done. Whether the issue centers on participation by the United States in an international treaty or proposed changes in the speed limit on Main Street in your hometown, public policymakers have the responsibility of resolving differences. If they are able to reach a decision, these policymakers must ensure that the intentions of the new policy are carried out. Usually, bureaucrats are given the responsibilities for putting decisions into play in accordance with the intentions of public policymakers.

As the policy is put into motion, some people will be happy about the decision, while others may attempt to get the policymakers to change their minds (and decisions). In other cases still, those disgruntled with a particular policy will take the issue to other policymakers located elsewhere in the government hierarchy. All of this underscores the point that public policymaking is a dynamic, fluid process. It also makes clear that relatively few decisions at any level of public policymaking are permanent.

Accountability, the two-way linkage between policymakers and the public, is a critical element that distinguishes constitutional democracies from authoritarian regimes. In authoritarian political systems, policymakers conduct their business irrespective of public concerns or involvement; their sheer might or military prowess allows such individuals or groups to do almost anything they desire. But in a constitutional democracy, the political process is attentive to the expressions of individuals, organized interest groups, the media, or even competing centers of power within government. In fact, the health of a democracy depends upon the participation of individuals who are willing to say what is on their minds as well as the ability of leaders to respond to those sentiments. This free exchange between those of us outside of government and those within it assures that the public policymaking process is fluid, dynamic, and malleable.

What Public Policy Is—and Is Not

So far we have discussed the public policymaking framework. But expansive as it is, the framework has boundaries. At a minimum, public policymakers attempt to resolve public issues, questions that most people believe should be decided by officials at the appropriate level of government—national, state, or local. Depending upon the extent of disagreement, some issues are resolved over time, whereas others drift aimlessly with little hope for agreement because of their charged nature or controversy.

All public policymaking involves government in some way. Thus, it is distinguished from those many initiatives affecting the general welfare that are undertaken by that portion of the private sector we sometimes refer to as *civil society*. By civil society we mean that autonomous, self-organized portion of a free society that is outside formal political and legal institutions. In most free societies the institutions of civil society play a very important role in realizing a wide variety of opportunities and addressing a wide variety of problems affecting the general welfare. Chambers of commerce, parent–teacher associations (PTAs), and trade unions are typical examples of such institutions in the United States. A dynamic civil society, in fact, has always been an outstanding characteristic of American democracy. Alexis de Tocqueville, the great French interpreter of American democracy in the early nineteenth century, noted that "in no country in the world has the principle of association been more successfully used or applied to a greater multitude of objects than in America."[3] Yet, whatever the merit of such private initiatives, they do not constitute public policymaking unless government is somehow involved.

Defining Public Issues

Law, convention, and societal expectations may go a long way toward providing a general framework of what public policymakers may or may not do (and how they may do it), but the specific roles of policymakers are hardly set in stone. Those roles change as the standards and expectations of society change. Many of the major public policy issues of today, from homelessness and domestic violence to environmental pollution and energy, were considered beyond the responsibility of government two centuries ago. Moreover, the framers of the U.S. Constitution could scarcely have imagined the impact of such technological innovations as nuclear power, cloning, or fiber optic communication networks, all of which have generated public policy issues in today's world. But as social, economic, and technological changes take place, so do the demands upon the policymakers and the policymaking process.

Public policymaking can also be daunting because, as part of their responsibility, policymakers may give benefits to some and place burdens on others. For example, if state legislators vote to increase funds for public education, they may decrease commitments to other sectors such as prisons, highways, or recreation areas. With this scenario, one group "wins" a larger piece of the budget pie, while another group gets less. Alternatively, if legislators decide to spend more money for public education without curbing expenditures in other areas, they may decide that the best way to fund the new commitments is by raising taxes. In this case, the education community may "win," while taxpayers—or at least their pocketbooks—may "lose." Added to this basic formula is the awareness that any public policy commitment can change at any time if different, stronger coalitions of policy advocates emerge inside or outside of government.

Defining Private Issues

We have distinguished public policymaking from the actions of civil society. It must also be distinguished from those matters that belong exclusively to the private world of individuals, families, and other groups. Public policymakers are responsible for resolving important questions, but they do not decide all questions. This is because many issues are private and, as such, remain outside of the public policymaking process. So, even though children in some families may watch television or be "online" until late at night, it is not the task of public policymakers to set standards or rules for such matters. Only in cases of child endangerment do authorities even consider stepping in, and only if there is a clear case of a violated law such as child abandonment. Likewise, if people spend large proportions of their income on "foolish" purchases, wear seemingly bizarre clothing combinations or pray to the devil, these activities are outside of the public policymaking process, which focuses on the relationship between the governed and the governors.

Much of the reluctance of public policymakers to deal with private issues stems from the well-established value of limited government. Our constitutional democracy sets boundaries on what governments can do, leaving considerable autonomy for individuals. But these boundaries are sometimes challenged, and occasionally rearranged. Thus, if leaders of local public schools decide to make school uniforms mandatory, their decision makes policy in an area where it previously did not exist. Conversely, when the U.S. Supreme Court ruled in 1973 that government could not restrict a woman's right to terminate her pregnancy during the first trimester, the decision narrowed considerably the role of government in this area of public policy.

Public/Private Issues in Perspective

Simply put, the public and policymakers constantly debate and reconsider the lines between public and private. Different interests will demand that governments "get in" or "stay out" of the issue, depending upon the values of the competing groups or interests and the extent to which they benefit or suffer from such action. Furthermore, division between what is "private" and what is "public" may well change along with the evolution of society's dominant values. That goes for you and your values as well. Nevertheless, whatever the determination, the debate over public policy issues takes place in an environment that is prescribed by basic constitutional guarantees, rights, and obligations.

Constitutionalism: The Architecture of Public Policymaking

To appreciate the dynamics of public policymaking today we must first understand the legal and institutional architecture in which public policymaking occurs. And to do that we need to take a step back into history. The essentials of that architecture were put in place two centuries ago with the framing and adoption of the United States Constitution. The *Constitution*, together with the constitutions of the individual states, established the procedures and norms by which public policy is made at all levels of government.

With all of the success America has enjoyed over two centuries, it may be difficult for us to appreciate today what a gamble our nation's founding represented. Our country began as a novel experiment in republican *self-government*. The founders rejected the monarchical form of government that was almost universally accepted in the Western world at that time. Instead, they opted for a *republic*—something that had never been tried before in history on so large and ambitious a scale. Moreover, the track record for the small city-state republics that had existed in the past was not good. Such governments had failed sooner or later as a result of political instability and an absence of civic-mindedness among their citizens.[4]

Our first experiment in republican self-government (the Articles of Confederation) seemed to confirm the founders' worst fears. The confederation of largely autonomous states provided by the Articles failed. This form of government lacked sufficient power at the center and, as a result, allowed many of the worst features of small-scale republics to flourish in the individual states. Though Americans at that time would not have used the phrase, effective public policymaking was not working at either the national or state level. The national government lacked the ability to carry out its policies. Factionalism, popular passions, and poor leadership undermined public policymaking in state government.[5]

A second and ultimately more successful attempt at republican government began in Philadelphia during the late spring and summer of 1787 with the drafting of a new constitution. As James Madison, one of the principal architects of the U.S. Constitution, explained it, the great challenge in framing any government "administered by men over men" was to provide sufficient authority and power to achieve its legitimate objectives, but to so constitute that government as to prevent the abuse of power and authority.[6]

The solution worked out by the framers in 1787 provided for both an "extended" and a "compound" republic. It was, as Madison said in his *Federalist 10*, an effort to "provide a republican remedy" for the "diseases most incident to republican government."[7] A large republic, it was hoped, might avoid the problems of small republics by means of an effective balance of both national (centralized) and federal (decentralized) features, as well as a system of shared powers among three co-equal branches of government. And a large republic had one other advantage. Its institutions of government at the national level would be representative of the people and ultimately accountable to them but sufficiently distanced by geography and indirect elections (e.g., the Electoral College) so as to be shielded from popular passions. For Madison, a national republic so contrived was a representative or indirect democracy.

Though many of its features have been imitated and adapted by other countries during the last two centuries, our form of *constitutionalism* remains distinctive to this day among the governments of the world. To understand how public policymaking operates in the United States, we must consider our system's outstanding features:

1. separation of powers;
2. federalism;
3. judicial review; and
4. chartered rights.

Separation of Powers

The framers of the U.S. Constitution created a strong national government, but one whose powers were shared among three independent and equal branches of government: the legislative, executive, and judicial. Though this arrangement is sometimes described as a *separation of powers*, it is really a system of shared powers among three co-equal branches of government.[8] The executive and legislative branches, for example, share the power of passing laws and making treaties. The framers created this arrangement to provide a check upon the power of government through a system of *checks and balances*. Accountability to the people through elections, the framers believed, was a necessary but insufficient way of limiting government. "Additional precautions" were needed in the way of internal mechanisms that would enable government to limit itself. Our system of three separate branches with shared powers was intended to provide this.

There was, however, a price to pay for such precautions. The framers placed a high premium on compromise in order for public policy decisions to be made and carried out. Without agreement among the branches of government, policies usually will not emerge. Because of this unique "consensus or nothing" form of organization, some people today consider the American system both undemocratic and inefficient. Most of the world's constitutional democracies have adopted a parliamentary system, where the policymaking process incorporates the executive and legislative branches almost simultaneously. But our system, with independently operating branches, does not always respond quickly to the popular will, especially when the legislative and executive branches are controlled by different political parties. Divided government, as it is sometimes called, often results in "gridlock" along the public policymaking "highway."

Defenders of our constitutional traditions point out that the structural requirements for compromise and delay help to assure proper and comprehensive consideration of public policy. Even in today's fast-paced world, rapid response to complex problems is not always good policymaking. In any event, prolonged and, it is hoped, careful deliberation is built into the public policymaking process by our constitutional system.

Controversial issues have often separated the nation. Abortion, gun control, and gay rights represent a few such modern-day examples. At times, divisions have run so deep that public policymakers have found it almost impossible to find precious common ground, creating considerable tension as a result. But these are exceptions. Why? For the most part, the separation of powers doctrine and the concept of checks and balances moderate political differences among disputing interests. The consensus reached by public policymakers on a thorny political issue may not be universally pleasing to everyone concerned, but it may be enough to discourage the opposition from working against the decision.[9]

Federalism

Our federal or combined system of both national and state governments is sometimes described as the vertical expression of the system of shared powers. Under *federalism*, some powers are reserved by the Constitution for the federal government; some for state governments; some powers these two levels of government share; and some powers are reserved for the people.[10] The framers of the Constitution considered this compound of the centralized and decentralized systems of government the best way to secure a balance between centralized and localized power. They feared alike the despotic tendencies of all centralized systems and the chaos that often arose in systems where power was decentralized among member states of a confederation.

The nineteenth-century British jurist James Bryce spoke of the "immense complexity" of the American federal system, which provided two semi-independent spheres of government "covering the same ground, commanding with equally direct authority, the obedience of the citizen."[11] The balance has shifted very much in favor of the national government in the last century, but it remains a balance nonetheless. In fact, state and local government have enjoyed a resurgence in recent decades in what has sometimes been called the "New Federalism." As we shall see, most of the public policymaking that directly affects our lives takes place at the state and local levels. We may discuss at length our opinions about whether the Supreme Court should outlaw capital punishment, but we are much more directly affected by policies that direct local police to control traffic and school safety.

The complex arrangement of our federal system has often mystified American citizens and foreigners alike, but it has also attracted great interest in recent years among other constitutional democracies seeking to find the best mixture of centralized and decentralized government.

Like the system of shared powers among different branches of government, our federal system requires a large measure of cooperation and compromise among the different levels of government. Achieving such cooperation has not always been easy. Indeed, relations between national and state government have been a source of conflict throughout our nation's

history, as the great battles over trade policy, slavery, and school desegregation illustrate. So serious was the conflict over slavery that a civil war ensued.
Fortunately, that was the exception. In other instances of disagreement,
our constitutional system has found more peaceful paths to solutions, the
most important of which has been judicial review—another of America's
important contributions to modern constitutionalism.

Judicial Review

"Scarcely any political question arises in the United States," Alexis de
Tocqueville observed, "that is not resolved, sooner or later, into a judicial
question."[12]
    With that statement, Tocqueville noted the great importance that law
played in American public life and in the shaping of our public policies. He
characterized lawyers as the American democracy's version of aristocracy,
given the immense importance of law in American life. The legal profession
continues to dominate our public institutions today.
    Judicial review, the greatest expression of what Tocqueville called the
"legalistic spirit" of American public life, is another unique element of
our constitutionalism. Defined narrowly at first as the power of a court
to determine the constitutionality of a legislative act and, if found to be
unconstitutional, to render it null and void, judicial review now applies this
same authority to all actions of the legislative and executive branches, as
well as those of lower courts. It even applies to the actions of the people
themselves, when expressed in plebiscites, referenda, and other initiatives.
Judicial review has become perhaps the most important expression of our
commitment to constitutional government.
    Yet this preeminent expression of constitutionalism is not even mentioned
in the Constitution at all. It is a power taken unto itself by the judiciary,
first and foremost in the famous case of *Marbury v. Madison* (1803), in which
the Supreme Court for the first time declared an act of Congress to be
unconstitutional.[13] Simply put, Chief Justice John Marshall argued in this
landmark decision that, because the Constitution was (as stated in Article
VI) the highest law in the land and because it was the undoubted function of
the judicial branch to interpret the law, courts had the authority to interpret
the Constitution—and to determine whether or not the actions of the other
branches of government complied with the Constitution.
    Marshall's argument did not go undisputed at the time he made it. Ever
since, in fact, some Americans have believed that granting an unelected

branch of government such power over the actions of the more representative branches of government violates the principles of democracy. The courts' use of judicial review has been frequently challenged, especially when they make controversial or unpopular decisions. Recent court rulings nullifying referenda in several states, for example, have been very controversial.

Why is judicial review important to the study of public policymaking? Because it assures that all public policy in the United States is *justiciable*, a fancy way of saying that such policy must comply with legal norms and, when it fails to do so, can be overruled or modified in a court of law. Policymaking in the United States is made with the knowledge that any policy decided upon is subject to constitutional scrutiny.

Many of the great court cases in our nation's history began as otherwise obscure public policy matters. In *Barron v. Baltimore* (1833), for example, the Supreme Court ruled that the Bill of Rights applied only to the national government and not to the states. Yet this fundamental decision sprang from urban improvements initiated by the city of Baltimore, which resulted in damage to a private wharf owned by a gentleman named Barron. Who would have imagined that such a seemingly small issue would bring about such huge implications?[14]

Although the framers of the Constitution envisioned the judicial branch as playing a passive role of interpreting the law rather than becoming involved in political matters, the power of an independent judiciary has involved the nation's courts in public policymaking. Court decisions themselves can have a profound effect on public policies. Look at what happened to state and local school policies when the U.S. Supreme Court ruled in 1954 that school segregation by race was unconstitutional.[15] Courts have become even more directly involved in the public policymaking process by assuming administrative responsibilities in the enforcement of their decisions. For example, in recent decades courts have taken over the administration of school and prison systems so as to ensure compliance with their decisions. By prescribing what government cannot do and also what it must do in order to comply with constitutional norms, the nation's courts (state as well as federal) have become major players in the public policymaking process.

Chartered Rights

Many of these constitutional norms are found within the Bill of Rights. Written or chartered declarations of individual rights are one of the oldest expressions of constitutionalism, within our own tradition as old as the

Magna Carta. Many of our colonial charters and most of the original state constitutions contained such explicit guarantees.

The U.S. Constitution was ratified with the understanding that a "bill of rights" would be added upon the document's implementation. As to the U.S. Bill of Rights, it has since been widely copied by other nations. Indeed, the inclusion of a bill of rights in a nation's charter of government has come to be accepted as an essential feature of modern constitutionalism. Enforced by an independent judiciary armed with the power of judicial review, a bill of rights provides yet another mechanism of limited government.

With its protections of individual conscience and expression, privacy, and due process of law, the U.S. Bill of Rights establishes certain norms and procedures that government may not violate. Originally intended as a limitation only on the national government, most of the provisions of the Bill of Rights have become "nationalized" (i.e., applied to all levels of government) as a result of the Fourteenth Amendment. Sometimes called the Great Amendment because of its far-reaching impact in the protection of individual liberty and equality under the law, the Fourteenth Amendment was intended to prevent individual states from violating the rights of their citizens. By judicial incorporation through the *due process clause* of the Fourteenth Amendment (forbidding states from depriving their citizens of life, liberty, or property "without *due process of law*") most of the rights guaranteed in the U.S. Constitution have been applied, as well, to the states.[16]

As much as any other provision in the Constitution, it has been the *equal protection clause* of the Fourteenth Amendment, prohibiting states from denying their citizens "the equal protection of the laws," that has prompted the nation's courts to become involved in many areas of public policymaking, from electoral districting to affirmative action. The equal access facilities that have become commonplace in our world—curbless corners, access ramps, sound-keyed traffic signs, and Braille inscriptions—are obvious examples of the continuing importance of the equal protection clause in today's public policymaking.

Chartered rights also illuminate one other very important aspect of the public policymaking process: the dynamic role played by beliefs, convictions, and passions. Politics has been defined by Harold Lasswell as "the process of who gets what, when, and how" in a world of limited resources.[17] The "what," however, should not be defined narrowly—simply in terms of power or material gain. That is because our needs and desires tend to be more complicated than that. Values and ideas matter to most of us. They help us compare the world as it is with the world as we would like it to be. Bearing that in mind, words like "equality," "due process," and "freedom" are not just the fluff of Fourth of July speeches. They have a significance of their own in public policymaking because they help us see the chasm between the empirical (the way things are) and the normative (what we want). The struggle over slavery, the women's vote, McCarthyism, the civil rights movement, abortion, affirmative action, and countless other political struggles in our nation's history have little meaning as public policy issues without an understanding of the important role ideas and beliefs play in our lives.[18]

Where Public Policies Are Made—Vertical Relationships

Public policies are developed and carried out at all levels of government, as provided for by our federal system. Although the issues may vary, the process of resolving them is remarkably similar regardless of where decisions occur. Article IV of the Constitution guarantees a "republican form of government" to each of the states. Although the meaning of this guarantee has never been tested in the courts, in effect it has meant that our state governments have adopted much the same system of shared powers among three co-equal branches of government. (The one notable exception is Nebraska, which has a unicameral, or one chamber, legislature.) Of course, the responsibilities of public policymakers vary with their level of government. Nevertheless, the common denominator for the public policymaking process centers on the legitimate exercise of power by those in authority, accountable always to the people they serve.

Public Policymaking at the National Level

The most sweeping public policies are developed at the national level of government, where the actions of national public policymakers tend to affect almost everyone. Sometimes, a single branch can bring about a public policy, such as the president issuing an executive order that defines affirmative action or sets aside land as a national preserve, but usually such efforts emerge from the cooperation of all three branches with the assistance of members of the bureaucracy.

The passage of a new immigration law known as the H-1B bill in 1999 typifies the public policymaking process at the national level. In this case, leaders from high tech and other specialized industry sectors argued before Congress that the law permitting no more than 50,000 immigrant specialists each year did not provide them enough expertise to offset the long-standing

U.S. labor shortage. The consequences, they claimed, would be the inability of American industry to compete with other nations. Some representatives from organized labor countered that shortages could be solved by retraining unemployed workers for the unfilled technical positions. After committee hearings and on-site visits to particularly impacted areas, Congress enacted new legislation that expanded the number of immigrant specialists to 115,000. President Clinton signed the bill and it became law.

Resolution of the Social Security crisis has not been so easy. Since the mid-1990s, the Social Security Administration has warned that the Social Security Trust Fund, the money set aside for Social Security recipients, would run out by about 2032 because of retiring "Baby Boomers" living longer than anticipated. Although aware of the problem, national leaders have not agreed on a solution. Some members of Congress believe that Social Security should be voluntary rather than mandatory. Others think the program should adjust various benefits or raise the ages of recipients. Still others would increase the Social Security taxes paid by all workers and employers in order to keep everything intact. Though public policymakers are divided, Americans are largely ambivalent about the Social Security issue. Most say that the system should remain in place without new taxes—an impossibility given the changing demographics. Clearly, the issue is significant, but policymakers and the public have yet to reach any consensus on resolution.

Public Policymaking at the State Level

Despite their organizational similarities, the fifty states provide fifty different public policymaking environments for their populations. In many instances, the states have been remarkably consistent in their approaches to the same issue. Policies on marriage, public safety, and automobile registration are a few such examples; the specifics may vary from state to state, but the public policy commitments in these and other areas are similar. In other cases, states have acted differently on the same issue, creating controversies within the state as well as between the states. State policies on teenage abortion, gambling, and taxation illustrate issues with contrasting responses, with residents sometimes going from state to nearby state to take advantage of or to avoid such policies.

Although states are responsible for public education, their leaders and populations do not always agree on the best way to manage it. The development of school voucher programs stands out as a recent example of such disagreement. Vouchers are checks given by the state government to parents for educating their children. Parents may use these public funds to send their children to the schools of their choice. Voucher advocates have praised the concept as a means for parents to pick the best school for their youngsters, whether it is private or public. Opponents argue that the concept permits public funds for private religious schools, thus violating the *establishment clause* of the First Amendment, which prohibits a government establishment of religion. Proponents, however, point out that the G.I. Bill of Rights, which provides government scholarships in higher education for military veterans, has established a solid constitutional precedent. School vouchers have been adopted in Florida, but rejected in Maine. They were also passed in Ohio, only to be declared unconstitutional by a federal district court. Sooner or later, the issue will end up in the U.S. Supreme Court, where the justices will decide whether the Constitution permits school vouchers as an educational tool that does not violate the separation of church and state.

In some states, the public may become directly involved in the policymaking process through their participation in *initiatives*, statewide elections where voters decide the fate of issues. An initiative appears on the ballot after sponsors gather signatures from voters, the amounts of which are determined by state law; its fate is decided through an election campaign similar to those conducted by candidates. People and organizations raise money, air television commercials, and mail campaign literature for and against the issue. Depending upon the issue and the state, initiative campaigns can cost $100 million or more and dramatically alter state public policies. Twenty-two states have this process, thereby allowing voters to decide what legislators and other public officials would otherwise be expected to do. As we have seen, however, even the results of this most direct expression of the wishes of the people are liable to constitutional scrutiny and can be overturned by court rulings.

The initiative process is used extensively in California, where voters have decided questions ranging from interest rates to the legalization of marijuana. One such contest occurred in 1998, when entertainer and social activist Rob Reiner led a campaign to add fifty cents in new taxes to each pack of cigarettes sold in California to help children who are victims of tobacco-related illnesses. Medical, environmental, senior citizens' and children's rights groups united in support of the initiative. Tobacco forces, joined by smokers' rights groups, outspent Reiner's allies by a ratio of more than ten-to-one, but the initiative, known as Proposition 10, squeaked by with a narrow majority and became public policy.

Public Policymaking at the Local Level

Although public policymaking occurs at all levels of government, its impact often is most visible in communities. The public policy decisions of state, county, and city or town government most directly affect our daily lives. They determine in large measure how we educate our children, how fast we can drive our cars, where and how we can build our homes and offices. Whether it is a city council or school board, these governments are physically close by, and thereby afford you the opportunity to "have your say" without trudging to Washington, D.C., or other faraway places. This "proximity factor" adds a unique dynamic to the relationship between citizens and public policymakers, for we can see firsthand how they respond to issues directly affecting us. Thus, for many of us, local issues serve as the entry levels for participation in the public policymaking process.

Fees associated with the use of automated teller machines (ATMs) have become controversial issues at the local public policymaking level. In California, the city council in Santa Monica, located west of Los Angeles, banned fees in an ordinance, or city law. Shortly thereafter, voters in the City of San Francisco reached the same conclusion in a citywide election proposal to eliminate ATM fees. Stunned, the major banks declared their ATMs off-limits to users without accounts and took their concerns to a U.S. federal court, where a judge prohibited implementation of new laws until a full hearing could be held on the matter. Whatever the outcome, this example shows how citizens and city councils at the local levels can become engaged in the public policymaking process.

Sometimes, different communities will respond to the same public policy issue in decidedly different ways. Smoking in public places is an excellent example. Recently, the city council of Santa Fe, New Mexico, decided to ban smoking in restaurants, but not bars. At about the same time, the city council in Corvallis, Oregon, banned smoking in all public places, including bars. To make matters even more confusing, there are still thousands of communities throughout the United States that permit smoking almost anywhere. These different patterns result from several factors, including local values, the kinds of organized interest groups arguing for or against change, and the attitudes of elected local officials. Many consider such diversity one of the strengths of our federal system, allowing people to determine policies according to their own values and local circumstances.

Empowerment, the idea of "owning" one's destiny, is an important component of citizen participation, particularly at the local level of the public policymaking process where the outcomes are readily visible. One such example occurred recently when the residents of Leisure World, a senior community in California, voted to incorporate as their own city. "This gives us the right to take care of ourselves and govern ourselves," said one of the leaders of the independence movement.[19] With that decision, Laguna Woods (the city's new name) became the oldest city (in terms of the average age of residents—seventy-eight) in the nation. Moral to the story? Whatever the issue, there is no age limit on people becoming involved in the public policymaking process.

Does Citizenship Matter?

Justice Louis Brandeis once described *citizenship* as "the most important office" in the land.[20] Many Americans today would have trouble taking Justice Brandeis's remark seriously. Citizenship as the most important office? When government seems so aloof and removed from the people? When policymaking seems dominated by special interests and nameless bureaucrats?

It may seem a bit bizarre, but perhaps we should pause to consider Justice Brandeis's remark before moving on. He notes the special place accorded to citizenship and civic engagement within the American tradition. Our experiment in republican government was an experiment in self-government. The nation's founders believed that this experiment could not succeed without an enlightened and engaged citizenry. Which is why public education became a major public policy priority in the early days of the republic and why civic education became a centerpiece of that public schooling.

Government aloof and far removed? Maybe, but as we have already mentioned, most of the government (and public policy) that affects our lives is no further away than the local city hall or county building. Though we do not take advantage of the opportunity as much as we might, Americans have more opportunities to vote in more elections—local, state, and national—than any people on earth. There are over a half million elected officials in the United States. From a constitutional perspective, citizenship has become more important than it was during the time of the founders. Many of the landmark amendments added to the U.S. Constitution since the Bill of Rights have focused on widening participation in the political process by extending the franchise, or right to vote. The Fifteenth, Nineteenth, Twenty-third, and Twenty-sixth Amendments gave the vote to former slaves, women, residents of the District of Columbia in presidential elections, and eighteen-year-olds, respectively. The Seventeenth Amendment provided for the popular election of U.S. senators and the Twenty-fourth Amendment removed poll taxes and other economic requirements for voting. In the course of 200 years we have become far less distrustful of democracy than the nation's founders were.

Although there is debate today about the nature of volunteerism and community service in the United States, we remain very much as Tocqueville described us over a century and a half ago, a nation of joiners and doers. Associations continue to energize America's civic life. As we have noted, there has been a significant increase in the amount and variety of community service performed by younger Americans in recent years—by college students and even younger citizens. We may not think of such activities as expressions of our citizenship, but they are.

The influence of interest groups? Whether we like to acknowledge it or not, all Americans are represented in one way or another by the thousands of associations and other interest groups who seek to influence government policy. All of these groups are exercising one of our oldest constitutional rights: the right to petition government for the redress of grievances. Many of them represent *you*, although you may not realize it. Do you belong to a ski club, a homeowner's association, an automobile club, a church choir, or a student body organization? These are organized interests.

So, whatever problems there may be in our political system and whatever our frustrations as citizens with the "system," we may be deluding ourselves by seeing these difficulties as a question of "us" versus "them." We might do well to remember the words of the cartoonist Walt Kelly in his comic strip *Pogo*: "We have met the enemy, and he is us."

What Does Citizenship Mean?

Americans have taken citizenship very seriously over the last 200 years. We have never agreed, however, about what the ideal citizen is or the role the citizen should play in public life. In general, two very different models have shaped this debate, and both have influenced public policymaking. Indeed, one can detect these two different views on opposite sides of many of the great public policy issues today.

The Rights-Bearing Model of Citizenship

What is the fundamental basis of citizenship? One of the classic models defines the citizen as a *rights-bearing individual*, one of many such individuals who make up a given society. It is a highly individualistic, consumer-oriented view of citizenship. The duties or responsibilities of the citizen in this model are narrowly defined by his or her obligations under the law (e.g., pay one's taxes, serve on juries when called, etc.). Government's obligation, in return, is to secure each individual's rights. Citizenship takes its legitimacy and its purpose from those natural rights (e.g., the rights to life, liberty, and property) that are inherent, or within, each individual member of the political community, and which is the duty of the government of that society to secure.

This is sometimes referred to as the traditional "liberal" view of citizenship, not in the sense in which we often use the word "liberal" today, but rather because of the word's long-standing association with principles of individual liberty. This model of citizenship has deep roots within the American tradition. It is closely associated with the natural rights philosophy articulated by John Locke in his *Two Treatises of Government*, which had a considerable influence on the nation's founders.[21] Thomas Jefferson enshrined Locke's views in the stirring words of the Declaration of Independence. Advocates of this view of citizenship would argue that because of its emphasis on the freedom of the individual it is a realistic model for the large, complex, and diverse nation of today. And even its detractors concede that the rights-bearing model is perhaps the most widely accepted view of citizenship among contemporary Americans.

The Citizen as Community Loyalist

Very much different is the view of the citizen as the member of a team working for the common good. This aptly describes the ***communitarian model of citizenship***, in which the citizen takes his or her identity from membership in a community defined by common values and a common concern for the welfare of all. If the liberal model is defined primarily by rights, this alternative view might be defined as the "responsibilities-bearing" model of citizenship. It emphasizes the obligations and responsibilities owed by citizens to the community of which they are a part. Whereas the first model emphasizes the relationship between the citizen and government, this model emphasizes the relationship between the citizen and community.

The communitarian model of citizenship has deep historical roots that find their way back to the ***classical republicanism*** of the ancient Greeks and Romans, which also influenced the political thought of the founders. The very word "citizen" takes its original meaning from this tradition.[22] Central to classical republicanism is the belief that the best kind of society is one that promotes the common good over the private interests of individual citizens or groups. A key element of classical republicanism is the idea of *civic virtue* in every citizen, a quality that today we might call "public-spiritedness." Good citizenship means putting personal or private interests secondary to the common good.

Advocates of this model see the communitarian spirit as essential to solving many of the complex problems of modern society that all members of that society share in common. Environmentalists tend to be communitarians. So, too, generally are those who promote volunteerism and other forms of community service. It would not be surprising to discover proponents of the individualist and communitarian models of citizenship on opposite sides of many public policy issues. School prayer is one such dividing issue. Government regulation of the Internet or the entertainment industry might be another.

Citizenship as Public Work

Harry Boyte of the University of Minnesota suggests a third model of citizenship, one that combines certain elements of the first two models but adopts a different focus: *citizenship as public work*.[23] This alternative view sees citizens as "practical agents" who work together in public ways and spaces to solve problems they collectively face. This model establishes a close connection between citizenship and proactive, pragmatic problem-solving in the public arena.

This model, too, is a legacy of the American experience with its rich traditions of local self-government from the earliest colonial days. It is a model very much in line with Tocqueville's appreciation of the role of civic associations in the American democracy. Through widespread participation in public life, Tocqueville observed, citizenship in the United States ceases to focus on either individualism or group conformity. It becomes, instead, an "enlightened self-interest" because citizens can see a connection between their individual needs and the common good.

Consistent with the practical, proactive character of this third model of citizenship, the work of solving problems of mutual interest takes individuals off the sidelines as passive observers and moves them closer to the center of the public policymaking process. Through public commitments, citizens are able to deal with a problem from beginning to end, achieving a sense of satisfaction and ownership in the very process of doing so. Building or achieving something—for example, a homeless shelter or an after-school recreational program—provides a legacy, an identifiable result of citizen efforts in their community.[24]

Practicing Citizenship Through Public Policy Analysis and Advocacy

This book takes its cue from the third conception of citizenship as practical problem-solving of public issues within one's community. It will help you learn how to monitor and influence public policies as such policies relate to those issues. It is about influencing and bringing about political change through government action, and about using the tools of public policy analysis and advocacy to do so. Such a focus has obvious connections with the many other forms of civic engagement—for example, volunteer service, internships, field research, or service-learning opportunities associated with academic courses. Community service can take the form of direct service to the needs of your community, as, for instance, the building of a homeless shelter. Or it can be in the form of indirect service through supportive activities (e.g., collecting food or clothing for those in need). And alternatively, it can take the broader form of trying to cause a change in the system of service (or lack of service) itself, through public policymaking.

These different types of community service efforts often go together. Perhaps a direct or indirect service experience in your community has highlighted the need for a change in public policy. The knowledge and insights gained from such an experience can provide an excellent platform for trying to bring about systemic change. Alternatively, work on a public policy issue that began as largely a classroom exercise might be followed by community service, perhaps in the role of helping to implement a change in policy. And, of course, community service and public policymaking can also go hand in hand. Moreover, getting involved with public policymaking offers its own form of community service and experience, through the researching and analyzing of a community issue, contacting government officials and civic leaders, devising, advocating, and helping to implement a plan of action, and evaluating the results of implementation.

There is a word we sometimes like to use to describe the acquisition of such basic knowledge, dispositions, and skills of civic engagement. You read it earlier in this chapter: *empowerment*. Empowerment is about intelligent action, about exerting influence in one's community in effective ways.

Citizenship empowerment does not mean necessarily devoting one's life to public service. Many citizens decide to do just that—and make a career of it. Other citizens choose to remain largely uninvolved in the public life of their community. That is their right. Empowerment does mean, however, the capacity (and the awareness of that capacity) to have an impact when we choose to do so, when an issue comes along that arouses our inspiration or our ire.

Putting It Together

Service learning is a form of education that encourages empowerment through civic engagement. Simply stated, you as a student undertake an activity through which you contribute a skill, knowledge, or other resource to the "community" beyond your immediate world. As part of your activity, you receive benefit from your contribution. Usually, this exchange is carried out under the watchful eye of a professional, in this case your instructor.

So, where does public policy fit in? Contributing to the public policymaking process can be a powerful element of service learning. In this situation, the objective is for you to become more involved in your community by embracing an issue of importance to you that needs attention. Perhaps it is working with other students in your class to change the way your student government allocates money for various projects. Perhaps it is a matter of you looking into the way your city council zones areas for housing. Your service-learning experience might be focused at the state or national public policy levels, although the proximity of local government makes it easier for you to get your hands around an issue closer to home.

The important thing is that through service learning, you can be a player in the public policymaking process. This book is designed to help you not only learn about the policymaking process, but also get the tools for participating in the process. Richard Battistoni notes that "[d]emocratic and the arts of self-government are not things that we know innately. Like reading, writing, and mathematics, they are qualities acquired through the learning process."[25] That is where the empowerment idea comes in; by getting involved, you become part of the process and practice citizenship at the same time.

When and how you choose to have an impact will be up to you. It is hoped that this book will help you to acquire the means to do so. In the pages that follow, we will cover the public policymaking process in all its steps, explain the tools that are involved, and suggest by way of example how those tools can be used in addressing a community issue. The rest is up to you.

Case Study: Immigration Reform

In 2007, some congressional leaders introduced the Comprehensive Immigration Reform Act to overhaul a series of issues ranging from porous borders to foreign high-tech workers. Nearly 400 pages in length, the bill was co-sponsored by the unlikely pair of senators: Massachusetts Democrat U.S. Senator Ted Kennedy and Arizona Republican John McCain. Rarely have these two individuals voted on the same side of any legislation. Yet, a series of mutual concerns regarding the immigration question brought the two leaders together to spearhead an improbable coalition, which, if successful, would go to the House of Representatives for passage.

There were many reasons for the legislative attempt. The fact that more than 12,000,000 undocumented residents were living in the United States in the post-9/11 era was a cornerstone, to be sure; with the recent memory of terrorist infiltrators who had entered the United States with ease, government officials more than ever spoke about the need to identify who comes to the United States and why. Open borders to our north and south suddenly seemed a luxury that the nation could no longer afford at a time where terrorism knows no borders. Then there was the consideration that different cities and states were enacting their own laws on illegal immigration, creating a patchwork of uncertainty throughout the nation.

Much of the nasty debate in the Senate centered on whether illegal immigrants were helpful or harmful to the well-being of the country. But there were other concerns that folded into the illegal immigration question, many of which centered on the question of resources. Some people worried about American workers losing their menial jobs to foreigners who would work for less, while others fretted that without undocumented workers, there wouldn't be enough people to pick crops and work in service industry positions. Still others warned that without high-tech–trained immigrants, skilled positions in the United States would go begging. Some critics claimed that undocumented residents were sponging off public services such as schools, food stamps, subsidized housing, and free medical attention, while others were troubled that the newcomers were afraid to get proper health care lest they be discovered and sent back to their countries of origins.

Finally, there was serious division on what constituted fairness. Some opponents contended that the legislation would provide "amnesty" for people who came into the United States illegally; surely, this would be a slap in the face to those who had sought citizenship by adhering to the rules. Proponents countered that applicants could be considered for citizenship only after those already in the citizenship pipeline and after they paid taxes and fines amounting to as much as $15,000.

As the Senate attempted to find common ground, lobbyists from hundreds of interest groups weighed in with their opinions, adding further congestion to the discussion. President George W. Bush, an advocate of immigration reform, attempted to dispel the fears of congressional doubters, saying in late June 2007, "I view this as an historic opportunity for Congress to act, for Congress to replace a system that is not working well with one that will work a lot better."[26] Yet, with a low standing in the nation's public opinion polls, his influence carried little sway. Ultimately, Bush convinced only about one quarter of his fellow Republicans to vote for the bill. And that was its death knell as much as anything else.

Ironically, virtually everyone in the Senate agreed that immigration loomed as a large problem for the United States. However, so contentious were the issues surrounding the illegal immigration question that legislators found it impossible to craft a public policy. Although immigration reform was the number one issue on the domestic agenda, the parties on all sides agreed that the next opportunity for action would not be until after the 2008 national elections. And so, the issue that so many wanted resolved remained without resolution because of the inability of the various sides to find common ground.

1. How does the illegal immigration issue stack up in terms of the definition of public policy?
2. What does the illegal immigration issue tell you about conflict and consensus? What keeps public policymakers from addressing an issue that almost everyone wants resolved?
3. We hear a lot about "gridlock" in government. Is gridlock part of the price we pay for living in a democracy, or is it a benefit?
4. If the Congress is unable to manage the illegal immigration question, are there other institutions that might forge public policies on the issue? How might they work?

Reflection

Here are some additional questions to consider while reflecting on what you have learned in this chapter. What do you think about the concept of public policymaking? Does it seem *real* or just another academic exercise far removed from everyday life?

Where and how do you fit into the public policymaking framework? Which of the various models of citizenship best appeals to you? Why? What personal values and interests influenced your selection?

Think about service learning in the context of your role as a citizen. Have you ever been involved in service learning or some other form of civic engagement? If so, did that activity pursue any public policy? What were the constitutional dimensions of that issue?

Take a moment to write your answers to these questions. When you are finished, share your ideas with others in your class. You might also want to keep these initial impressions and compare them with your thoughts at the end of the class. Remember: there are no right or wrong answers to these questions—only your answers.

Student Projects

Long-term group—Choose a public policy issue in your institution or community that you will work on over the next few weeks or months. Why is it a public policy issue, rather than the private concern of a person or group? What makes this issue important to your group? On what basis did you make your selection? What should be your group's first steps in dealing with it? What might get in your way?

Short-term individual—Write a one-page summary of a current community issue. What makes it part of the public policy framework? Which community resources, opportunities, or costs are at stake? Why is it important to you?

Discussion Questions

1. What factors determine when an issue or problem becomes a public policy issue?
2. How does public policymaking in an open, democratic system differ from that of an authoritarian, or closed system?
3. In many respects, most public policies are compromises. How do this country's constitutional principles influence the need for compromise?
4. Think about your involvement with local public policymaking authorities such as teachers, police officers, or local city council members. Have you ever attempted to work with them on a particular policy issue?
5. How would adherents to the rights-bearing and communitarian models of citizenship differ in their views on public policy regarding school prayer? On censorship of the Internet or the entertainment industry? Can you think of other examples?

Notes

1. All definitions of public policy include government activity. Beyond this, the most significant distinction involves the extent to which others outside the immediate decision-making arena participate in the process. In his relatively straightforward approach, Thomas Dye refers to public policy as "whatever governments choose to do or not to do." See Thomas R. Dye, *Understanding Public Policy*, 7th ed. (Englewood Cliffs, NJ: Prentice-Hall, 1992), p. 3. In a more expansive definition, James Anderson describes public policy as "a relatively stable, purposive course of action followed by an actor or set of actors in dealing with a problem or matter of concern." See James E. Anderson, *Public Policymaking*, 3d ed. (Boston: Houghton Mifflin, 1997), p. 9.

2. For an early contemporary discussion of this relationship, see Carl J. Friedrich, *Constitutional Government and Democracy* (New York: Blaisdell, 1950). Among the numerous current textbooks that continue this theme, see Christine Barbour and Gerald C. Wright, *Keeping the Republic: Power and Citizenship in American Politics* (Boston: Houghton Mifflin, 2001).

3. Alexis de Tocqueville, *Democracy in America*, 2 vols. (New York: Vintage Books, 1945, 1956), vol. i, p. 198.

4. In their views of republican government, the founders were greatly influenced by the writings of the eighteenth-century French aristocrat Charles de Secondat, Baron de la Brède et de Montesquieu, in particular Montesquieu's *Spirit of the Laws*. For additional reading on the legacy of classical republicanism, see Forrest McDonald, *Novus Ordo Seclorum: The Intellectual Origins of the Constitution* (Lawrence: University of Kansas Press, 1985), Paul Rahe, *Republics Ancient and Modern: Classical Republicanism and the American Revolution* (Chapel Hill: University of North Carolina Press, 1992), and Thomas Pangle, *The Ennobling of Democracy: The Challenge of the Postmodern Age* (Baltimore: Johns Hopkins University Press, 1972).

5. See founder James Madison's documentation of the lessons to be drawn from previous experiments in confederated and republican governments in two research memoranda he wrote just prior to the Constitutional Convention of 1787: "Ancient and Modern Confederations" and "Vices of the Political System of the United States." Both can be found in *The Papers of James Madison*, 17 vols. (Chicago: University of Chicago Press, 1962–1991), vol. ix.

6. Federalist No. 51, *The Federalist Papers*, Clinton Rossiter, ed. (New York: New American Library, 1961), p. 322. Among the several excellent and readable histories of the Constitutional Convention are Catherine Drinker Bowen, *Miracle at Philadelphia: The Story of the Constitutional Convention May to September 1787* (Boston: Little, Brown, 1966); Christopher Collier and James Lincoln Collier, *Decisions at Philadelphia: The Constitutional Convention of 1787* (New York: Random House, 1986); and Richard B. Morris, *The Framing of the Federal Constitution* (Washington, DC: National Park Service, 1986). For a more direct and detailed look at the framers, see Max Farrand, ed., *The Records of the Federal Convention of 1787* (New Haven, CT: Yale University Press, 1966). Madison's role is described particularly well in Robert A. Goldwin, *From Parchment to Power* (Washington, DC: AEI Press, 1997).

7. Rossiter, ed., *The Federalist Papers*, p. 84. The *Federalist* essays, eighty-five in

all, were written by Madison, Alexander Hamilton, and John Jay in 1787 and 1788 as individual tracts in the campaign for the new Constitution's ratification in New York State. They are now widely regarded as America's greatest contribution to political philosophy. In addition to Rossiter, several editions of *The Federalist* are available, including those edited by Gary Wills (Toronto: Bantam Books, 1987) and George W. Carey et al. (Dubuque, IA: Kendall/Hunt, 1966).

8. This refinement of the definition is generally credited to Richard E. Neustadt in *Presidential Power and the Modern Presidents: The Politics of Leadership from Roosevelt to Reagan* (New York: Free Press, 1959, 1990), p. 29.

9. Separation of powers has been perhaps the most distinctive and controversial feature of American constitutionalism. For a closer look at the contrary views about this principle and its relationship to the effectiveness of the policymaking process, see Robert A. Goldwin and Art Kaufman, eds., *Separation of Powers: Does It Still Work?* (Washington, DC: AEI Press, 1986), and Bradford P. Wilson and Peter W. Schramm, eds., *Separation of Powers and Good Government* (Lantham, MD: Rowman and Littlefield, 1994).

10. For a more detailed look at the origins of federalism, its resurgence, and its implications for public policymaking, see Raoul Berger, *Federalism: The Founders' Design* (Norman: University of Oklahoma Press, 1987); Michael S. Greve, *Real Federalism: Why It Matters, How It Can Happen* (Washington, DC: AEI Press, 1999); Jeffrey R. Henig, *Public Policy and Federalism: Issues in State and Local Politics* (New York: St. Martin's, 1985); and David C. Nice and Patricia Fredericksen, *The Politics of Intergovernmental Relations*, 2d ed. (Chicago: Nelson-Hall Publishers, 1995).

11. James Bryce, *The American Commonwealth*, 2 vols. (New York: Macmillan, 1899), pp. i, 37.

12. Alexis de Tocqueville, *Democracy in America*, pp. i, 290.

13. Judicial review in all its aspects, from the role of an independent judiciary in a democracy to contrary theories of constitutional interpretation, has generated an enormous bibliography. For an excellent and recent account of the development of judicial review in this country, see William Nelson, *Marbury v. Madison: The Origins and Legacy of Judicial Review* (Lawrence: University Press of Kansas, 2000). For a rich discussion of judicial review in different countries, see Donald W. Jackson and C. Neal Tate, eds., *Comparative Judicial Review and Public Policy* (Westport, CT: Greenwood, 1992).

14. Marshall's decision confirmed the very limited status of the Bill of Rights in the early republic. Because the federal government had only a marginal role in people's lives before the twentieth century, courts rarely had occasion to invoke the protections of the Bill of Rights. Not until the Fourteenth Amendment allowed courts to apply those protections against the actions of state and local government did the Bill of Rights assume more than a symbolic significance in the nation's life. See David G. Barnum, *The Supreme Court and American Democracy* (New York: St. Martin's, 1993), pp. 150–151.

15. The long and bitter struggle to implement the 1954 and subsequent desegregation decisions demonstrates the limitations as well as the power of policymaking by a judiciary in a democracy. As Alexander Bickel observed, court decisions represent the beginning, not the end, of the conversation between the judiciary and

the people. See his *The Supreme Court and the Idea of Progress* (New Haven, CT: Yale University Press, 1978), p. 91. For a history of this landmark decision, see Richard Kluger, *Simple Justice: The History of Brown v. Board of Education and Black America's Struggle for Equality* (New York: Knopf, 1975).

16. For more information on the impact of the Fourteenth Amendment, see Richard C. Cortner, *The Supreme Court and the Second Bill of Rights: The Fourteenth Amendment and the Nationalization of Civil Liberties* (Madison: University of Wisconsin Press, 1981). See also J.W. Peltason, *Corwin and Peltason's Understanding the Constitution*, 8th ed. (New York: Holt, Rinehart and Winston, 1979), pp. 196–220. In his book *We the People: The Fourteenth Amendment* (New York: Oxford University Press, 1999), Michael J. Perry examines some of the more controversial policy areas in which courts have applied the Fourteenth Amendment in recent years.

17. Harold Lasswell, *Politics: Who Gets What, When, How* (New York: World, 1958), p. 13.

18. Irving Brant's *The Bill of Rights: Its Origin and Meaning* (Indianapolis, IN: Bobbs-Merrill, 1965) and Bernard Schwartz's *The Bill of Rights: A Documentary History* (New York: Chelsea House, 1971) remain standard references on the subject of rights in the American experience. For a fresh interpretation of the Bill of Rights and its constitutional significance, see Akhil Amar, *The Bill of Rights: Its Creation and Reconstruction* (New Haven, CT: Yale University Press, 1998).

19. Quoted in "Vote for Cityhood Shows Seniors' Political Power," *Los Angeles Times*, March 4, 1999, p. A-1.

20. "The most important office and the one which all of us can and should fill is that of private citizen. The duties of the office of private citizen cannot under a republican form of government be neglected without serious injury to the public." Quoted in Alfred Lief, *Brandeis: The Personal History of an American Ideal* (New York: Stackpole Sons, 1936), p. 72.

21. John Locke, *Two Treatises of Government*, ed. Peter Laslett (Cambridge: Cambridge University Press, 1960, 1998). Because of his articulation of the principles of natural rights and government based on popular consent, Locke's work was widely regarded as the "Bible" of political thought in eighteenth-century America and Western Europe.

22. From the Latin word *civitatem*, citizen meant originally an inhabitant—and more specifically—a free person—of such a city-state. Classical republicanism developed in the ancient city-states of Greece and Rome. "Public" and "policy" also come from this same tradition. "Public" derives from the Latin word *publius*, referring to those matters that concern the people as a whole, as distinguished from *privatus*, which refers to concerns that are private in nature. "Policy" stems from the Latin word *politia*, which referred to general matters of citizenship and government.

23. See, for example, Harry C. Boyte and James Farr, "The Work of Citizenship and the Problem of Service Learning," in Richard M. Battistoni and William E. Hudson, eds., *Experiencing Citizenship: Concepts and Models for Service-Learning in Political Science* (Washington, DC: American Association for Higher Education, 1997), pp. 35–48; and Harry C. Boyte and Nancy N. Kari, "Renewing the Democratic Spirit in American Colleges and Universities: Higher Education as Public Work,"

in Thomas Ehrlich, ed., *Civic Responsibility and Higher Education* (Phoenix, AZ: Oryx Press, 2000), pp. 37–59. See also Boyte, *Citizen Action and New American Populism* (Philadelphia: Temple University Press, 1986).

24. The meaning of citizenship has been a lively and controversial subject throughout the nation's history. Among the excellent surveys of this subject are Michael Schudson, *The Good Citizen: A History of American Civic Life* (Cambridge, MA: Harvard University Press, 1998) and Rogers W. Smith, *Civic Ideals: Conflicting Visions of Citizenship in U.S. History* (New Haven, CT: Yale University Press, 1997). Renewed interest in civic engagement in recent decades has produced a wealth of titles. A good beginning read might be Benjamin R. Barber's *Strong Democracy: Participatory Politics for a New Age* (Berkeley: University of California Press, 1985). A more detailed examination of the various models of citizenship in contemporary American society can be found in Don E. Eberly, ed., *Building a Community of Citizens: Civil Society in the 21st Century* (Lantham, MD: University Press of America, 1994). For an interesting debate on the possibilities of civic engagement, see Robert D. Putnam, *Bowling Alone: The Collapse and Revival of American Community* (New York: Simon and Schuster, 2000) and Everett Carll Ladd, *The Ladd Report* (New York: Free Press, 1999). Ted Becker and Christa Daryl Slaton examine the impact of the telecommunications revolution on civic engagement in *The Future of Teledemocracy* (Westport, CT: Praeger, 2000).

25. "Service Learning and Civic Education," in Sheilah Mann and John J. Patrick eds., *Education for Civic Engagement in Democracy* (Washington, DC: Educational Resources Information Center, 2000), p. 30.

26. "President Bush Discusses Comprehensive Immigration Reform." The White House, Office of the Press Secretary, June 26, 2007, p. 1.

2 IDENTIFYING PUBLIC POLICY ISSUES

As we discussed in chapter 1, public policymaking takes place when people with authority make decisions or commitments on important public questions. The effect of those decisions may or may not disrupt the status quo, depending upon the extent of change connected with the decision. Thus, if a city council decides to establish a needle exchange program for drug addicts to discourage the spread of infectious diseases, its policy decision will be important for the immediate area; for the addicts who frequent the area; for people who live and work nearby; and for physicians and hospital personnel, police, and others with an interest in the policy. Conversely, if the same city council decides to leave the troubled area as is, the decision to do "nothing" will still impact all of the aforementioned groups, although in a different way.

The resolution of public policy questions can occur at all levels of decision making, ranging from international matters to local government issues. Even the classroom can be a public policymaking environment. Whatever the level of governance, the decisions made by public policymakers affect the distribution of public resources in one way or another, and that change—or lack of change—usually affects everyone, although some of us more than others.

Just as decision making takes place at numerous levels of government, the range of issues under consideration is equally vast. An issue may affect a few people or many, regardless of where it occurs. Its potential for change can cut across all kinds of lines ranging from geography (one area affected more than another) to income (one group benefiting or suffering more than another). All of this leads to a simple, but important question: how do we figure out whether a problem is weighty enough to be a public policy issue?

In this chapter we will examine the criteria for determining public policy issues and how to go about researching them. In the process we will begin to assemble the necessary tools that will allow you to identify public issues at your college, city, or other public policy arena.

Triggering Mechanisms: Indicators for Determining Issues

How do we separate legitimate public policy issues from nonissues or private predicaments? It is not the easiest thing to do because many of us are bothered by different problems. In addition, we have different views of what should or should not be appropriate government activity. This in itself has always been a great source of divisiveness. Most of the reform movements in our history, such as the abolition of slavery and child labor, the safety regulation of food and drugs, prohibition, Social Security, and the civil rights movement, involved a minority of citizens attempting to persuade the public policymakers that matters beyond the responsibility of government should be added to the public agenda. Many of the current controversies surrounding abortion, cigarette smoking, and sexual harassment turn on this same dilemma.

Conversely, some reform movements take the opposite direction: namely, the demands to remove government activity from matters in which it has traditionally been involved. Laws regulating private sexual conduct, reproductive rights, and the "right to die" come to mind. The framers of the Constitution, our most fundamental public policy guide, attempted to draw basic, though inconclusive, boundaries of the public policy environment, defining in broad strokes what governments could or could not do. By virtue of those decisions, they also defined what citizens could or could not do. Yet, "the devil is in the details," as the saying goes, and since the earliest days of the republic, public policymakers have attempted to apply those guidelines in concrete policies.

With changing values, different policymakers, and competing interpretations, many public policies have traveled a "zigzag" course—adopted at one point, only to be revised or reversed at another. As we saw in chapter 1, changing approaches to welfare is one example; whereas the national government had virtually no role in the 1800s and early 1900s, it became much more active during the Great Depression and the 1960s, only to pare back commitments during the 1990s.[1] Such policymaking flexibility was built into the process by the framers. As we approach the end of the first decade of the twenty-first century, universal health care may be an example where public policymakers are considering a greater role for government at the national, local, and even local levels. In 2006, Massachusetts became the first state to mandate health care coverage for all, with several states contemplating similar programs. One year later, San Francisco embarked on a program to provide health care coverage for anyone not insured. And in 2008, health care was a key discussion area of the presidential campaign.[2]

Disagreements notwithstanding, some issues become public and thus available for resolution, while many others do not. Still, we ask, on what bases do such developments occur? In fact, there are basic indicators, or events, that are the spawning grounds of what constitutes a public policy issue. Called *triggering mechanisms,* these factors show an issue with enough strength to capture the attention of public policymakers.[3]

In the next few pages we examine scope, intensity, duration, and resources, which are the components of triggering mechanisms. The more that all of these elements apply to a particular problem, the more we can be reasonably certain that the problem becomes part of the *public agenda,*[4] the list of issues awaiting resolution by policymakers at their respective levels of governance.

Scope: How Widespread a Problem

The first test of a public policy question centers on the scope of the issue, which refers to the numbers of individuals who are connected with the topic. *Scope* tells us much about the universality of a problem; it is a quantitative variable. If a large percentage of the potentially affected population is influenced by a dilemma or matter of concern, then the problem has widespread scope. However, if only a small percentage of the population is worried, then the issue will fail the scope test because of its inability to generate enough attention. More often than not, people in decision-making positions are very sensitive to scope. Without this critical mass, the issue remains a private "problem" for a few concerned individuals.

Although scope is numbers-based, it always takes place within a geographic framework. Depending upon the location of a problem, scope can be just as important at a "micro" or local level, as it can be at a "macro" or broad level. For example, suppose that a university student government decides to raise student body fees permanently by $500 per semester to help pay for a new athletic facility. In this case, such a plan may well raise an issue for a large segment of the school student body, even though it is an insignificant number compared to the population of the state or nation. With so many people now affected within a relatively small environment, the scope of the student fee issue takes on large proportions.

State and national questions become important through scope as well. For example, if a state legislator proposes a bill to lower the highway speed limit by ten miles per hour, such a potential change can affect virtually everyone who drives! Likewise, if the head of the U.S. Environmental Protection Agency (EPA) calls for tighter controls on automobile emissions, this proposal can impact the more than 275 million motor vehicles and their owners throughout the nation. On another level, lower emissions can potentially affect the health of millions of people suffering from asthma and other respiratory disorders. In other words, scope is a matter of proportionality—the larger the percentage affected in a particular area, the more likely that the issue will pass the scope test.

How can you tell when a scope is significant? The first thing to do is to take note of how many of the potentially affected people with a particular policymaking jurisdiction are aware, or perhaps even agitated, about the issue that is important to you. Whether it is an informal "head count" or a formal survey, you can determine the scope of a potential problem and, as such, gauge its magnitude.

Intensity: How Troublesome a Problem

The second triggering mechanism component centers on *intensity,* or the extent to which people feel psychologically invested in and affected by the issue. Intensity can be positive or negative; either way, it refers to the degree to which people become concerned about a potential problem. Because it deals with affect, or emotion, intensity is a qualitative variable. Is there ever an issue that keeps you from sleeping at night? Do you know others who are bothered about the same question? Sometimes, an issue may attract strong reactions from people. In a world where all kinds of problems arise every day, intensity helps to separate public policy issues from nonissues. If sizable numbers are not engaged or "worked up" about a particular situation, then the likelihood is that the concern will not emerge as a public policy issue. As such, intensity is part of the triggering mechanism mix.

As with scope, intensity can occur at all levels of public policymaking. At the local level, intensity on particular issues can be profound because the public experiences them firsthand. Questions ranging from the plight of homeless people to school uniforms can churn stomachs and move citizens to make themselves heard at city council meetings, school board meetings, or wherever policymakers have the ability to decide an issue that has generated deep public concerns. At the state level, populations are often bitterly divided about whether there should be toll roads, legalized gambling, or other changes that impact public resources or values. Thus, when hundreds of Hells Angels motorcycle club members descend upon a state capitol to protest a helmet law, they are reorganizing several days of their lives to speak out on an issue that they have to deal with every day.

More times than not, intensity is fleeting, thereby reducing the likelihood that an issue will become part of the public agenda. That's because our lives are crowded with everyday problems, making it likely that we will have little time for or interest in a pressing concern that is outside of our day-to-day routine. In general, it is pretty hard to get worked up and *stay* worked up over problems; it is easier to focus on more pleasant matters. Even when such intrusions occur, they are usually brief interruptions.

Take the issue of gun control, for example. Virtually every time there is a shooting or other well-publicized abuse of firearms, public opinion surveys show the widespread demand for immediate action in the form of tighter restrictions. When relative quiet follows such outbursts, public intensity tends to die down. Even the well-publicized Columbine High School tragedy in Colorado failed to move national or state policymakers, principally because public intensity faded.[5] Or consider the helmet issue we discussed earlier. Although hundreds of people may object to what they believe is interference by government, by next week they will likely be back at work or in their regular routines.

It's when the protests fail to subside that the eyebrows rise and that public policymakers are more likely to pay attention. Thus, during the 1950s and 1960s, thousands of activists across the nation kept the civil rights issue on the front burner through protests, marches, and mass arrests for civil disobedience. Similarly, during the 1980s, pressure from within and abroad mounted on the U.S. Congress and President Ronald Reagan to impose economic sanctions on South Africa as a tool to get that country to do away with apartheid. In 2006, public intensity surged when the owners of several major ports decided to sell them to a company headquartered in Dubai, a small Arab nation in the Middle East. Frustration with the war in Iraq and terrorism fueled public anger at unprecedented levels. Despite the reassurances by President Bush that U.S. security would not be jeopardized, congressional committees scheduled hearings on the transfer. Ultimately, the resentment was so strong that the Dubai-owned company decided against the purchase.[6] From these examples we can see that intensity is an important, if unpredictable, ingredient of the public-agenda-building process.

As you try to determine intensity about a potential public policy issue, check the "mood" of those people around you. Are they stirring about the same issue with a passion, or level of intensity, similar to yours? Has the issue been churning in the pit of their political stomachs to the point of anguish? If you see these kinds of reactions, chances are that the issue within you has generated intensity in others as well and, therefore, become part of the public agenda.

Duration: How Long a Problem

So far we have discussed quantitative (how *many* people know?) and qualitative (how *much* do they care?) components of triggering mechanisms. A third element, *duration,* centers on the length of time that an issue has bothered people. As with scope and intensity, duration is determined by a simple formula: the longer that an issue attracts the interest of an affected population, the more likely that sizable numbers of that group will demand change from public policymakers. Should an issue come and go, then it fails to capture enough momentum to resonate as part of the public agenda.

Duration forces policymakers to take a long hard look in the "public policy mirror." Should an issue become a long-standing part of the public agenda, policymakers feel growing pressure to deal with it. The longer the issue remains without resolution, the more that the capabilities of policymakers may be called into question. Such reservations are the first signs of reduced public support for decision makers. Wise public policymakers pay attention to matters that stay on the public agenda for long periods of time.

There are countless examples of concerns or irritants growing into public policy issues over time, as well as even more examples of would-be public policy issues failing to emerge because they "go away." One case concerns the emergence of AIDS (acquired immunodeficiency syndrome) as a serious problem, particularly at the national level. Viewed twenty-five years ago as a bizarre malady affecting relatively few people in Africa, AIDS has attracted public attention with its assault on tens of millions throughout the world. Today, AIDS is considered an international epidemic of immense proportions. With this issue only growing in scope and intensity over time, it has drawn increasing attention from both the general public and from policymakers.[7]

The duration element is important at other public policymaking centers as well. Consider a troublesome intersection, where large numbers of automobile accidents occur on a regular basis in the absence of a traffic signal or stop sign. The longer that this danger zone goes without corrective action, the more likely that those individuals who are affected by or who live near the intersection will remain concerned about the issue and demand resolution. Should public policymakers fail to take action over time, the intensity of opinions will in all likelihood increase, showing once again the connection among the various triggering mechanism elements. But if traffic patterns change because of a new nearby interstate highway that alleviates local pressures, then the troublesome intersection may well become less of a concern. Either way, duration tells us much about whether an issue has the "legs" to climb the triggering mechanism rungs.

Let's say you are troubled by an issue and don't really understand why nothing has been done about it. If you are still bothered after a prolonged amount of time, the duration of your concern will give momentum to your issue. If, after awhile, you are no longer concerned, or are now worried about something else, then your decreased attention will probably mean that the problem has passed as a potential public policy issue.

Resources: Costliness of the Problem

The final triggering mechanism component, *resources,* completes the set of conditions necessary to place an issue on the public agenda. Resources center on what or how much is at stake with the emergence of a potential public policy issue. Commonly, resources include dollars, or the financial costs attached to a growing issue. But sometimes, as we learned in chapter 1, resources include personal values, ideals, and loyalties. Although not necessarily costly in terms of money, such commitments can exact a price as well. Some public policy analysts prefer to consider such factors as constraints rather than resources because they place limits on what public policy can do.[8] In contrast, values, ideals, and loyalties can also provide powerful support to policies that are in accord with them.

In many cases, resource issues develop over a long period of time. Thus, a city's need for a public transportation system emerges as a consequence of increased population, traffic congestion, and increased pollution. As more and more people struggle with long, costly commutes, they begin to realize the serious issue on their hands. As expensive as it may be to build a public transportation system, citizens and policymakers sometimes conclude that the benefits will outweigh the costs; on other occasions, they may decide that the costs exceed the benefits.

Sometimes, resource questions arise with incredible speed. For example, when a massive hurricane suddenly descends upon a southeastern or gulf coast state, the financial damage from the devastation can run into the billions of dollars. Such was the case when Hurricane Katrina ravaged Louisiana and several other states in 2005, leaving the region in disarray for years. With this abrupt intrusion, repairing the infrastructure of the state becomes an instant issue on the public agenda.

Resources can also be contested with respect to values or nonfinancial questions. Think about the issue of high school locker searches. Here, competing values are at stake—the question of one's right to privacy versus the school's need to keep order and promote safety. If school violence threatens the well-being of the students and teachers, school officials may elect to search lockers or remove the storage units altogether. As education representatives debate the issue and work their way through the public policymaking process, the administrators may decide that the more important resources lie with protecting the public good. Such are the difficulties when competing rights are at issue. And given that ours is a society that honors many different rights, it is not surprising that clashes occur.

Whether financial or otherwise, the question of resource use is critical to putting an issue on the public agenda. People are much more likely to get worked up over the question of cameras at busy intersections (the concern about unnecessary government intrusion) than traffic congestion; likewise, they are much more likely to argue over whether public library computer Web sites should be blocked (the issue of pornography versus free speech) than whether the library should start carrying videos. The problem is particularly delicate with respect to the distribution of values or rights because we do not "see" these as easily as we see a new highway or government building.

Combined, scope, intensity, duration, and resources are the ingredients of the agenda-building process. Together, they fuel the engine that brings issues to the attention of public policymakers, who must decide what, if anything, to do about them. That's what happened with welfare reform, an issue that reached a crescendo in the early 1990s because the triggering mechanism ingredients became too substantial for public policy to ignore any longer. These factors, together with the election of a president who pursued the issue as a state governor and the election of Republican majorities in both houses of the Congress committed to welfare reform, pushed the issue into the forefront of the policymaking process.[9]

But few triggering mechanisms contain the drama of the September 11, 2001, terrorist attacks on the World Trade Center in New York and the Pentagon near Washington, DC. These tragic events took more than 3,000 lives, disrupted the nation's air transportation system, and cost more than $40 billion in losses. Within weeks, President George W. Bush and the Congress committed more than $100 billion to dealing with various aspects of the terrorist attacks, ranging from beefed up antiterrorism efforts to relief for laid-off workers. Most of all, however, the attacks shook Americans to the core, removing our naïve perception of invulnerability.

Just how many triggering mechanism ingredients are necessary to jolt the public policymaking process is always hard to say—every issue has its own set of factors pushing it in one direction or another. But this much is certain: the more we see of these elements, the more likely it is that public policymakers will be compelled to respond. Why? The reason is simple: the longer and more complicated the agenda, the more that various individuals and groups scream out for action because of their increasing discomfort. All of this is complicated by people often clamoring with different responses to the same issue, leaving policymakers sometimes unable to resolve complicated issues, or responding to them in ways that leave more people disappointed than satisfied.[10]

Ultimately, the pressure to resolve public problems falls squarely upon the shoulders of public policymakers. The more they feel the public's concern about an issue, the more that they are compelled to act. Avoidance usually will not work, for if policymakers fail to solve enough problems within a reasonable amount of time, then those who put them there may well lose patience and, you guessed it, throw them out at the next election.

On the other side of the public/public policymaker relationship, policymakers don't always wait for a public policy issue to gain prominence before acting on it. Occasionally, they take it upon themselves to act without getting much public input. Think about the city council that annexes nearby and unincorporated vacant land or the state legislature that raises water purity standards.

Sometimes public policy is made more in response to an excellent opportunity rather than a compelling need: the right combination of resources becomes available to address a matter that otherwise would likely not be given a high priority. For example, when the U.S. government released Department of Defense–controlled land in the post–Cold War era, city and county governments throughout the country quickly lined up to convert these sites into parks, schools, low-cost housing, and other uses critical to local needs. Federal welfare reform legislation in the 1990s was inspired by pilot programs initiated in some states during the previous decade. In these or other cases, public policymakers may define issues on their own—often without the knowledge or concern of others. When this happens, it simply means that these authorities have decided to do something because *they* think it is important. By acting in this preemptive manner, sometimes policymakers "solve" a problem before it draws the public's attention.

But What If My Issue Is Kept Off the Public Agenda?

So far, the discussion in this chapter has been based upon an important assumption, namely that the agenda-building process is open to any issues that acquire the four properties associated with triggering mechanisms. But is the system really open? Some people argue that small groups of leaders are so powerful that they keep issues from ever getting on the public agenda. They do this in various ways such as controlling the press, outmaneuvering those with fewer resources, "paying off" key policymakers, or wielding power selfishly in key elective positions.[11]

It's difficult to prove that leaders keep issues off the agenda because there is no way to show what cannot be seen. Still, when some people promote an issue that never seems to attract serious attention of those in power, they may attribute such unresponsiveness to the ability of people in policymaking positions to keep the issue off the public agenda. Thus, the argument goes, homeless people are marginalized and ignored not because of their small numbers or an inconsequential issue, but because policymakers never allow serious consideration of their plight. Likewise, some would say that people die young in certain communities because the local government refuses to allow examination of any water contamination sources. Others might claim that we remain dependent upon oil because of a conspiracy between the automobile industry and energy producers to prevent the development of alternative engines or fuels. Could such perceptions of the public policymaking process be true?

One way to decide the credibility of the "hidden agenda" argument is to ponder those issues you know about and the extent to which they have been considered by public policymakers. If you believe that the system is relatively open, you probably would reject the idea that people could keep significant issues off the public agenda. Particularly in the age of the Internet, there are just too many opportunities for information to become public. Conversely, if you believe that policymakers are removed from public input, then you may be among those who view the policymaking process as a closed, unresponsive environment. Regardless, the system is hardly perfect. Since some people are much more likely to speak their minds than others, public policymakers may take their cues from an "unrepresentative public" and make "unrepresentative public policies."[12] So before we leave this discussion, think about the issues important to you and the extent to which policymakers have at least acknowledged them on some level. If they have, then you are likely to view the public agenda as the result of an open, dynamic process.[13]

Deciding What Is Important—How and Why

So, you're steaming over an issue that you feel those in charge—probably public policymakers, if they really *are* in charge—should do something about.

Maybe the area immediately surrounding your campus is overrun with graf-
fiti and no government organization—city council, college administration,
or anyone else—has done anything about it. Maybe a new college policy
has increased the cost of parking or, worse yet, has made fewer parking
spaces available to students during construction. Then again, maybe a state
law now denies a driver's license to any driver under the age of twenty-one
who police find has any alcohol on his or her breath (even if well under the
official intoxication threshold), a public policy that you and others like you
may believe is unfair.

If you are bothered about something that is not being done right, needs
to be changed, or deserves the attention of public policymakers, you may be
part of the earliest stages of agenda building and not even know it! Check it
out. Bearing in mind triggering mechanisms and how they work, think about
some of the critical questions that you need to ask:

- Are you alone in your concern, or are there others who feel as you
  do?
- Exactly what is at stake here, anyway? Are your values or important
  resources threatened?
- Do your ideals and principles lead you to believe that there is a gap
  between the world as it is and the world that you want? Is closing that
  gap doable? Does closing the gap call for a public policy?
- Is this a minor irritant or a major concern?
- Who created this problem and, equally important, who can do something
  about it?
- Which level of public policymaking authority is "in charge"?
- Just what can be done about the issue that has you so worked up?
- How can you participate in solving the problem that you have identi-
  fied?

Asking such questions will help you answer two others: whether an issue
is authentic (i.e., whether it is a plausible candidate for public policymaking)
and whether it actually interests you. There are other considerations that you
might want to address. Is your potential issue an enduring one, that is, an
issue whose problems and questions invite comparison with similar public
issues at different times and places in the past? Such a comparison is likely
to enrich the context of the issue. Along these lines, you would probably
want to avoid transient or exotic themes. Second, does the issue suggest the
importance of values and foundational principles and, better still, conflicts

between them? Again, this takes you away from the trivial and moves you toward matters of substance.

In any event, your first step is to investigate the problem to get your hands around the issue. In fact, the kind of investigation leading you to identify an issue is also the first step to *solving* the issue. When you have completed this assessment task, you will be in a far stronger position to know what to do next, how to attempt change, and which level of the public policymaking process to address.

Doing Research

The best way to learn whether your concern is a public policy issue or has the potential to become one is by doing research. Much of what you learn will be in response to the triggering-mechanism components we discussed earlier. Think of those basic four questions: How many people feel as you do (scope)? What is the strength of their convictions, and are there deep divisions (intensity)? How long has this issue been festering, or has it just come up (duration)? Does the issue suggest major change, minor change, or is it much ado about nothing (resources) as Shakespeare would say? To answer these questions, you will want to investigate a variety of *social indicators,* from the statistical to the anecdotal, that will help you get a handle on the legitimacy and extent of the issue you are considering. As you develop the answers to these questions, you will also want to know which public policymakers are capable of responding as well as which important organizations and interests have taken positions on the problem you have identified.

There are many ways to investigate a public policy issue. They range from intensive library work to personal discussions. Either way, there is a simple rule for doing research—the more information you get from different sources, the more you know. And the more you know, the more that you become empowered to do something about the issue, and become part of the public policymaking process.

Library Work—Doing It the Old-Fashioned Way

Libraries are huge depositories of knowledge. In fact, they are so huge that sometimes libraries are overwhelming. That said, they are excellent places to find all kinds of valuable information. In many ways, libraries are equivalent to "one stop" convenience stores. In addition to containing endless shelves of books, they house journals, magazines, newspapers from far and near, historical records, and government reports. Most important, libraries are likely to have information to present many sides of the same issue.

Some libraries are more sensitive to student needs than others. High school and college libraries, for example, are likely to have abstracts and other indexes that organize information by subject area, thereby making it easier to find than if you just went aimlessly from shelf to shelf. The *Social Science Abstract* is one such collection that provides information on journals that focus on issues relevant to political, social, economic, psychological, and related sources. *Lexus Nexus,* another compendium, is a clearinghouse for hundreds of newspapers and magazines. By entering the "issue" or a series of key words at a designated computer terminal, you can gather significant amounts of information within a short time. Public libraries are also important depositories, but they usually contain more generic information that appeals to the wider, general audience. Moreover, such libraries usually specialize in publications that have a local interest, from government documents to a variety of civic and community materials. Whatever the extent of their resources, all libraries have librarians, resource experts who can be instrumental in pointing you in the right direction.

Going "Online"

In recent years, the Internet has become an excellent tool for obtaining all kinds of information, including material on just about any public policy issue. Today, more than three-fourths of all households have personal computers, giving them access to the Internet. Some people operate these sophisticated machines to write term papers, balance checkbooks, play games, and keep records. But personal computers can also be used as research devices for uncovering information about almost anything.

By connecting to one or more online information sources known as "search engines," you can become immersed in virtually any topic. Some skill is necessary to the extent that the search engine responds to the topics it is asked to investigate. So, if you ask the search engine to find information about "public parks," you may find yourself going through more than a million sources. However, you can make your task much more manageable by limiting your search. For example, you may ask the search engine to retrieve information sources between January 1, 2003, and December 31, 2007, on "dumpsites" and "parks" in the English language only. By narrowing your topic, you may get information that is closer to what you need.

As with libraries and newspapers, online research can help you get information without going far. These forms of "secondary research"—information you learn from reports or printed accounts, rather than firsthand exploration—can go far in helping you to understand an issue and its various sides without being overly entangled in the dispute. By the way, most colleges and universities teach students how to use the Internet either in special classes or at the library. Tapping into this resource can save you lots of time over and over again.

One cautionary note: Unlike newspapers or magazines that have known authors and publishers, many online sources are written anonymously. That means it may be hard to verify the accuracy of the information you gather. Web sites such as Blogs may give you a feel for an issue you might not have otherwise, but they may be biased or one-sided. To the extent that you rely upon information you retrieve online, you need to be extra vigilant about the claims associated with the material.

Newspaper Tracking

If you are interested in a local issue, relying upon a local community or daily newspaper is an excellent way to track its development. Often, a local newspaper will print stories not only about your issue, but also related topics of significance. Let's say you are interested in a proposed ordinance (local law) concerning the conversion of a garbage dump into a city park. As the issue grows in importance, the newspaper will carry a stream of stories about the area, its contents, neighbors, and conversion costs. The paper may also print "sidebars," or related stories about the original owners of the dump, any health risks associated with the proposed new use, how the proposal came to be, or tax benefits if the land is donated to the city. Also, if the issue has attracted interest from the paper's editors or publishers, you may see an editorial or op-ed (opposite editorial page) article written by someone with a strident point of view. Such additions help to show why an issue may be controversial; in other words, they illustrate the nuances that aren't so obvious at first glance. If the issue is campus-related, keeping close tabs on the college newspaper is a great starting point for information gathering. Questions such as alcohol on campus, local crime, and plagiarism are among the many public policy issues that have a tremendous impact on the student community. Nowhere will you find more information on such issues than in the campus newspaper.

Sometimes a newspaper or other media will decide not to report on an issue that seems important to you. That may be because members of the media have their own values about what is or is not an important story.[14] Such occurrences—or lack of occurrences—invite a series of questions, such as why isn't the paper writing about an issue affecting so many people? Is there something the television station wants to keep quiet? What relationship, if any, exists between the issue and local media sources? Perhaps the local radio station or newspaper is reporting extensively about the activities of one of its advertisers but not the competition. Maybe the reporter assigned to the story knows some of the participants, and thus is unable to write with objectivity. The simple point is that all information sources, even members of the press, have their biases. You might think of such linkages as conspiracy or collusion, but the fact is that everyone writes or reports from a point of view. Knowing this, you will be wise to "consider the source" as you gather your data.

Government and Community Organizations

In addition to providing lots of local information, newspapers publish calendars of upcoming events such as hearings, forums, or city council meetings that will discuss the proposed local public policy. By attending these meetings, you can learn more about the other "actors," people who are close to or part of the decision-making process. Some examples include:

- interest groups, such as an environmental organizations, homeowners, chambers of commerce, unions, or even the local PTA;
- bureaucrats, such as the head of the planning department, public health officials, the chief of police, or the city manager;
- powerful, well-connected individuals, whose opinions might not be publicly known except for the fact that a public policy proposal affects their needs or values;
- community leaders, such as scoutmasters, Little League coaches, senior citizen groups, members of the clergy, philanthropists, or others who may have ideas about responding to a public policy issue;
- interested private businesses whose welfare may be affected by the outcome of a public policy issue;
- service clubs and organizations, such as Rotary, Kiwanis, or the United Way, with members who might feel impacted by a proposed policy or threat to community value;
- local political parties, whose members may well take positions on controversial community topics;
- competing government agencies either at the same level (such as police and fire departments with different views on the same issue) or at different levels (federal, state, or local agencies with their separate views on the same issue).

The more you learn about an issue, the more you realize that the issue may have many sides as well as many people interested in its outcome. Their priorities and points of view will differ, and even if they agree that a particular issue or problem warrants attention, they probably will favor different solutions.[15]

Such a discovery may be disconcerting, especially if you have already formed your own views in the matter. Welcome to the realities of democracy. Public policymakers may find themselves in increasingly difficult positions because of competing values or struggles over public resources. Like them, you would be wise to keep an open mind—to be not only tolerant of other people's points of view, but also understanding of the differing values and circumstances that shape them. Tolerance and open-mindedness are virtues of democratic citizenship.[16] They can also help assure that whatever public policy you espouse will be a realistic one that has taken all relevant factors into consideration. And trying to see "where the other fellow is coming from" has one other benefit: it forces you to reexamine your own opinions—and the values and assumptions on which they are based—in a new light.

Personal Interviews

Thus far we have discussed acquiring information through reading about an issue, the information or data of which is gathered by the reporter or writer. But there is a difference between digesting a dry, clinical account of something and actually talking to an individual involved with it firsthand.[17] It is the difference between relying upon what others write or say and learning about it yourself. In the first instance, you are depending upon the values, assumptions, and conclusions of someone else; in the second instance, you are establishing your own criteria for what you want to know and your own assessments of what you learn.

In addition to getting information firsthand, personal investigations can go far toward closing the gap between "theory" and "reality." They can also help you understand what's "behind" (or who's behind) an issue as much as the issue itself. They point you toward truly independent conclusions based upon what you have been able to learn.

Suppose that some city leaders propose to turn a garbage dump into a public park in an effort to convert questionable land into something for the public good, and you are given the task of determining the merit of this proposal. In this scenario, you might learn much by talking to the people who are part of or most directly affected by the process. The obvious choices would begin with the actual public policymakers, the city council members and mayor, or perhaps the city manager, police chief, planning director, or director of parks. But there are others to search out as well. For example, you might want to meet with neighbors, nearby school organizations, business people who might have something to gain or lose from the proposal, or the owner of the garbage dump. Perhaps more impartial interview resources would be journalists who tend the city desk or who cover particular community issues.

By asking questions directly, you can gain a sense of how people feel not only through their words, but through their expressions or "body language." You can also learn about their alliances and capabilities as well as the reasons for their concerns. Also, these individuals, in turn, may refer you to someone you had not thought of otherwise. On another level, you get a sense about not only the competing individuals and groups but also conflicting values such as the virtue of community open space versus the desire to keep a neighborhood intact.

To continue with the proposed public park theme, perhaps a local developer who is attempting to get the park conversion contract has made political campaign contributions to some of the city council members. Or maybe a company owns a nearby land parcel that, if adjacent to a public park, will become more valuable than it would have been next to a garbage dump. Neither of these circumstances is necessarily bad or illegal, but they help to explain the contexts, motivations, and behavior of individuals who are closer to the process. As you search for interview sources, it will be worthwhile to consult campus experts. With respect to the park issue, here's a list of some of the academic disciplines where professors or teachers may provide information:

- environmental studies—impact of the land use changes on traffic, the environment, and other social patterns
- economics—development costs, tax implications
- political science—issue conflict, interest group involvement, public policymakers, and possible solutions
- urban planning—values, patterns, and methods by which local governments determine the placement of resources
- health sciences—toxics studies in and near the affected area
- recreation and leisure—possible recreational uses of the land, uses elsewhere
- public administration—needs and public sector costs related to the project build-out, maintenance, and police services

- sociology—people and public values as they relate to recreation sites such as parks
- history—previous uses of the land and related areas

Instructors in these areas may have independent studies that they can share with you. Through these sources, you may gain yet another perspective about who may "win" or "lose" from a new public policy.

Polls and Public Opinion Surveys

Another way to learn about an issue is by conducting a poll or public opinion survey. These instruments are handy devices for learning what "the people" think about various questions; they can be utilized at any level of investigation, from a classroom to the nation. If you are interested in how people feel about welfare reform, depletion of the ozone layer, or another national issue, the expense involved will make it just about impossible to do your own survey. Instead, you will want to look up information gathered by professional survey research organizations such as the Gallup Poll, the *New York Times*/CBS Poll, or several others. These organizations use various scientific methods to ensure that the few hundred people in their surveys are near mirror images of society as a whole. But if you want to know the knowledge level of a class of students about a particular issue or set of core values, the gathering of that information can come in the form of a simple survey—in this case, a poll asked of a rather "limited" public.

Surveys allow you to get information from large numbers of people who may have opinions about all kinds of issues. With this data, you can see firsthand how much people know about an issue and whether it is even important to them. You can also learn the extent to which the opinions of those who participate in your surveys have any impact upon the decisions of public policymakers. Although professionally administered surveys can cost thousands of dollars, an individual effort to get survey data can be pretty effective and cost little more than an individual's time. Using our hypothetical garbage dump-turned-public park proposal as a case in point, imagine what you might learn by asking the neighbors or city's residents how they feel about the proposal.

Just because most of the people you talk with may feel one way or another about a question does not mean that their answers are the basis for making public policy. Consider a survey on crime. If asked about the importance of public safety, most respondents might answer that the police should do whatever is necessary to keep our streets safe. But what does that answer say about the rights of individuals to be protected from an unconstitutional search or police behavior that chases people off the streets because of crowded conditions and nothing more? Surveys may tell us how people feel, but they do not necessarily confirm what is right. For this we must always keep in mind the seminal ideas that frame our values. Here, again, we see the tie between our constitutional and political traditions and the public policymaking process.

There is a precise methodology to organizing a survey, and if you want to do it right you should read a book or two on the process.[18] Well-written surveys gather data through carefully crafted questions that avoid showing bias. As such, the most reliable surveys are usually designed and conducted by trained people. But assuming you have the help to carry out this task, a poll or survey can give you information that you would never have from asking just your friends or people who you believe know most about the issue at hand.

Even if you do not have the resources to conduct a "scientific" survey, you still can learn quite a bit by just asking people about the issue of concern to you. If nothing else, a few probing questions can at least tell you what others may be feeling, their reactions to your concerns, and what they believe should be done. And even though this type of survey analysis may not be truly scientific, it may well enhance your awareness nonetheless.

Research is a valuable part of understanding and becoming involved with the public policymaking process. Research takes you from your own perspective to a more complete understanding of an issue, the participants, and various possibilities for resolution. Most of all, research provides the power of information, and nothing is more important than information in defining and coming to terms with public policy issues.

Considering What to Do

Now the plot thickens. Having done much of your homework, you have decided that there is an issue of importance that requires attention by public policymakers. The next question is, "What do I do now?"

In a few situations, such as a local or state ballot (initiative), you may actually be able to participate directly in the public policymaking process by campaigning for (or against) the issue and casting your vote if you are old enough to participate. Initiatives are public policy proposals that are put on the ballot by individuals or groups that gather enough signatures of registered voters required by state or local law. Twenty-four states and hundreds of local communities permit public policymaking through this "hands on," policymaking tool. That is what happened in a 2004 California election, when voters decided to purchase $3 billion in bonds to underwrite stem cell research. A public policy decision of another sort also was made in 2006 when South Dakota voters overturned the most restrictive antiabortion law in the nation. Voters also initiate actions at the local level such as in 2006, when 70 percent of the townspeople of Waldoboro, Maine, voted 747 to 456 to cap the size of retail stores, in effect boxing out a proposed Wal-Mart. These and other instances of direct participation put citizens right into the public policymaking seat.[19] By deciding to do or not to do something, voters create important conditions of governance.

More times than not, however, citizens are more likely to attempt to influence elected officials than actually make decisions directly. That is the basis of *representative government,* the system designed by the framers of the Constitution wherein we elect people to make most decisions on our behalf. There are just too many issues at too many levels of government for all of us to take on, extraordinary circumstances or compelling questions notwithstanding. Nevertheless, the close relationship between the public and policymaking authorities is constantly fused through public input, the stream of statements that flows from citizens to public policymakers.

Knowing Where to Go, Whom to See, and How to Get There

Are you familiar with the phrase, "You can't tell the players without a scorecard"? It refers to the difficulties of understanding tangled situations where large numbers of people or interests are involved. Sometimes, that applies to understanding the public policymaking process as well.

Earlier we discussed the complexity of American government, an elaborate system with different levels of operation (national, state, local) and different branches of responsibilities (executive, legislative, judicial). It's important to understand these distinctions because not all public policies can be made at the same levels or by the same branch of policymakers. This takes us back to the discussions of federalism and separation of powers, both of which serve as organizational principles of the Constitution.

For example, let's say you are concerned about a city subsidized day care center that city council members decide they can no longer afford to support, potentially leaving hundreds of working parents without a safe place to leave their children. Perhaps funding has been cut because the council members decided to build a municipal parking lot, reduce taxes, or effect public policy changes that led to their abandonment of day care support. Change in this situation will not come from you communicating with your member of Congress because Congress does not have jurisdiction over such issues; instead, you would probably need to speak with officials at City Hall about the importance of keeping open the day care center. In the process, you need to show them the social, economic, and political costs of their actions.

Or, consider the question of meat quality at a local supermarket. Even though you are convinced that the label incorrectly describes the type or cut of meat, there is no way to get the local city council to legislate quality control or characteristics that address this issue. Such requirements are more likely to fall under the federal government's Food and Drug Administration (FDA), an agency that Congress has assigned responsibility for labeling and package descriptions, or perhaps your state's agriculture department. There is no use in attempting to change policy at the local level when that level does not have any jurisdiction over the issue.

The bottom line is this: It's not enough to know that you want to get something done; it's equally important to know *where* to go. Without knowing the appropriate public policy authority, you are not likely to get much of anything accomplished and may become frustrated in the process.

Determining What Should Be Done

If you are prepared to make your case and have a sense of where to go, you may be ready to try to influence those in authority to act. In the following chapters we will learn how to develop and advocate a public policy initiative. But here are some easy and preliminary steps that can be taken, either on an individual or group basis:

- *Talk with a school official, your city council member, county supervisor, state legislator, or member of Congress.* Campus public affairs officials or service-learning coordinators can point you in the right direction particularly with respect to local issues; it is their job to know who in government has responsibility for particular local policy issues. If you want to talk with local officials directly, it is pretty easy to call for an appointment. Even if the elected official is unavailable or too far away, you can usually meet with a staff member at a nearby office. Don't underestimate these "staffers," for they are the "eyes and ears" of their bosses. Either way, the fact that you take the time to meet with leaders and/or staff tells them that your issue is important to you.

• *Write a letter or send an e-mail to someone who can do something about your issue.* Direct communications are important; they not only put policymakers "on notice" about a problem but they serve as a written record of your concern. That you take the time to communicate about an issue shows the public policymaker that you are invested in that issue and its resolution. In addition to sending a letter or e-mail to the appropriate public policymaker, you may also decide to send a copy to the local newspaper, which may publish it as a "letter to the editor." This can both spur additional discussion and add pressure to the official you seek to influence. The effect here is to make your concern very public, something that, in turn, may encourage others to become involved as well.

• *Meet with others like you.* Local neighborhood or "town hall" meetings are excellent vehicles for airing concerns and seeing how many people are bothered about the same issue or whether there are different opinions about that issue. Sometimes, these encounters are little more than gripe sessions; at other times, they may include local officials who, after hearing about the issue, may be in position to join with their colleagues to do something about it. Organized protests and marches are variations of public meetings, but because they are out in the open, they tend to attract more attention from the press and passersby. Without hearing from the community, public policymakers often don't realize there is a problem.

Several years ago, Congressman Thomas "Tip" O'Neill, then the powerful Speaker of the U.S. House of Representatives, said that "all politics is local." By that, O'Neill meant that elected officials should not become so involved in broad national and international issues that they overlook or ignore the concerns of the folks back home.[20] And why? Because more times than not, we are more concerned with local problems than national dilemmas or international crises. Day in and day out, we are more likely to worry about homelessness than abstract global warming patterns, important as they may be. Likewise, we are more likely to see gender inequality in the workplace than we are in India, China, or other developing nations. Most of the time, local problems seem the most important and manageable. The questions then arise, What do we do? Who do we go to? This gets to the matter of expressing our concerns to those who can do something about them.

Whether it is in person or by letter, alone or with others, citizens have the right to express themselves. In a democracy such as the United States, the ability to do so is by design. We may not think about constitutional guarantees such as free speech, a free press, or freedom of assembly on a daily basis, but those rights and others guarantee the opportunity for citizens to take part in the public policymaking process. Whether tractor-driving farmers surround the White House in protest of low government farm supports or residents in Santa Fe, New Mexico, jam City Hall over a smoking ban in local bars, our political system encourages and benefits from citizen participation.

The Consequences of Inaction

Where is it written that you *have* to participate in the public policymaking process? The fact is, it is not and you do not! Actually, on any given day, most of us decide not to become engaged in the process rather than assume a role in the process. Yes, we often have opinions about issues and the people we choose to manage them, but about the only time that many of us do something about our concerns is when (or if) we vote. On a smaller scale, some of us write to a public policymaker, attend a meeting, or occasionally participate in a public protest by attending a rally or signing a petition. Otherwise, we are usually pretty removed from the actions (or inaction) of decision makers.

Students of public policy vary in their opinions about the rather docile American public. Some say the public is usually quiet because large numbers are alienated by the irresponsible actions of policymakers and feel helpless to do anything about it; others argue that the public is not expressive because it is basically satisfied with the actions of decision makers.[21] Either way, of significance here is that people *can* participate in the process if they wish, and it is that right or opportunity that separates the American political system from so many others.

The more that people participate, the more that public policymakers see the connections between those who put them in office and what they—the policymakers—must do in office. But here's the fundamental point: by knowing more about the issues and how the policymaking process works, you become more empowered to have an impact.

Should you decide to get involved in the process, you are choosing to weigh in on a public policy issue or issues important to you. Should you decide not to say anything or become involved, others will act and speak in your absence. It is up to you; the system works either way.

Case Study: Community Development Project

The president of your university or college has announced that the university will work with local government agencies, civic groups, businesses, and other constituencies on a comprehensive renewal of surrounding neighborhoods. The president has promised to commit the full range of the university's resources—intellectual as well as monetary and physical—to this effort. As part of the initial steps in this enterprise, faculty have been asked to research the problems, needs, and opportunities in the community. Your instructor has enlisted your class in this effort, asking you and your fellow students to investigate and analyze the community and to produce a report outlining problems, needs, and opportunities.

Actually, such initiatives have become common in recent years as many institutions of higher learning are redefining themselves less as ivory towers removed from their neighbors and more as engaged citizens, using their assets to improve the civic life of their communities. Collaborative efforts in these new town-gown relationships have included housing developments, environmental cleanup, the creation of new business zones, recreational and cultural facilities, libraries, transit facilities, and an expansion of volunteer outreach in areas such as education, health care, and legal services. This new role, however, is not altogether "new." A century ago, during the Progressive Era, the resources of higher education were very much involved with community service and public policymaking.

Consider the following questions in preparing such a project for your particular college or university:

1. How and where would you begin? What sources of information would you first explore? What sorts of statistical evidence might you seek about your issue? What anecdotal evidence? What groups might you want to survey or interview?

2. From what you know personally about your community and your institution's relationship to it, what potential issues first come to mind? What in your own experience might be useful in uncovering them? Those of your friends and classmates?

3. Characterize your institution and its community setting. Small college in a rural setting? Large university in an urban setting? How would different settings explain the issues one might want to consider?

4. What offices or individuals at your institution might be valuable

contacts for this initial research? What community contacts first
come to mind? Do you know anyone who might be helpful?

5. How would you begin to use the Internet as a research tool? What
would be the first words you would put into your Web browser's
search engine? Why?

6. After you have determined the potential issues, how would you go
about setting priorities? For each issue, indicate the potential role
of government, the private sector, and your own institution.

Reflection

Identifying issues brings you close to the public policymaking process and
gives you insight into that process. Still, what appears as an obvious problem to you may not be an issue to anyone else; in fact, sometimes what you
perceive as a problem may actually be thought of by others as a virtue or
benefit! Either discovery does not necessarily minimize the validity of your
concern or interest, but it may suggest that you have some work to do before
getting others to see the issue the way you see it. Remember the significance
of scope.

When researching your issue, think about what drew you to the problem
in the first place. Do you feel wronged by a certain condition? Are you of-
fended by the way some people are treated, compared to others? What is it
that draws your passion into the public policymaking arena?

It may be that as you "mine" your data and explore the issue further, your
feelings about the issue may change. Does this mean that you should walk
away from the problem? It all depends upon how important the issue is to
you and what you are prepared to do about it. In other words, your intensity
may determine what you decide to do. Either way, you have choices to move
ahead with your concerns or pursue other issues upon reconsidering your
initial observations. It is one of the benefits of an open political system, and
one that we should not take for granted.

Student Projects

Long-term group—Bearing in mind the issue you have selected at the end
of chapter 1, gather information about the problem. As you pursue your
research, ask yourself what indications point to your designated problem

as a public policy issue. Who/what is affected by the problem? How long has the problem persisted? Who/what will be affected by change? What, if anything, should be done, and at what price?

Short-term individual—Spend a couple of hours observing a problematic condition in your community such as a crowded traffic intersection or an open/closed campus policy. How do you know your concern is a public policy issue? What are the key elements that should be addressed? What might keep any action from taking place?

Discussion Questions

1. What happens when the rights of the individual collide with the needs of the community? How do we reconcile these differences in the effort to make public policy? Is it possible that there are times when the best public policy is *no* public policy?

2. How do you distinguish your own private issues from public policy issues? Discuss the criteria that transform individual problems into public policy issues.

3. Regarding the issue that you are considering, what triggering mechanisms have put it on the public agenda? How can you determine whether the key factors of *scope, intensity, duration,* and *resources* exist? What resources would you look for to answer these questions? Whom would you talk to?

4. Do you see any obstacles in carrying out your research? If so, what can you do to overcome them? How can you assure yourself of success in the information-gathering phase of the public policymaking process?

Notes

1. Gary Bryner traces the changing patterns of American welfare in his *Politics and Public Morality: The Great American Welfare Reform Debate* (New York: W.W. Norton, 1998). Mary Ellen Homb's *Welfare Reform: A Reference Handbook* (Santa Barbara, CA: ABC-CIO, 1996) is another useful introduction to the subject.

2. See "States' New Health-Care Prescription," *The Wall Street Journal,* January 13–14, 2007, p. A11, and "S.F.'s Bold Foray into Health Care Ready to Start," *San Francisco Chronicle,* June 28, 2007, pp. A1, A7.

3. Not everyone uses the same term. For example, Thomas A. Birkland refers to these defining moments as "focusing events." See his *After Disaster: Agenda Setting, Public Policy, and Focusing Events* (Washington, DC: Georgetown University Press, 1997).

4. Identifying potential issues is the first step to agenda building. For a thorough discussion of this process, see Roger W. Cobb and Charles D. Elder, *Participation in American Politics: The Dynamics of Agenda-Building* (Boston: Allyn and Bacon, 1972).

5. For an excellent review of the gun control issue, see Robert J. Spitzer, *The Politics of Gun Control,* 4th ed. (Washington, DC: CQ Press, 2008).

6. "GOP Allies Abandon Bush in Fight Over Arab Port Deal," *Los Angeles Times,* February 23, 2006, pp. A1, A14, and "Dubai Firm Bows to Public Outcry," *The Wall Street Journal,* March 10, 2006, pp. A1, A17.

7. The emergence of AIDS as a public policy issue is discussed in Stella Z. Theodoulou, ed., *AIDS: The Politics and Policy of Disease* (Upper Saddle River, NJ: Prentice-Hall, 1996).

8. Robert Bellah and his colleagues write about "values" being even more fundamental than "laws" in structuring the public policymaking environment: "A good society . . . depends in the last analysis on the goodness of individuals, not on the soundness of institutions or the fairness of laws." See Robert N. Bellah, Richard Madsen, William M. Sullivan, Ann Swidler, and Steven M. Tipton, *Habits of the Heart: Individualism and Commitment in American Life* (New York: Harper and Row, 1985), p. 183. For a constraint approach that relies upon an economics-based "choice" model, see Milton and Rose Friedman, *Free to Choose* (New York: Avon Books, 1979).

9. For a chronology leading up to the 1996 Personal Responsibility and Work Reconciliation Act, see Gregory R. Weiher, "Post–Cold War Social Welfare Policy: Limited Options," in William Crotty, ed., *Post-Cold War Policy: The Social and Domestic Context* (Chicago: Nelson-Hall, 1995), pp. 335–354. Theresa Funiciello offers an indictment of the pre-1996 system in her *Tyranny of Kindness: Dismantling the Welfare System to End Poverty in America* (New York: Atlantic Monthly, 1993). With respect to debate on the outcomes of the new policy, see William H. Miller, "Surprise! Welfare Reform Is Working," in Gregory M. Scott and Loren Latch, eds., *21 Debated Issues in American Politics* (Upper Saddle River, NJ: Prentice-Hall, 2000), pp. 226–231, and Ruth Conniff, "Welfare Profiteers," in Gregory M. Scott and Loren Latch, eds., *21 Debated Issues in American Politics* (Upper Saddle River, NJ: Prentice-Hall, 2000), pp. 232–237.

10. In a different approach that reaches much the same conclusion, Thomas A. Birkland writes of "focusing events" as the prerequisite events to agenda setting. See his *After Disaster: Agenda Setting, Public Policy and Focusing Events* (Washington, DC: Georgetown University Press, 1997).

11. Among those who have made such claims regarding American politics are C. Wright Mills, *The Power Elite* (New York: Oxford University Press, 1956) and Michael Parenti, *Democracy for the Few,* 7th ed. (New York: St. Martin's Press, 2002). Regarding the manipulation of local politics, see Peter Bachrach and Morton S. Baratz, "The Two Faces of Power," *American Political Science Review* 56, no. 4 (December 1962).

12. Russell Brooker and Todd Schaefer make this point in *Public Opinion in the 21st Century* (Boston: Houghton Mifflin, 2006), pp. 278–279.

13. Most students of political participation argue that the political system not only encourages, but is dependent upon citizen participation. For an excellent synopsis of this approach, see Steven J. Rosenstone and John Mark Hansen, *Mobilization, Participation, and Democracy in America* (New York: Macmillan, 1993), pp. 228–248.

14. Whether print, broadcast or electronic, reporters and editors do have a say on what goes or does not go in print, on air or online. For a discussion on "gatekeeping," see Doris A. Graber, *Mass Media and American Politics,* 6th ed. (Washington, DC: CQ Press, 2002), pp. 99–117.

15. In their discussion of the policy analysis process, Walter C. Parker and William Zumeta emphasize the importance of "mapping the stakeholders," that is, doing a careful analysis of the competing interests and perspectives involved with a particular issue. Such analysis also considers the arenas in which the important decisions are likely to be made and where the different stakeholders will likely make their influence felt. See Parker and Zumeta's "Toward an Aristocracy of Everyone: Policy Study in the High School Curriculum," in *Theory and Research in Social Education* 27, no. 1 (1999): 9–44.

16. One reason that tolerance blooms in American democracy lies with widespread consensus over basic values. See Robert S. Erikson and Kent L. Tedin, *American Public Opinion,* 7th ed. (New York: Longman, 2006), pp. 153–155.

17. For further information on interviewing techniques, see Raymond Gorden, *Basic Interviewing Skills* (Itasca, IL: F.E. Peacock, 1992).

18. For a "user-friendly" guide to polling, see Celinda C. Lake with Pat Callbeck Harper, *Public Opinion Polling: A Handbook for Public Interest and Citizen Advocacy Groups* (Washington, DC: Island Press, 1987). To learn about formulating questions and interpreting results, see Herbert Asher, *Polling and the Public,* 7th ed. (Washington, DC: CQ Press, 2007).

19. Initiatives are used in California to address endless substantive public policy questions. See Larry N. Gerston and Terry Christensen, *California Politics and Government: A Practical Approach,* 9th ed. (Belmont, CA: Thomson, 2007), pp. 23–27. Also see Elizabeth R. Gerber, Arthur Lupia, Mathew D. McCubbins, and D. Roderick Kiewiet, *Stealing the Initiative: How State Government Responds to Direct Democracy* (Upper Saddle River, NJ: Prentice-Hall, 2001).

20. See Roger H. Davidson, Walter J. Oleszek, and Frances E. Lee, *Congress and Its Members,* 11th ed. (Washington, DC: CQ Press, 2008), p. 139.

21. For a discussion on the nature of political participation, see Oliver H. Woshinsky, *Culture and Politics: An Introduction to Mass and Elite Behavior* (Englewood Cliffs, NJ: Prentice-Hall, 1995), pp. 106–121.

3 DEVELOPING A PUBLIC POLICY PROPOSAL
Inventing the Better Lightbulb

Think back to when you were young—very young, like four or five years old. In those days, the only people you viewed as "public policymakers" were your parents or teachers. They were quintessential authority figures with undisputed power. Whatever the issue, you knew that these people would fix the problem; it seemed that they could do almost anything. Whether you were angry with someone for sending you to your room or upset because you did not get your share of school snacks, you knew that there was someone you could go to for help to make things right. In other words, you saw solutions taking place in a simple, "one-stop shopping" policymaking environment.

As we become adolescents, and later adults, sometimes our sense of the public policymaking environment remains almost as simplistic as it was during our childhood. The only difference lies with the person in charge of fixing the problem that bothers us. Instead of looking to our parents or teachers, we often turn—almost in desperation—toward the president, governor, mayor, or some other public official to make all things right.

Gasoline costs too much money? The president should make the oil companies charge less!

Unsafe streets? The governor should put away all the criminals!

Dirty drinking water? The mayor ought to make it safe!

Too much school violence? The school board should enforce proper behavior!

In actuality, different public issues require responses from different public policymakers—usually several sets of policymakers, in fact—depending upon the nature of those issues and who is empowered to do anything about them. Even more startling is that in many cases we can either have a role in the discussion of those issues or influence the policymakers who do make decisions. That simple reality serves as the basis for this chapter.

Everyone has the ability to influence change, but change occurs only through action. After you have researched an issue enough to be convinced that there is a public policy problem, some more research and some hard thinking are in order. Remember, public policymaking is essentially problem solving by someone in an authoritative position to get the job done. As such, policies are responses to defined needs and proposals to address those needs. Therefore, it helps to consider different potential solutions (or policy alternatives) to the problem and then settle on the one you believe is best. To do this, you need to examine an issue in all relevant aspects, which include the objectives you have in mind, alternative solutions, criteria for determining whether a particular alternative will achieve those objectives, and, finally, what you believe is the best policy approach. In short, you will be doing the same kinds of activities carried out by public officials, their staffs, and researchers: policy analysis.[1]

Connecting Issues with Public Policymakers

Many things in life are more complicated than they seem at first glance. A spider's web may initially appear as little more than an interesting geometric pattern; yet, upon closer examination, it is a mechanism for catching food, replete with a precise design and a sticky substance that keeps unsuspecting prey in place. A roller coaster at first appears to be little more than a series of curves and lifts for moving people swiftly through a predetermined traffic pattern; but after taking a few rides, we realize that every angle and curve is carefully designed to allow maximum speed without the train leaving the track. It's no different with the public policymaking process, which has more webs and traffic patterns than we can possibly imagine. But whereas the absence of knowledge about a spider web or roller coaster does not threaten our well-being, ignorance about the public policymaking process leaves us without the tools to affect our lives in major ways.[2]

The results of a recent national student test on the workings of government show that about one-third of the high school seniors in the United States do not understand the webs and traffic patterns of American government. They know little about constitutional guarantees and rights, and little about which issues are settled where. In the same study, less than one-tenth of the respondents were able to give two reasons why citizens need to be involved in a democratic society.[3] Among other things, these and other data suggest that students do not understand the relationship between public policymaking and democracy.[4] Part of the problem stems from the ignorance of who does what. If we can connect the issues with those who can do something about them, we not only begin to understand more about the process, but see where we fit in.[5]

Whatever the level of American government, all policymakers must make laws and rules in accordance with the U.S. Constitution. Other sets of rules such as state constitutions or city charters (local sets of governing regulations) may also come into play, but first and foremost, public policymakers do things by the broad guidelines prescribed in the U.S. Constitution. Sometimes, these decision makers may not be entirely sure of what they are permitted to do, so they flounder; on other occasions, they may make a law that replaces a previous one because they believe it was wrong. In either case, a primary function of the American court system, particularly the appellate courts, is to deal with challenges to the rules and regulations enacted by policymakers. This judicial exercise applies to the actions of all levels of government.

Assuming that you are concerned about (or assigned to learn) a particular topic or issue, you will need to get a handle on who makes which public policies. This is an important place to start because unless you know the areas of responsibility, it is hard to know where you can turn to be heard, should you wish to do so. These vertical relationships were outlined in chapter 1. Nevertheless, moving from the general to the specific can be difficult. So, what can you do and how can you do it?

Learning What Can Be Done by Whom

Virtually every public issue is connected with one or more levels of public policymaking authority. Whether you are concerned about nuclear waste or household garbage, there are public policymakers who can respond to your concern. Nevertheless, learning *who* can do *what* about a particular problem can be a difficult task. When delving into an issue, you may wish to work with others in a team effort, thereby sharing the load and bringing different perspectives and talents into your endeavor. It is also possible to get information on an individual basis. Either way, here are a few steps you can take to figure out how and where you can participate in the public policymaking process.

1. *Check the local newspaper or go online to see which public officials and well-known opinion leaders have spoken out on your issue.*

   If the issue of concern to you has been mentioned a lot by local leaders or public officials, in all probability it is because they are involved with efforts to deal with it. Even if it is discussed at other levels of government, chances are that leaders at the local level will have some experience with a major public policy problem. For example, national health insurance has captured quite a bit of attention from Congress lately, yet local governments bear much of the burden of paying the health care costs of indigents who use county hospitals.

Sometimes, policymakers at several levels of authority attempt to deal with the same issue when it includes more than one jurisdiction or authority. Staying with health care for the moment, the city of San Francisco moved forward with a mandatory employer-based health insurance program while state and national leaders struggled over a variety of approaches and potential solutions.[6] Another case in point: In recent years, leaders at the federal and state levels have not only struggled with environmental issues such as clean water or smog, but they have differed over which level of government should be in charge of solving such problems.[7] Similarly, policymakers at the state and local levels routinely debate over which level should bear the largest burden for maintaining transportation systems. Each, of course, would prefer funding from the other![8] Why should it matter? Answers such as funding sources, political control, and standards come to mind. On an issue that cuts across government jurisdictions, you may have to approach people at several levels until it is determined which policymaking authority will have the most significant role in solving the problem. You may even have an opinion on which level of government *should* be in charge; that can be as important as the issue itself. The point is that a local newspaper can direct you to the sources. This works for college issues as well, where reports in the campus newspaper may help you figure out whom to approach.

2. *Do research on which interest groups have taken positions on your issue.*

Interest groups often make public statements for or against issues of importance to their members. In the process, they not only provide information, but points of reference as well as connections with other groups that feel strongly about the same issue.[9] You do not have to be a member of a particular interest group or agree with it to learn its point of view. For example, you can learn how a neighborhood association feels about a local school bond election without living in the area. Likewise, you do not have to join the National

Rifle Association or the American Association of Retired Persons to learn how they feel about gun control or Social Security reform. The point is that interest groups provide information as well as their own interpretations of information.

By examining these sources, you can learn the underlying subtleties, uncover political allies, ascertain competing political values, and determine the sticking points to resolving the issue. Though the knowledge gleaned from interest groups should be augmented by other points of view, such information provides a valuable starting point for determining whom to talk to about an issue. An appendix in this book contains the Web sites of several prominent interest groups.

3. *See if you can find public policies that already have been made on your issue.*

Few issues are truly new or without any history; that is because most debates are over values or resources that are constant reservoirs of public dispute. Whatever your concern—homelessness, health care, pollution, equality—the likelihood is that it has attracted the attention of policymakers before. By finding out the level at which the issue has been handled in the past, you will have a good start on where to begin your own search for information. If you learn that nothing has been done about a controversial issue, it may be because there are elements about the issue you did not understand.

For example, suppose you want city leaders to restrict parking in a neighborhood to local residents because of traffic congestion. You may learn that the city council has done nothing about it because a church in the middle of the neighborhood needs that parking, leaving the council with concerns about First Amendment rights related to freedom of religion. With the collision of rights and needs, suddenly it becomes clear why no action has been taken, and a harder problem to solve.

Taking the time to learn about an issue's history is the first step in determining what can be done (and what cannot be done) about that issue. By engaging in this exercise, you begin to appreciate many points of view and the obstacles that may interfere with the attempt to make change. For instance, consider the neighborhood parking issue discussed above. Does the neighborhood have a right to "peace and quiet"? Yes, according to a series of Supreme Court decisions referring to the Fourteenth Amendment. Conversely, do people have the right to be part of religious activities? Absolutely, as proclaimed in the First Amendment. How do we attend to the needs of the many without trampling on the rights of the few? Sometimes, there is no answer. In other instances, there may be an answer, or compromise, which appears as a result of the airing of differences and needs. So, on the neighborhood traffic congestion issue, it may be that the best policy is one where parking is restricted during the week but allowed for certain hours on Sunday. Dilemmas such these emerge over and over again as we delve into issues that initially seem to be "no brainers."

Starting at the Bottom of the Ladder

As noted above, many of the thorniest public policy issues capture the attention of policymakers at several levels of government. Because of that, it is sometimes difficult to figure out a course of action or which public policy authority to approach. Consider something like changing the speed limit on a busy local street because of the many accidents that have occurred within a short period of time. It seems relatively simple to develop such a policy, until you learn that many jurisdictions are involved with the management of automobile traffic. Here is a list of the various levels of public policymaking authorities and some of their activities in this particular policy area:

National

- Congress and its creation of the interstate highway grid
- Driver safety programs developed and monitored by the Department of Transportation
- Rules created by the National Highway Traffic Safety Administration and Environmental Protection Agency (EPA)

State

- The state legislature that authorizes construction or maintenance of roads and speed laws
- Highway construction authorized by voters via initiatives and/or referenda
- Interpretation and enforcement of laws by state police or highway patrol officers

Local

- Local ballot measures passed by the voters to permit special taxes for transportation programs or a larger police force

- Ordinances ranging from speed limits to traffic lights enacted by elected county supervisors and city councils
- Interpretation and enforcement of state and local laws by local county sheriff deputies and police
- Administration of justice in traffic cases (finding of innocence or guilt) by local judges

Suddenly, decision making about a situation affecting almost everyone—automobile use on a particular stretch of road—has multiple sources of authority.

Another example might revolve around the proposal of temporary housing for homeless people during the winter at a local National Guard armory. Here, too, numerous levels of government and agencies come into play as we struggle to solve this problem, among them:

National
- The Department of Defense
- The Department of Health and Human Services
- The Department of Homeland Security
- Congressional actions on multiple uses of defense facilities
- Occupational Safety and Health Administration

State
- State adjutant general of the National Guard
- State Office of Homeland Security
- Governor's office
- Key state legislators whose districts include the proposed armory-turned-shelter

Local
- County board of supervisors or city council, depending on the armory's location
- County sheriff's office or city police department, depending upon jurisdiction
- Local health agency
- County child protection services agency
- Local public education authority
- Local zoning authority

Like the speed limit example, suddenly a seemingly straightforward matter of housing the homeless in an unused public facility is not so easy to address.

Still, you are left with the basic, yet compelling, question: Whom do I talk to about this problem?

A good place to start is the resource closest to you—your university or college. At these centers of knowledge, professors, researchers, administrators, and even fellow students may be experts in the issue you are trying to understand. If not, they may be able to point you in the right direction a lot sooner than you would learn otherwise. Nearby, you might find a religious or nonprofit organization that works closely with homeless people. These groups may add to your knowledge base.

Assuming that you want to discuss your issue with someone who can do something about it, it is usually wise to start at the bottom of the public policymaking ladder. The local level is less complicated and more accessible than the other levels of the public policymaking process. At the local level, you are physically near public policymakers; hence, you can make contact fairly easily. By approaching policymakers closest to home, you have the best opportunity of interacting with people directly who may know something about the issue and be able to do something about it. It is also helpful to seek out an elected official, because he or she has a special responsibility to constituents who have put him or her in a position to get things done. In part, the ability to get reelected depends upon citizens feeling good about the way elected officials respond to their needs. An elected official who fails to listen may be perceived by the voters as insensitive, and thus not worthy of reelection.

Direct contact provides potentially powerful linkage between the citizen and the public policymaker. For the citizen, contact connects the individual and issue with someone able to do something about that issue. For the policymaker, contact provides public input, or pressure, on something that he or she may not have known about, viewed as unimportant, or even opposed. Also, the informality that comes with contacting a local policymaker may allow you to learn things that you would not learn by asking questions of other policymakers who, while knowledgeable, may not feel compelled to talk with you.

A lot of this is common sense. If we go back to the traffic discussed earlier, it's a good first step to approach public officials who have some responsibility for managing the problem. After all, chances are that they already know something about it and, it is hoped, have some ideas about what can and cannot be done. If, by chance, the issue is new to the people you approach, they will probably want to look into it, especially if others feel as you do.

After talking with local officials, you may decide to attend a city planning commission meeting or city council session. In the process, you may get a sense of whether others have strong feelings about your issue, as described in our discussion of triggering mechanisms. Remember the triggering mechanisms criteria discussed in chapter 2:

- Are large numbers of people as concerned about the busy road as you are?
- How upset or worried are they about the speeding traffic issue?
- Has this issue been troubling your neighbors and you for a long time?
- How much will it cost to remedy the problem, and at whose expense? And what is it costing—in lives or other resources—not to fix it?

Starting out at the bottom of the public policymaking ladder is a "no-lose" situation. Even if it turns out that you eventually need to take "your case" somewhere else or to someone else, in all likelihood your contacts with local officials will open doors to those elsewhere who can do something about your issue. If you approach a city council member who says that you need to see Mr. X, the city planner, about your highway issue, the council member may offer to go with you or write a letter on your behalf. If your issue is more appropriate for state or national authorities, the city council member may offer to contact such people on your behalf. Either way, early contacts can be the first step to forging important alliances, and the informal vertical network among policymakers in the same areas can be instrumental in helping you find the right people.

By talking with local experts, you will also get a sense of history about the issue and begin to develop your own expertise. As you learn what local leaders have or have not done in the past, you will probably gain insight into the various sides of an issue that once seemed simple to resolve. Information is power, and by making a preliminary investigation, you will be able to use what you learn for your own efforts down the road.

Clarifying Objectives

If you have gathered enough initial information about your issue to move forward and want to take an active role in the management of that issue, you next need to think about approaching those who have the capability to respond. This is the point where you want to connect the issue with the appropriate public policymaking authorities.

But wait. Before you take that step, it may be wise to "touch base" with others who can help you with your effort. Why? Two reasons. First, by coordinating with those close to your issue, you have the opportunity to benefit from other insights and, perhaps, build alliances. Second, even if those who you consult disagree with your plan, you will have the advantage of knowing ahead of time the nature of their concerns. This, in turn, will enable you to make adjustments, and perhaps win them over to your point of view.

Why should you care about getting people on your side? Because the larger the group on one side of a particular issue, the more difficult it is for policymakers to turn away from considering the problem. Numbers do not necessarily guarantee the outcome of a proposal, but as we learned in our discussion of scope, they go a long way toward capturing the attention of policymakers.

Anywhere between one and four components may be included in your effort to consult others. They are: other students, your class instructor, your parents or other role models, and outside parties who may be interested in working with you in pursuit of the same objective.

Other Students

If you have been working on your public policy issue with other students, you do not want to move forward until everyone is ready. To do otherwise would make your efforts unnecessarily complicated and possibly undermine your objectives. Moving early might also jeopardize the teamwork, another factor that ultimately could interfere with your success.

Suppose that five of you are looking into whether your college should enact a public policy that forbids financial compensation to speakers from countries that deny basic human rights to their populations. Chances are that you have divided up responsibilities to get more research completed in a shorter amount of time. Perhaps one person has looked into the rules for bringing speakers to campus (in terms of jurisdiction and appropriate campus policymaking authorities); another has carried out research on previous campus government actions or precedents in the policy area at your school and elsewhere; someone else has looked into policies at other universities; and another has talked to student body officers, campus administrators, and local civil rights attorneys about the policy proposal. So far, so good.

But maybe the last person in the group was assigned to find out whether there was any opposition to the proposal on campus from other groups— perhaps groups from some of the countries in question—and he or she has yet to complete the research. These kinds of information gaps can cause serious problems down the road. To move forward without all of the possible knowledge could lead to a problem, especially, continuing with this hypothetical case, if it turns out that there is organized opposition to the change. If such information is known in advance of the influence effort, then you may decide to hold off, attempt to build an alliance with the group, or devise another strategy altogether.

Class Instructor

The instructor leading your class can be a valuable resource. Whether because of firsthand experience, academic knowledge, or both, this individual may well be a source of much needed information and contacts. Because of the nature of their work, instructors often have independently gathered data touching on pressing policy questions. Thus, as you get ready to move on your issue, it will be wise to consult with your instructor about your effort. It is one of your last opportunities prior to contacting public policymakers to ensure that the work you are doing is "on the money" in a variety of respects ranging from assumptions to direction to objectives.

Even if your instructor does not know specifically about your issue, he or she can guide you to important sources, assist with the organization of your effort and, sometimes, help you connect with others you need to meet. In addition, he or she may be able to tell you about some of the key decision makers as well as the process, or how the "system" works. Finally, your instructor can help you organize your project in terms of its relationship to the "big picture," the public policymaking process.

Family, Friends, and Acquaintances

It never hurts to get the advice of acquaintances and contacts we might otherwise be inclined to overlook—perhaps a work colleague, friend of your family, the parent of a classmate, perhaps even your own parents! It is possible, for example, that such individuals may have firsthand knowledge about your potential public policy issue. If you are trying to change a law and that family member or friend is a police officer, attorney, or social worker, there may be a valuable knowledge base worth tapping. If you are interested in a water pollution matter and you know a chemist, biologist, or engineer, you may have access to some pretty worthwhile information. If you are concerned with overcrowded prisons and you know someone who has "done time" or worked at a corrections facility, your access to that experience can be invaluable, helping you to learn information you would never find in any book. Acquaintances and personal contacts, then, can contribute to your general knowledge base.

Outside Parties

While researching your issue, you may consult with outside experts, people who have extensive knowledge about your issue area. Suppose that you are interested in the issue of protecting a reporter from revealing sources in a story he or she writes about a trial, a problem in court cases because such "shield" laws pit First Amendment "freedom of the press" rights against a defendant's Sixth Amendment right to a fair trial. In this instance, you may want to solicit opinions of the local journalists' organization about the issue, in addition to interviewing law enforcement personnel, judges, prosecutors, and someone from the public defender's office; maybe you will find experts at your college who have experience with your topic as well. Cumulatively, these individuals can provide a wealth of opinions and data.

Outside experts provide you with different perspectives that you may not always find on your own. If you have been concerned about something like the disappearance of dolphins in tuna nets, you may want to talk to environmental groups, animal rights groups, fishing association representatives, and even the people who make the nets. Whatever your topic, you will fare best if you cast your own "sizable net" to capture information from a wide variety of sources.

With your information in hand, you have the opportunity to assimilate all that you have learned. If you use many sources, chances are you will find contradictory information. That is not necessarily bad, because it shows the extent to which your issue may have many sides or different interpretations. Nevertheless, it is better to sort out the differences now rather than later. You will want to know the reasons for the contradictions as well, perhaps requiring further investigation. In the process, you may well discover that many sides have merit, thereby increasing both your sensitivity and knowledge. The result is that you will be further empowered to present your case before public policymakers and with a greater understanding of the many ramifications of your issue.

Inventing the Better Lightbulb

So now that you have thoroughly scouted the issue you are considering, researched its diverse aspects, and consulted with a variety of interested parties, in both government and the private sector—where do you go from here?

Don't be discouraged if all this research has left you more confused than you were at the outset, or if some of your initial assumptions now seem less certain. In fact, that's a good sign. If you have done your homework, your issue should seem more complicated than it did when you decided to jump in. Having had the opportunity to explore the issue in depth and to listen to people whose views on it may be very different from your own, you would be less than intellectually honest or curious if you did not feel a little bit unsettled at this point. "Don't confuse me with the facts" may seem like the best way out, but it leads us nowhere (and certainly gets in the way of our being effective citizens).

Here's a little perspective. The incandescent lightbulb has been a fixture of modern society since its invention by Thomas Edison in 1879. This light source shines as a result of an electric current heating a filament. That means the lightbulb uses energy, a commodity that has become increasingly scarce and expensive in recent years. Because of the need to use energy more efficiently, scientists have sought to improve upon the incandescent lightbulb. A breakthrough occurred in the 1990s with the invention of the compact fluorescent lightbulb (CFL), which uses 75–80 percent less energy than its predecessor and lasts years longer. The use of one CFL in each U.S. household would save enough energy to light up a city of 1.5 million people for an entire year.[10] So efficient is this energy breakthrough that Australia is phasing out all traditional lightbulbs beginning in 2010, followed by Canada in 2012. There you have it—a breakthrough in technology has led nations to alter their energy policies. So, what's a new lightbulb have to do with pursuing information about political issues? Sometimes, new knowledge has a way of acting as a catalyst for change.

Asking the Tough Questions

This is where some honest and hard thinking is in order. Before going ahead, you must ask some challenging questions. Is the matter concerning you really a public issue or problem, or does it fall into the realm of a personal problem or nuisance? If the former, is it something that government can and should address?[11] Could your issue be better dealt with in another way, such as individually or by the private sector? If this is a matter for public policy, what should that policy be? What specific objectives is that policy to achieve? Are there different alternative solutions that a new policy might take? What are they? What criteria should be used for determining the preferred outcome?

Which among the several alternatives is the one these criteria support more than others?

Why do you need to go through this analysis? Policy analysts, whether government officials and their staffs or scholars working at "think tanks," go through the process all the time in weighing the many aspects of a policy issue. For one thing, it is the only way to make sure one has properly understood the issue. For another, it helps to ensure that whatever policy you eventually decide to embrace will be credible—an important consideration when you get to the advocacy step (chapter 4).

Rarely does a policy issue call for one obvious and problem-free solution. In Hollywood movies with happy endings, perhaps, but not in the real world where no particular policy is perfect or best for everyone. The simple fact is that every plausible alternative carries with it both an "upside" and a "downside." That is because different "policy communities" are approaching the same issue from distinctly different points of view and, in all likelihood, with distinctly different objectives.[12] Accordingly, each alternative is connected to a series of variables—financial, legal and constitutional, political, and others—that, more often than not, diverge in terms of their priorities. Weighing the feasibility of each alternative involves a cost/benefit analysis, where the cost or price for any public policy commitment is measured against its anticipated benefits. The exercise helps to determine whether the policy alternative is worth all the effort.

Tobacco Regulation as an Example

Let's take these various steps of analysis in turn and use the issue of tobacco as an example. Assume for a moment that you view tobacco use as a serious public health problem, and that you want to do something about it. You believe that tobacco smoking is harmful to both individuals and to society as a whole, and that public policymakers should discourage tobacco use by the adoption of a new public policy. You have probably discovered as well that different people and interests—health care officials, tobacco farmers, tobacco companies and stockholders, libertarian activists, educators, lawyers and bar associations, insurance companies, and others—have different views on the matter. But what, precisely, is your objective? What do you want to have happen as a result of a change in public policy? More effective control of teenage smoking? Of prenatal smoking? Of smoking in public places? The rapid disappearance of smoking altogether? What are you after?

The answer to that question will go a long way in determining possible policy alternatives (as well as which level and agencies of government should be most directly involved with the effort). If you are interested in reducing tobacco consumption, should it be through legislative restrictions on purchasing or on advertising? Or should the policymaking authorities increase cigarette taxes as a means of discouraging purchases? Should you lobby the FDA to declare tobacco a "dangerous drug," or demand that the city council make all public facilities "smoke free"? What about more education on the health problems associated with smoking? Or should solutions look instead to the judicial branch through civil action against the producers of tobacco products?

Each of these proposed solutions suggests different areas and degrees of government responsibility. Any outright ban of tobacco or restrictions on tobacco advertising, for example, would likely get the federal government involved.[13] Lawsuits have thus far been primarily a state matter (though they could well end up in federal courts). Further restrictions on smoking in public places would probably involve local ordinances.

Each alternative, moreover, carries costs as well as benefits. An outright and immediate ban of cigarettes might seem warranted to you in terms of tobacco's health risk, but it would likely generate a firestorm of protest from many quarters—and not only the producers of tobacco but also the many companies involved with its distribution and sale, the millions of dependent smokers, civil libertarians eager to rally to their cause on philosophical or constitutional grounds, and perhaps even state officials who have come to rely on the revenues of tobacco taxes (perhaps even the beneficiaries of those additional revenues, such as public schools). What might seem politically feasible and legally permissible could prove to be impractical from an administrative or financial point of view.

Alternatively, what may be legal and financially feasible could be too politically explosive to work—the extent to which it addresses the values and concerns of one group of people may in proportion run against the grain of another group. The various aspects of the issue and the relative importance you attach to each of them in terms of reaching your objective will provide the criteria for determining an alternative. The weighing of policy alternatives is a little like riding a seesaw: when one side goes up, the other side goes down.

Finding the best policy—particularly in a democratic society with divergent claims and interests—is a little bit like trying to level the seesaw, that is, striking a balance. Sometimes there must be clear winners and losers, for instance, when the issue at hand involves a clash of fundamental principles (school integration might be one such example). Most public policies, however, are unavoidably the result of compromise and trade-offs.

Equally important, as you search for the best solution to the tobacco issue, it may be worthwhile to consider the public policy actors you will have the best chance of influencing. Outlawing tobacco altogether may take an act of Congress or new regulation by the FDA—both tough audiences to reach from a class project. On the other hand, getting your university president to establish a "smoke-free" environment on campus or the city council to enact an ordinance that declares smoking illegal at public parks may be much more within the realm of possibility.

A Checklist for Policy Analysis

Consider the following checklist as a set of questions associated with your need to get to the bottom of the issue:

- Viability—is it doable? Can anything realistically be done to address your concern? Can government do anything about it? If so, which level of government?
- Community benefit—What are you providing to the community with your policy initiative?
- Value proposition—What are your objectives? What, precisely, do you want to achieve? Are you proposing significant change or a modest alteration of the status quo?
- Options—what are the policy alternatives?
- Criteria—What factors will determine which of the policy alternatives is best for you?
- Anticipated consequences—What changes may occur as a result of your efforts? What are the trade-offs? The likely benefits and costs?
- Unforeseen consequences—Is it possible that the new policy or arrangement will create new problems even more challenging than the ones you are attempting to solve?
- Constitutionality—does the project fit within constitutional guidelines?

One last suggestion: your policy analysis can be helped by researching comparable situations elsewhere. Where have there been similar circumstances involving the same issue? What policy alternatives were considered in those cases? Why was one alternative selected and how did it work out?

By using these and other questions as an internal checklist, your instructor can help you analyze your efforts thus far and possibly avoid pitfalls that others have encountered.[14]

Doing a Reality Check

Acquiring information about and acting on a public policy issue can be an intimidating experience. But it does not have to be. By relying upon others for guidance and support, you can work your way through what John Kingdon calls the "policy window,"[15] or the process of pursuing your action step. Three valuable sources of support are faculty at your institution, other experts in the field, and your peers.

Scheduled Meetings with Your Instructor

Periodic meetings with your instructor will help you organize how you will deal with your public policy issue. By working with such an individual, you can get

- guidance on whom to approach in the earliest stages of information gathering;
- help with determining a schedule of activities;
- direction on where to go for source material;
- feedback on your strategies for engagement.

Your college faculty can be invaluable resources. Particularly if members have some awareness of or experience with your issue, they can advise you on many points ranging from early contacts to political pitfalls. On another level, they can help you stay "on task" and on schedule. Most significantly, they can help you understand your issue in the context of the "big picture," the public policymaking process. Do not hesitate to ask for help or guidance; being a resource is part of the reason that your professor is paid the big bucks!

Seeking an Expert in the Field

You can get close to the specifics of an issue through consulting someone who is close to that issue. His or her indirect involvement and knowledge may well help you get an "inside feel" much faster than if you were to begin research at "square one." So, if the policy question centers on downtown redevelopment, you might seek the assistance of a member of the local redevelopment agency, a prominent developer, or a local historian who is familiar with the area. If the policy question is about whether the city should permit smoking in restaurants, you might try to spend time in a nearby city that has such a policy or with interest groups who favor and oppose the proposal.

One way to learn about your issue is to ask someone already dealing with it for permission to "shadow," or follow him or her around, for an extended period of time.[16] Thus, if your issue was the question of racial profiling, where police may use race or ethnicity as the basis of stopping someone, you may want to ride with police and/or spend time in a community where this type of treatment is alleged to exist. By placing yourself close to the individual, you may gain an enhanced sensitivity to the nuances associated with your concern. Such effort does not replace the research necessary to become familiar with your concern, but it can add a level of reality you might not appreciate otherwise.

Working with Your Peers

Finally, working with peers, others in positions similar to yours, is another way to do a reality check of your take on a public policy issue. Sometimes, an individual can get so involved that he or she loses all objectivity about that issue as well as what can, or should, be done about it. Have you considered all of the possibilities? Is there an obvious alliance or information source that you have overlooked in your haste to find answers? Are the possibilities for change realistic? These are some of the questions that others can ask you (and you ask others) as you go through the effort to influence the public policymaking process.

To Influence or Not to Influence—That Is the Question

It goes without saying that the public policymaking process is most often dominated by those "in the know." Simply put, people close to the process understand it best. Nevertheless, the process is more porous than you might think, and usually open to new ideas and proposals. In some areas, especially those affecting budgets, policymaking moves incrementally and seems impervious to substantive change. Yet, in other areas, particularly those representing new challenges, the policymaking environment is open to new ideas and proposals. You might be surprised how many times ideas for a "better lightbulb" draw attention.

What you do about this opportunity is another story. You may or may not choose to participate in the influencing effort, but by developing the tools to acquire information, cultivate alliances, and determine the appropriate recipients of your ideas, you at least have the choice. What happens from there is up to you. While public policymakers may hold most of the power to make change, what you tell them may have some impact upon what they do.

Journal Writing

When you and the others in your group are working through a public policy issue, there will be much to remember. Sometimes, critical meetings, observations, or realizations are forgotten as you identify your policy area, scurry about to do research, consider alternatives, and reach conclusions on the best approaches to a proposal. Here is where journal writing is important. Keeping a journal will help you remember things you might otherwise forget— some of which may contribute to your overall understanding of your public policy journey. Observing a brief conversation between the mayor and a major contributor at the side of the room or watching the way police fail to enforce stop sign violations may not seem important at the time, but such events may prove valuable as you piece things together. If you account for what you see, experience, and feel every day you are on your public policy project, then you will have valuable information at the end of the process.

Case Study: Campus Security

Suppose that campus security has become a major issue at your institution. In recent months there have been several well-publicized incidents of robbery and assault involving students, both on campus and in the surrounding neighborhoods. The president's office is troubled by worried inquiries from parents. The admissions office is concerned with the possible effects of these well-publicized incidents on the institution's image and on its recruiting. Seeing themselves as especially vulnerable to campus crime, women's groups organized a "Take Back the Night" march that drew hundreds of participants and spectators.

All the while, various community constituencies have not been happy, either. In fact, they believe that your institution's population is as much a contributor to as a victim of the situation, thanks, in part to its congregated, relatively affluent, and sometimes careless population providing an attractive target for criminals. Many in the surrounding community also resent the way some students engage in illegal parking, rowdy acts, and other inappropriate behavior.

Whatever the respective culpabilities involved, your class has decided to do something about the problem: to look into it, determine its nature, and produce some alternative policy solutions. As policy problem solvers you would likely consider the following questions and tasks:

1. How would you go about "getting a handle" on the problem? What evidence would you seek out to measure its nature and extent? What sorts of data might you want to look at? What individuals and groups would you want to talk to?

2. What might your specific objectives be? What would you consider the precise goals of a successful policy to be?

3. Either individually or with fellow students, try to brainstorm at least three alternative policy solutions to the problem. Do they address the same specific goals or different ones?

4. What values and assumptions does each proposed solution embody? How is financial cost a factor? What competing interests and values are involved? What groups might favor each solution? What groups might oppose?

5. For each alternative solution, define the potential roles of the public sector and the private sector.

6. Are potential constitutional and jurisdictional issues involved? What might they be?

7. How would you go about deciding on one favored policy solution? What would be your criteria for selection?

8. Share your selection with your classmates. Do they favor different solutions? If so, why?

This exercise is particularly valuable if you are working with others in a class setting to identify an issue and pursue a public policy.

Reflection

You now know how to take part in the agenda-building process, with the ability to put forth issues for public policymakers to consider. This knowledge in itself is valuable. Still, important questions related to your role in the agenda-building process remain. To what extent do you want to participate in building the public agenda, and what would be the benefit of such involvement? What does such involvement mean to you as a member of the political system? Conversely, is it better to leave the contents—and outcomes—of the public agenda for others? The important fact to remember here is that the power is yours to move forward alone, with others, or stay on the sidelines. But just as the choices are yours, the consequences of your action or inaction are yours as well. It is just part of the responsibility we share as citizens in society.

Student Projects

Long-term group—Using the information you have gathered to understand your issue, prepare a plan of action. Whom will you work with to gain support (a) within your class and (b) in the outside community? What kind of alliances can help you to succeed? Specifically, how will you go about such an effort? Whom will you use for a reality check?

Short-term individual—Observe a city council discuss a particular issue and proposals for resolution. Try to talk with some council members and interested parties about the issue. Decide how you would resolve the issue. How does your plan match up with the ultimate decision?

Discussion Questions

1. What do you do if you try to put an issue on the public agenda and are unable to find anyone else to work with you? Do you pursue the matter anyway or drop it? If you decide to move forward, what alliances can you try to build, and how?
2. Suppose an expert expresses concerns about your project that you had not anticipated. How do you deal with the new information? What should you do?
3. During your research, what sources and experts proved most valuable in refining the information you learned for your project? How have you benefited?
4. How would you go about determining whether your issue is one that can be addressed by creation of a public policy?
5. What factors helped you to define your precise objectives? Feasibility? Personal values and priorities? Other considerations?
6. How did you go about determining various policy alternatives for your issue? Do they fairly represent the different aspects and perspectives involved with the issue?

7. Why did you select one policy proposal over others? What criteria determined your selection?

Notes

1. For a thorough treatment of this topic, see Robert A. Heinman, William T. Bluhm, Steven A. Peterson, and Edward K. Kearny, *The World of the Policy Analyst: Rationality, Values and Politics* (Chatham: NJ: Chatham House, 1990).

2. Richard Rose refers to policymaking as a "reflective" process that moves through time and space. See his *Lesson-Drawing in Public Policy* (Chatham, NJ: Chatham House, 1993).

3. "35% of High School Seniors Fail National Civic Test," *New York Times,* November 21, 1999, p. 1.

4. Several studies reach similar conclusions with respect to the political knowledge of American students and adults. According to a 1994 National Assessment of Educational Progress (NAEP) study, 57 percent of high school seniors do not have a "basic" knowledge of American history. The NAEP's 1998 study of civics education revealed that only 26 percent of twelfth-graders had at least a proficient understanding of the subject. Seventy percent fell below the desired standard and 35 percent lacked even a basic knowledge. The same report, however, noted that almost 60 percent of high school seniors had performed community service. See U.S. Department of Education, Office of Educational Research and Improvement, National Center for Education Statistics, *The NAEP 1998 Civics Report Card Highlights* (Washington, DC: NAEP, 1999). An eight-nation study of adults commissioned by the *Los Angeles Times* shows Americans knowing "less about current events than any of the nationalities polled." See "Trust in Media High, but Curbs Favored, Poll Finds," *Los Angeles Times,* March 16, 1994, pp. A-1, A-9.

5. Thomas A. Birkland refers to the connection between issues, people, and authoritative structures as the "policy domain." See his *After Disaster: Agenda Setting, Public Policy, and Focusing Events* (Washington, DC: Georgetown University Press, 1997), pp. 15–16.

6. For a summary of San Francisco's program, see "Universal Coverage Program Expands," *San Francisco Chronicle,* September 18, 2007, p. D2.

7. These issues are discussed in Jacqueline Vaughn Switzer with Gary Bryner, *Environmental Politics: Domestic and Global Dimensions,* 2nd ed. (New York: St. Martin's, 1998).

8. Martin Saiz and Susan Clarke, "Economic Development and Infrastructure Policy," in Virginia Gray and Russell L. Hanson, eds., *Politics in the American States,* 8th ed. (Washington, DC: CQ Press, 2004), pp. 430–436.

9. For an introduction to the various activities of interest groups, see Allan J. Cigler and Burdett A. Loomis, *Interest Group Politics,* 7th ed. (Washington, DC: CQ Press, 2007).

10. For information on the power of the CFL and its ability to change energy consumption patterns, see "How Much Savings Does it Take to Change One?" *Los Angeles Times,* February 24, 2007, pp. A1, A16.

11. As John W. Kingdon points out in his *Agendas, Alternatives, and Public Policies* (Boston: Little, Brown, 1984), there is a difference between a "condition" and a "problem." We put up with all sorts of undesirable conditions every day without perceiving them as problems to be solved. In a sense, a problem is a condition we have come to believe we should do something about. Of course, much of the debate in public policymaking centers on this distinction, with some people wanting a certain condition to become a problem, others believing that the condition is beyond practical solution or at least beyond the province of government action.

12. Ibid., pp. 128–137.

13. For a recent treatment on this issue from the viewpoint of regulation, see David A. Kessler, *A Question of Intent: A Great American Battle with a Deadly Industry* (New York: Public Affairs, 2001). For a look at tobacco as a long-standing public policy issue, see Cassandra Tate, *Cigarette Wars: The Triumph of the Little White Slaver* (New York: Oxford University Press, 2000).

14. For an interesting discussion of the policy analysis process and how it can be linked to classroom and community, see Parker and Zumeta, "Toward an Aristocracy of Everyone," (1999, Winter): 27 (1), especially pp. 25–30.

15. Kingdon, *Agendas, Alternatives, and Public Policies,* p. 173.

16. For approaches to observations of elected officials in action, see Richard A. Fenno Jr., *Watching Politicians: Essays on Participant Observation* (Berkeley, CA: IGS Press, 1990).

4 TAKING ACTION IN THE POLITICAL WORLD
How to Advocate a Public Policy

"Advocacy"—like so many words in the English language—has Latin origins. In this instance, the roots *ad* and *vocare* combine in a word meaning "to call to," or the idea of rallying people to a cause. The ancient Romans and Greeks viewed advocacy as an important responsibility of citizenship.

Advocacy also has an important role in modern settings. By calling for action, advocates place issues before policymakers. The struggle for civil rights by leaders such as Martin Luther King Jr., the defense of the right to bear arms by Charlton Heston, and the championing of migrant farm workers by César Chávez are all well-chronicled examples of advocacy. Less known but important forms of advocacy take place every day as well. Bicycle riders who disrupt automobile traffic in the name of safer riding conditions, animal rights activists who march in front of upscale department stores selling fur coats, and antiabortion activists who picket birth control clinics are also advocates. Advocacy is a vital part of the public policymaking process. Without it, many of the issues and problems requiring government action would never be noticed or acted upon.[1]

You become an advocate once you start trying to persuade others to take a course of action.[2] In the last chapter you learned about the process of creating a public policy for the issue you are considering. In this chapter, we will take up the next step in the policymaking journey: selling that policy proposal in the political arena. Unlike the research and analytical skills that were so important in investigating your issue and devising a solution, this next step will require you to focus on the skills of persuasion: using the best techniques and strategies for winning others to your cause.[3] As we shall see, some old-fashioned political savvy is also involved: the ability to survey and size up a political landscape, figure out who the key policy-change agents are, and identify potential allies and opponents.

Depending upon the outcome, advocacy may be a precursor to public policy. Regardless, it is a vital cornerstone of the representative democracy that connects the governors with the governed. As Russell Booker and Todd Schgaefer explain, "In order for political leaders to know what their constituents think, those constituents must let their leaders know."[4] Hence the value of advocacy.

Surveying the Policymaking Landscape

Now that you are ready to move forward with your issue, the question is— move where and with whom? Part of the answer to this question lies with the nature of your public policy issue and the public policymakers capable of dealing with it. For example, if you are interested in trade issues with China, it will serve little purpose to discuss the matter with your local city council member; such foreign policy issues are decided at the national level. However, if you are concerned about setting up a "free speech" area at your college, then you need to think about targeting appropriate college officials as the policymakers who can respond to your need; in such an instance, the president or Congress would be of no value. Likewise, if you have questions about establishing a safe haven for runaway teenagers, you will need to think about speaking with the mayor or city council members because state or national agencies will have little or no responsibility for solving local homelessness and runaway problems.

You already know that the public agenda consists of an ever-changing group of issues in various stages of resolution; these issues usually come to be as a consequence of triggering mechanisms. You also know that public agendas exist at any level of governance where people in positions of authority have the power to make decisions and see them carried out. Yet the questions remain— who places these issues before public policymakers? How does it happen? The answers to both questions lie with *agenda builders,* individuals or organizations with the capability of capturing the attention of public policy makers.[5]

Altogether, there are seven categories of agenda builders: public officials, the mass media, the World Wide Web, interest groups, political parties, the bureaucracy, and individual citizens like yourself. Agenda builders may work alone or in combination to place issues on the public agenda. Either way, they are the critical links between emergent issues and the public policymakers who can respond to those issues.

Public Officials

Public officials are among the most obvious and powerful agents of the agenda-building process. That is because as public policymakers, they are often in the unique position to place issues on the public agenda *and* do something about it in the midst of a chaotic political environment and competitive process.[6] Thus, if a public official assumes responsibility for bringing an issue to the attention of fellow policymakers, he or she is better positioned than anyone else who has to search for someone in authority to actually get something done. The power that comes from this connection cannot be duplicated anywhere in the policymaking process.

Public officials are found at all three levels of the agenda-building (and policymaking) process. Almost all are elected, with judges being the major exception at the national level and in some states.

National Government

The national government deals with the "big ticket" issues. Questions like defense and foreign policy are solely within the jurisdiction of the national government; indeed, this was clearly pointed out in 1787 when the framers wrote the Constitution. Some domestic areas such as the regulation of interstate commerce, postal service, and promotion of the "general welfare" are also clearly within the purview of the national government, although all levels of public policymaking address this broad issue in one way or another.

Basic Organization. Over time, public policymakers at the national level have assumed public policymaking roles that were not originally articulated as national responsibilities in the Constitution. Social Security, support for research and development, and environmental protection are three major areas that come to mind, although many others exist. As a means for these areas to be financed, Congress and the states established the income tax by enacting the Sixteenth Amendment to the Constitution. In other instances, the president sometimes assumes responsibility for policymaking either by proposals to Congress or, more directly, through use of tools such as the executive order.[7] Other areas such as the protection of civil liberties, food and drug safety, patent infringement, and regulation of the economy have all come under the jurisdiction of the national government.

The roles of these institutions often evolve. One area of change has occurred with the president's use of the "signing statement," a message that accompanies his signature to a bill passed by Congress in which the president indicates how the legislation will be carried out. Historically, presidents used signing statements to instruct bureaucrats about implementation. President George W. Bush, however, often used signing statements to disregard the new laws if, in his view, they infringed upon executive authority. During his presidency, Bush issued more than 750 such statements, a number significantly larger than those written by Ronald Reagan (71), George H.W. Bush (146), and Bill Clinton (105) during their presidencies.[8]

When we think of the national government, the presidency, Congress, and court system jump out in our minds as public policymaking institutions—and they are. But countless other agencies have been created by these public policymakers as well. The fifteen cabinet departments have resulted from joint presidential and congressional efforts. Many agencies such as the Central Intelligence Agency (CIA) or Social Security Administration also are the results of the same traditional public policymaking machinery, while others, such as the Environmental Protection Agency (EPA), emerged as a response to an executive order, a capability residing exclusively with the president. Simply put, the national government is a fairly complicated entity.

Access Points. Although large in size and extensive in organization, the national government has many points of entry for the individual or group seeking to influence the policymaking process. The access point most commonly used by people is Congress, where members of the House of Representatives or Senate introduce bills that they hope will be enacted into law. If majorities in both houses vote approval, they send the bill to the president for his signature, after which the legislation becomes law.[9] (Of course, if the president says "no" via his use of the veto, the bill dies, unless Congress manages to overturn the president's veto by obtaining two-thirds approval in both houses.) In addition to their public policymaker roles, the members of Congress (or their legislative assistants) reply to citizen inquiries either by proposing action or by referring them to appropriate arenas of authority. The latter is much more often the case than the former.

For example, if you object to the elimination of "old growth" redwoods in a nearby forest, you might ask a member of Congress to "do something" about it. The member might write back that he or she was proposing a bill to make the area a national forest, or the member might refer you to other individuals or organizations who feel as you do. The member might also provide you with a list of other bills he or she had proposed in the past or information from a government agency such as the Office of the Management of the Budget or the Department of the Interior. Government, particularly the national government, is huge, but congressional representatives can go far in helping you hook up with those who have responsibility in various policy arenas. In this very real way, you can be connected with the public policymaking process.

State Governments

In many respects, states are the workhorses of the public policymaking process.[10] Collectively, their budgets do not get nearly the amount of money collected and spent by the federal government, and they are spared responsibility for foreign policy matters. However, states have jurisdiction for a variety of activities and services, varying portions of which are assigned to local governments. Many more laws, court decisions, and administrative activities take place within the fifty states than at the national government level.

Basic Organization. States mirror the national government in their general organization; each has an executive, legislative, and judicial branch. But beyond these general comparisons, there is no single template that accounts for the specifics of the public policymaking within the states. For example, although most education issues fall under state authority, the heads of education departments are elected in some states and appointed in others. Moreover, great variations exist in what state education departments are permitted to do. In some states, they establish statewide standards for textbooks or high school graduation requirements; in others, they have no universal standards, leaving these and other decisions up to local school boards.

In addition to education, states are the major public policymaking authorities for prisons, highways (other than interstates, which are federal/ state projects), water systems, welfare, parks, agriculture, and wildlife preservation. In some cases, such as environmental protection or water quality, their public policies work in concert with nationally established minimums. In other cases, such as parks or state highway systems, states put together programs or services.

Because states are smaller units of government, they are often likely to be innovative in their policies, sometimes setting the stage for discussions. For example, during the 1990s and early twenty-first century, several states enacted restrictive abortion policies, followed by favorable U.S. Supreme Court interpretations. Likewise, while the federal government vacillated over the wisdom of funding stem cell research, California and other states moved forward aggressively in the research area.[11] Perhaps this is why one observer describes states as "laboratories of democracy" in the public policymaking process.[12]

Added to this maze are the different ways in which the states finance their efforts. Whereas the national government relies upon income and corporate taxes for most of its revenues, states cobble together different combinations.

Some have personal income and property taxes, but no sales taxes (such as New Hampshire); others have property and sales taxes, but no income taxes (such as Florida). Still others have all three (such as California). These different combinations help to establish each state as its own unique public policymaking environment.

Access Points. Each state has its own constitution, which, along with the U.S. Constitution and municipal charters, provides the framework for governance and policymaking within its borders. In fact, all of the state constitutions are more specific than the U.S. Constitution in spelling out fundamental principles such as the separation of powers and numerous civil liberties, concepts on which this country was founded.

Given the differing organizational patterns of the states, it is often difficult to know the individuals and institutions with responsibilities for various public policy areas; unlike the single national government, there is no road map. Thus, the advice for influencing the public policymaking process here is even more important than at the national level: start with a local legislator who, whether because of expertise or position as your elected representative, will be in position to recommend whom you should see and how you should go about making your case. You also may want to consult the governor's Web site as a way of learning about the agency or policymaking body that may have responsibility for managing your particular issue. Even interest groups can help you determine the appropriate body to approach on a public policy issue, especially since many have lobbyists well connected with events at the state capitol.

Once you know the best way to contact a public policy official or agency, you may wish to capture his or her attention by taking one of several steps. Writing a letter or sending a message via e-mail is an easy way to present your issue to public policymakers. Beyond that, you might join with others to testify before the appropriate committee, or demonstrate in front of a state building as a means of getting attention from policymakers as well as members of the press. You also may decide to coordinate your effort with the activity of a major interest group with objectives similar to yours, building alliances and collective strength in the process.

Given that most people live much closer to their state capital than to the nation's capital, it is relatively easy to "make your case" before public policymakers. One way is to travel to their offices at the capitol, where you might participate in legislative hearings dealing with issues important to you or discuss issues with a legislative staff member. By spending a day at the capitol before public policymakers, you can be heard and feel effective. For their part, most of the time, state leaders appreciate that you take the effort to tell them what you think. In fact, most have staff members available in local district offices, where you might find it easier to go. Either way, citizen contact helps legislators make decisions.

If you are seeking information on how your issue has been handled elsewhere, national organizations may help provide perspective. The National Conference of State Legislators and National Governors Association are two such organizations that come to mind. These, along with interest groups, political parties, and public interest groups, can provide you with information to pursue your issue with strength and conviction.

At the state level, governors and legislators stand out as agenda-building public officials. When the governor delivers the annual state budget to the legislature, he or she is putting countless issues on the public agenda, ranging from more money for education to new laws dealing with juvenile crime. Judges also sometimes place issues on the public agenda by virtue of their decisions that declare a state law unconstitutional. For example, if a state supreme court overturns a series of convictions because of a poorly written law, the decision of the justices may actually put the issue (in this case, a questionable law) onto the public agenda.

Local Governments

No level of the public policymaking process is closer to citizens than local government. Whether in the form of county boards of supervisors, city councils and mayors, school boards, special districts, or schools, local governments provide a "proximity" factor unlike any other level.[13] Because they are so close to us, local governments provide the easiest entry for individuals into the workings of politics and policy. And because we often feel so close to local government policymakers, we sometimes fail to see the extent to which some groups or interests succeed in the public policymaking process much more than others. It is likely that the project on which you are working will involve you more with local officials than with any other level of government.

Basic Organization. The best-known forms of local governments are county boards of supervisors (sometimes called "commissioners"), which serve both legislative and executive branch functions and city council/mayor arrangements, which may either share or divide legislative and executive responsibilities. Typically, these units of governments have administrative structures, led by city managers or county executives, who serve at the pleasure of the elected officials. Whether at the county or city level, local governments serve as appendages, or creations, of state governments. As such, they carry out responsibilities assigned to them by the state. Commonly, these include public policy areas such as education systems, zoning, and local traffic enforcement.

In addition to county and city public policymaking entities, there are more than eighty-five thousand local government jurisdictions, almost all of which have elected officials. Water districts, sewage districts, lighting districts, and, of course, school districts are some of the best-known examples of these specialized governments. Like cities and counties, these public policymaking institutions also have bureaucrats, mostly civil servants, who carry out various administrative tasks. Those elected to make policy in these special districts have responsibility for very narrow slices of the public policymaking arena.

Access Points. Unlike national or state units, local governments are truly in our backyards. Moreover, because they are confined to small areas and populations, we often know people who are elected to serve or selected to work in these institutions. They are our neighbors, people we went to school with, or individuals with whom we have had some contact. All of these elements fall into the "proximity" factor we discussed above, suggesting a relatively easy path to public policymakers. Want to see the mayor? Call his or her office and make an appointment. Want to have your say with the city council? Go to a city council meeting and ask the clerk to include you and your issue on the council agenda. It is that easy.[14]

Nevertheless, even dealing with local government can present certain challenges. The hardest thing to learn is where to go and whom to see. The best place to start is at the offices of the city manager or county executive. Because these are the chief administrative agencies of each elected local government entity, the staff there probably will know the public policymaker or office that should first respond to your issue. Another way to get some answers would be by seeing a city council member or county supervisor. Upon presenting him or her with your concern, this individual should be in a good position to either handle it or tell you any difficulties associated with resolving the issue. Sometimes a staff assistant to these individuals can be just as, if not more, helpful in providing information.

Although every city has its unique politics and public policy issues, you might be surprised at the number of common themes. One way to get a comparative handle on your issue would be to contact national organizations such as the U.S. Conference of Mayors or the National Association of Counties. As with their state counterparts, these associations have a lot of comparative information available.

Sometimes a public policymaker will allow you to "shadow" him or her for a day or so, an intense activity in which you follow the leader around from one meeting and event to another. Shadowing gives you great insight into the many aspects of the work of the policymaker. Not only do you have the opportunity to see the many sides to an issue that might be blurred if viewed from a distance, but you also have the ability to ask questions firsthand. At the end of the shadowing activity, you may well be much better prepared to pursue your public policy issue. Although shadowing can take place at any level of the public policy process, it is easiest to work out with local officials because they are nearby.

The most prominent local public officials with agenda-building capabilities are mayors, city council members, and county supervisors, although elected officials in special districts such as water districts or school districts also may exert leverage on issues relating to their areas of governance. Mayors and city council members put issues on the public agenda by calling for action by their peers on such matters as speed limits, zoning, and greenbelts. Or maybe a county supervisor will plead with his or her peers to raise fees at county parks with the proposal that the new revenues be used for better maintenance. Even college administrators can place issues on the public agenda with complaints about matters such as low funding, irresponsible fraternity behavior, or poor student preparedness.

The examples above show the "dual role" of public policymakers. They have the ability to place issues on the public agenda *and* act on it in their respective areas of jurisdiction. No other agenda builder has as much leverage in the public policymaking process, rendering public policymakers as unique participants in the mix. And because of this "dual role," no other agenda-building agent captures as much public attention from the media or the public.

Mass Media

The media, both print and electronic, have long been known as public agenda builders. When a story appears on television or in the newspaper, it often becomes an attention grabber because it is "news." People who might not have known previously about the issue described in the story suddenly become aware, and with that awareness, they may want to see change. For public policymakers, the media act as a microphone. By amplifying what otherwise might not be heard, the mass media force policymakers to focus on issues that they might otherwise just as soon avoid.[15]

Whether it is a national newspaper like the *New York Times* or a local television station, the media have the ability to bring substantial amounts of new information to large audiences. Sometimes the news can have national, or even international, implications such as in 2000 when President Clinton announced new scientific ability to map the entire genetic makeup of human beings, raising public policy issues from disease eradication to specialized human reproduction. The implications of this discovery were discussed at length on television and in the print media, and millions of people suddenly became aware of new challenges and opportunities. Just as often, the news may have powerful local consequences, such as the toxic waste at New York's Love Canal or the discovery of large numbers of illegal immigrants held against their will in makeshift, filthy garment factories, both of which were discussed initially by local media.

Occasionally, members of the media inadvertently create an issue on the public agenda for reasons unrelated to the story they report, especially if they rely upon a source who has given information with the explicit promise of "confidentiality." Political columnist Robert Novak set off a firestorm in 2003 when he exposed the name of a secret CIA agent as the result of a "leak" by someone in the White House. Novak's column was about issues related to an investigation into the unfounded charge that former Iraq dictator Saddam Hussein had access to nuclear materials, a cornerstone of the reasoning by President George W. Bush for attacking Iraq in March 2003. But his revelation spawned a series of issues ranging from the First Amendment right of the press to national security. Ultimately, I. Lewis (Scooter) Libby, chief of staff to Vice President Dick Cheney, was convicted of perjury, further eroding the already battered reputation of President Bush and his pursuit of the Iraq war.[16]

Some of the most interesting information provided by media is found in small communities. News such as a flawed public parking structure, a college cheating ring, homeless families, a polluted water supply, or a school built upon a toxic landfill can jolt a local population into demanding action from public policymakers, especially if there is the potential for harm. The local nature of such information is often more compelling than the big national stories because such stories are about the people we know.

The World Wide Web

In a sense, the Internet has created another class of mass media institutions, but those in which the traditional distinction between the provider and consumer of information has been blurred, if not erased. Anyone can become part of this mass media by establishing his or her own Web site, making this information center extremely accessible. During the 2000 election, some presidential candidates first turned to the World Wide Web as a site for both information dissemination and fund-raising. By the 2008 election, virtually all candidates used the Internet for Web sites, networking, blogging, and sizable portions of their fund-raising efforts. CNN and YouTube, a popular video-sharing Web site, actually teamed up to conduct presidential debates.

As both a medium and a host, the Internet has become in scarcely a decade a powerful tool of advocacy and a valuable ally of the "grassroots politics" that characterize so much of our agenda building today.[17] By overcoming the traditional barriers of time and space, the Web has nationalized (indeed, "internationalized") civic life and facilitated coalition building within and across communities.

Nevertheless, there is a potentially haunting element to the Internet. Unlike traditional media sources that identify authors, editors, and publishers, people who place "information" online can hide behind anonymity or deceit. During the 2008 presidential election, for example, a Web site called "Californians for Obama" purported to be a fund-raising group for Democratic presidential candidate Barack Obama. Yet, an investigation revealed that no one from the Obama campaign sanctioned the organization. Further, almost all of the money collected went to the "executive director" of the online group.[18]

Moral of the story: The World Wide Web can be a valuable source of information. Should you choose to use this media source, however, you must be aware of its limits as well as its benefits.

Interest Groups

In many cases, *interest groups* bring issues to the attention of public policymakers. These organizations of individuals with similar values or needs exist for the benefit of their members. Typically, interest groups express the views of their organizations as a way of protecting and promoting the concerns of their members. Nevertheless, their positions or concerns can also have an impact upon the public good. Therefore, interest groups can be powerful instruments for convincing policymakers to put issues on the public agenda.

Interest groups vary by objectives and constituencies, or the people they represent. Some, such as the American Bankers Association or Association of Trial Lawyers of America, have narrow objectives for their members. Others, such as the AFL–CIO or the National Organization of Women (NOW), have a broad agenda for a diverse membership.

When we think of interest groups, sometimes we focus only upon well-known organizations such as the American Association of Retired Persons (AARP), the National Rifle Association (NRA), or the International Brotherhood of Teamsters (Teamsters Union).[19] In each case, these and other large groups have huge staffs and budgets to make themselves heard; they also often make sizable campaign contributions to politicians who are sympathetic to their values. Even groups like Mothers Against Drunk Driving (MADD) and the National Abortion Rights Action League (NARAL) are large national forces, although their budgets are relatively small.

Interest groups at the local and state levels can also be powerful forces in placing issues on local and state government agendas. They vary in size as well as celebrity, but they number in the thousands. Here is a partial list of some categories:

- student body organizations
- children's rights advocacy groups
- carpenters unions
- local open space groups
- prayer groups
- scouting organizations
- realtor associations
- taxpayer groups
- county medical associations
- fraternities and sororities
- tenants organizations

These are among the countless examples of interest groups whose members attempt to influence local and state public policy. As with local media, these groups are close to home. Chances are that you know someone who belongs to an interest group, or you may belong to one yourself, even though you may have not thought of that particular body as an "interest" group. But the fact is if an organization seeks to affect the public policymaking process, then the likelihood is that it is an interest group.

Sometimes, interest groups refocus national issues at local levels of application. A recent New Hampshire case of gay high school student organizations demanding access to school facilities for their events represents a case in point. Relying upon the Equal Access Law passed by Congress in 1984 and upheld by the U.S. Supreme Court in 1990, these groups argued before the local school board that the same law allowing religious groups to meet in school facilities applied to them as well. The school board agreed.[20]

Sometimes, controversial interest groups use freedom of speech protection to offer values and ideas considered offensive by most people. Near St. Louis, Missouri, for example, lies a stretch of public highway that has been "adopted" by the Knights of the Ku Klux Klan, with a large sign placed along the highway announcing that organization's sponsorship. In the process of promoting the public good, the Klan, a self-described white supremacy organization, has put its message in a very public setting.

On other occasions, interest groups insert themselves into the public policymaking process. In Jackson, Wyoming, an organization known as Keep Yellowstone Nuclear Free sued the U.S. government to prevent construction of a nuclear incinerator ninety miles upwind from Yellowstone National Park. In Minnesota, a pro-business group known as the Fair Information Practices coalition successfully lobbied the state legislature to kill a bill that would have prevented companies from selling financial data and credit card information about their customers. In these and thousands of other cases, interest groups—some already organized, others newly organized—have taken their cases to public policymakers. Regardless of the outcomes, these groups carry out important tasks by raising the consciousness of policymakers.

In addition to gathering their members in public places and writing letters or sending e-mail, interest groups use their financial power to gain the attention of policymakers. In some instances, interest groups contribute to the election campaigns of candidates friendly to their issues; in other instances, interest groups may hold fund-raiser events for candidates or elected officials. These efforts often lead to close relationships between public policymakers and interest groups, leading some people to speculate about the independence of officials who take interest group money. Conversely, there are so many interest groups involved in the effort to lobby policymakers that it is usually hard for any one or two to have much influence.

Political Parties

Do not forget about political parties, which classically differ from the interest group in that their primary purpose is to gain public office rather than merely influence those who serve in public office. In this era of the independent voter, party organizations may not be as powerful or inclusive as they once were, but they still play a very important role in political life and, indeed, in building the public agenda at the local, state, and national levels. In fact, though we tend to think of the Democrats and Republicans as national entities, both major parties are really confederations of state and local organizations. Typically, they are joined by minor parties, which are often narrow in their issue orientation and without enough support—either in terms of voter appeal or financing—to win elections.

Political parties can have clout. If the party leadership is persuaded that your issue is consistent with its own agenda and that supporting the issue may further its objectives, the local or state party can be a powerful ally. Leaders may insert statements of support into the party platform, a long statement of legislative objectives; or some may take your ideas and propose them to legislators for consideration. In addition, the political party as a body of influence can help you by providing organizational and publicity resources—as well as its many contacts in government and the community.

Considerable disagreement exists today over the extent to which political parties remain vibrant as agenda builders. Some observers argue that diminishing voter loyalty and the growing strength of interest groups have helped to weaken parties as organizing agents of power. Others maintain that political parties remain critical depositories of partisan values.[21] Regardless of whether their influencing abilities have changed, political parties continue as organizations capable of placing issues on the public agenda.

Bureaucracy

We tend to view "the *bureaucracy*" as any unit of government with large numbers of people carrying out repetitive tasks in massive, faceless buildings. In some cases, bureaucrats do perform clerical functions and little else. But in other cases, they are not only deeply connected with the implementation of public policies, but also assigned by other public policymakers the responsibility for clarifying rules and regulations.[22] Even more frequently, bureaucrats are expected to provide expertise in their particular policy areas for those elected to make public policy. With their power to interpret the management of policies, bureaucrats are often public policy brokers. As such, they often contribute to the placement of issues on the public agenda.

Bureaucrats come in all shapes and sizes. Soil engineers who work for the U.S. EPA are bureaucrats. Upon learning from a test that a particular area is saturated with toxic chemicals, they may recommend that the area be closed off to inhabitation; upon receiving such a report, the EPA director may request authorization from Congress to move people out. He or she may also recommend to Congress standards for determining toxicity in other locations.[23]

State civil engineers are bureaucrats. If several should determine from a state-authorized study that too many bridges show signs of metal fatigue or stress, they may recommend to the governor or legislature special legislation authorizing repairs. Thus, the input from their expertise is valuable, particularly in terms of the potential to save lives.

City planners are bureaucrats. If a study they conduct indicates a need to set aside city land for construction of a homeless shelter, they may recommend a rezoning plan to the mayor and city council. Likewise, if planners determine that a local transportation system is inefficient, they may request local elected officials to make the necessary policy changes.

College faculty are bureaucrats. Routinely, they help to frame and carry out university or college policies ranging from academic instruction to student evaluations. Professors also act as agenda builders in their departments as well as in campuswide organizations. They may ask administrators to develop new course requirements or rules for graduating with department honors. Operating in the environment of academic freedom, they may speak out on controversial issues such as self-determination, discrimination, or other civil rights issues, attempting to persuade those in positions of authority to transform such pressure into new public policies.

Sometimes, it is hard to see the extent that bureaucrats affect our lives; in fact, they are in more places than you might think. The public school teacher seeking to implement new state or district curriculum requirements, the police officer attempting to comply with new guidelines against racial profiling, and the social services administrator adjusting to changes in federal or state welfare budgets are all bureaucrats. In their capacities to make the rules work, they all enjoy a large measure of flexibility and discretion in applying and interpreting public policies.[24]

Citizens as Individuals and in Small Groups

The ability to influence the public policymaking process extends all the way to the "ordinary" citizen, civically engaged as an individual or in collaboration with other equally "ordinary" citizens. Such a thought is difficult for some people to accept. Because individuals seem such a small part of the public policymaking environment, it is difficult to imagine that individual voices would ever be heard. Yet, it happens all the time. And when such a person connects with those who can get things done, his or her once quiet voice may suddenly become very loud.

When Rosa Parks, an African-American woman, refused to sit at the back of a bus in 1955, she not only expressed opposition to local segregation policies, but her actions influenced the public and public policymakers who made those policies. Soon others, acting as individuals or in small groups, carried out similar acts of defiance at diners, hotels, and other public venues. Cumulatively, these actions helped to change public perceptions and awaken the nation's public policymakers on the question of civil rights.[25]

Other examples are poignant in their own right. In 1991, a fourteen-year-old by the name of Ryan White testified before Congress about how he contracted AIDS through a blood transfusion. Until then, many had erroneously believed AIDS to be a disease restricted to adults who engaged in homosexual behavior. Ryan White's testimony showed the extent to which AIDS can impact anyone. After his remarks, Congress enacted legislation extending help to children with AIDS, putting aside for the moment the issues—and judgments—relating to homosexuality. Today several colleges and universities have programs that train students how to help individuals with AIDS qualify for government programs, find work, and obtain medical care.

Recently in California, a single individual sued the state because of a "smog impact fee" that was attached to cars coming to California from other states. He argued that the fee was arbitrary and discriminatory, and that people who brought cars into California from out of state were unjustly penalized. Ultimately, the state courts agreed, leading to a refund of $767 million for the owners of 1.6 million vehicles.

And ponder this: Over a fourteen-month period in 1999 and 2000, a ninety-year-old great-grandmother known as "Granny D" walked 3,200 miles from the West Coast to Washington, DC, to publicize the need for publicly financed election campaigns. She had neither a budget nor an organization behind her, yet with her arrival at the nation's capital on February 29, 2000, she brought massive public attention to her cause. No newcomer to activism, Granny D had previously fought to prevent the construction of a canal in Alaska and a highway in New Hampshire.

You may ask, what can I or my classmates accomplish by seeking to influence the public policymaking process? You never know. It might well be more than you imagine. Look at the impact that other young adults had on the nation's life in the 1960s, on issues ranging from the Vietnam War and civil rights to reforms in higher education. College students are continuing to demonstrate their empowerment through a variety of service learning and other initiatives at institutions across the country.

In recent years, students have served as effective policy advocates, helping to keep a host of issues on the local, state, and national policy agendas. They have participated in everything from sweatshop exploitation to environmental cleanup. Students at Pace University in New York State took a leading role in the passage of their state's Hudson River Marine Sanitation Act. Students at the University of Colorado at Denver have worked effectively in advocacy campaigns such as dezoning and fair housing initiatives, union organizing, and the reform of law enforcement practices. Student activism has provided an essential catalyst for many of the recent community outreach initiatives of the nation's colleges and universities.[26]

Sometimes, even young students can make a difference in the political process. The investigation of low-voter turnout by a middle-school class in Walnut Grove, California, brought about changes in voter registration procedures in both their county and state. A class of middle-school students in Michigan investigating concerns related to sexual harassment produced a set of policy guidelines that were subsequently adopted by their school district.[27]

The bottom line here is this: individuals, acting alone or with others, can be powerful forces in influencing the content of the public agenda and the policymaking process. The manner and degree of an individual's influence depends, in part, on that person's view of citizenship and civic responsibility.

As discussed in chapter 1, Americans have held very different views of what the "model citizen" ought to be. The nature of civic engagement will vary according to one's view. At one extreme, perhaps, are those who are fully disengaged from public process, including the completely alienated who have chosen to "opt out" of the system. That is their right. Such individuals have a minimal sense of *civic identity* and obligation. At the other extreme are those who are so involved with the policymaking process that they may even engage in *civil disobedience* if necessary. And that is *their* right. Most of us, however, are somewhere in the middle. When motivated by a particular concern or issue, we tend to interact with government in more conventional ways, which range from the writing of a letter to our representative in Congress to active involvement in the policymaking process. In this book, of course, we have been focusing on this last course of action.

But how do you fit in? Easier than you might believe. Think for a minute about public policymakers as agenda builders. Sure, they operate with a set of ideas and values, but many of them move on issues when they hear from constituents. So, by making an appointment with a local official or staff member to discuss your issue, you can have a role in help-ing the policymaker to put an issue on the public agenda. With respect to the mass media, something as simple as writing a letter to the newspaper editor can give visibility to your issue that it would not have otherwise. In the case of interest-group activity, a good first step is to take stock of the groups to which you already belong to see whether you should become more active with others in moving an issue to the attention of those who can do something about it. Even the bureaucracy is not without ability to hear your issues, although bureaucrats are often more likely to report your concerns to those with more direct public policymaking responsibilities. The simple but important point is that the political system is incredibly open to people making their case.

Agenda Building in Perspective

In a representative democracy, agenda building is a critical link to the public policymaking process. By serving as conduits between public issues and policymakers, agenda builders perform the important task of providing deci-sion makers with valuable information. By absorbing such information, public policymakers acknowledge the interests of others beyond themselves.

Just because an issue is put on the public agenda does not mean that public policymakers will do anything about it. After all, what one group or individual identifies as a serious problem may be viewed by another group as a desirable situation. Furthermore, even if several organizations or bureaucrats express concern about the same issue, they may have different solutions in mind.

Much like the material that descends through a funnel, agenda-building ingredients all fall into the political laps of public policymakers. They may or may not decide to act, depending upon a variety of factors that we will discuss later. What is important here, however, is to be aware that there are direct, unfiltered linkages between people and those who act on their behalf. That is the essence of representation in a constitutional democracy.

Preparing a Plan of Action—Carefully, and One Step at a Time

After you have completed your research, developed a policy proposal, and begun to survey the political landscape, you may be ready to prepare a plan of action for advancing your proposal. This is a critical moment, for you need to think through what you want to do, and whether you want to carry out your effort alone or with others. As you develop your approach, you will need to consider several options.

Whether to Act Alone or in Concert with Others

Your own initial awareness and knowledge about what others think might be the best guide in determining whether you act alone or with other individuals or groups.

- Sometimes, particularly in the case of a new issue, you may be the first person who wants to do something about it. If a storm drain near your house is routinely flooded, you will be the first to realize the implications of water spilling into the street; others more removed from the area may not see the problem as you do and, thus, may not be as motivated as you. Likewise, if you discover a garbage-riddled stream as a result of a route you take to work, you may see something that others do not. Under such circumstances, you may end up acting alone.

- Participation with others can be valuable as well, particularly if you find people with different perspectives on the same issue. Upon discussing the issue, you may decide that by compromising with others you can approach elected officials with a "united front." Consider the proposal of a police review board to make sure that law enforcement authorities respect the constitutional rights of individuals. You may be interested in this idea because of your concern about possible harassment by police officers. A local police organization or district attorney association may see the virtue of having an agency work with the police to ensure there are solid cases for conviction. Even though two or more groups come at the problem from different perspectives, there may be common ground for approaching public policymakers.

- The reality is that most major public policy proposals involve concerted and coordinated action from many participants. This is because most policy proposals are complex matters, affecting different interests. To succeed, policy proposals may also involve trade-offs. A policy comes into its own when its sponsors succeed in attracting a sufficient number of supporters, and this can sometimes be a difficult thing to do. If your issue and policy proposal are connected with a community service project (perhaps one on which you have been working), you would probably want to search for support of key individuals and groups interested in that project.

Determining Your Level of Involvement

As we have noted, the extent to which you participate in putting an issue on the public agenda depends upon how much you want to be involved. Some possibilities include:

- Circulating and/or signing a petition that will be forwarded to appropriate officials. This is a mild exercise and requires little energy, yet it allows you to align yourself to others. Sometimes, people will use petitions as a means of circulating formal policy proposals that eventually take the form of a ballot initiative. Each local or state government permitting this process has a different set of signature requirements and conditions.
- Writing a letter or sending an e-mail to an appropriate official or a local newspaper. By putting your opinions "on paper" you are expressing your thoughts directly and publicly to key decision makers or those who influence them. The fact that you "go public" may give you visibility and motivate others one way or another as well.
- Requesting the city clerk to place your issue on the agenda of an upcoming city council meeting so that it may be fully discussed and considered (with state and federal issues, you will need to ask a legislator to carry out this task).
- Speaking out on your issue at a city council, a county board of supervisors, or school board meeting. All local governments provide opportunities for public input. State legislatures frequently have public hearings on controversial issues as well; in some cases, they hold hearings in local communities. At the University of Vermont, students formed the Coalition for Responsible Investment, an organization dedicated to the protection of human rights. Concerned about "sweatshop labor," the group ultimately became the framework of a university-endorsed task force on labor and human rights issues.
- Forming or joining an already existing interest group that is actively involved in pursuing the issue. With larger numbers, you increase the likelihood of attention from the press and public policymakers alike. At Pace University in New York, students in a political science class formed the Hudson Environmental Legislation Project (HELP), a

service-learning project that drew enough support from the governor
and legislature to enact new clean river water legislation.

- Participating with others in a march or organized protest activity. The
right to assemble is a long-heralded provision of the First Amendment.
Sometimes, however, the statements made by one group may offend
another, such as when a Ku Klux Klan group marches near an African-
American church. To preserve calm and public order, the government
authority in charge may establish conditions that stipulate when a group
can exercise its right to free speech.

- Conducting an act of civil disobedience to protest the way the issue
has or has not been handled by public policymakers. This is a two-
edged sword in that civic disobedience—the intentional disregard of
law—could risk arrest; yet it's only by testing the constitutionality of
a law as a result of an arrest and conviction that it may be overturned
by a court.

These activities do not necessarily take place in any order. In fact, you
may undertake more than one at the same time. You may also get involved
for a while, only to discover information that you did not have previously.
To that end the information you derive from expressing yourself may lead
you to reconsider your position or abandon your involvement altogether. It's
all part of the learning process.

Preparing a List and Order of Activities

Upon deciding your course of action, you will need to determine the timing
and order of your activities. As with the public policymaking ladder analogy
discussed above, it's usually most beneficial to build alliances before moving
into a confrontational position. Here is a possible list and order of activities
to get your issue on the public agenda:

- Try to combine with others in a purposive (and public) way to both
broaden the base of participation and show policymakers the extent of
your support. Numbers can make a difference.

- Prepare a position paper that both builds on the knowledge you have
acquired and explains in clear, easy-to-understand terms the issue, its
history, what should be done, and why.

- Meet with a public policymaker to see about the possibility of him or
her being the "champion" or sponsor of your issue; such support can

be vital to getting early "buy in" from those who can do something about it.

- Circulate petitions, write letters to the editor, start a blog, and contact other appropriate public policymakers about your issue.
- Attend meetings of the public policymaking body charged with resolving your issue.
- If at first you do not succeed in capturing the attention of policymakers, review what went wrong, regroup, and change your approach as necessary.

It's important that these activities be carried out in sequence. Why? Because each one requires the expenditure of more energy than the one before it. Because political energy is tough to sustain, it's best to expend large amounts only when necessary.

Making the Most of Your Opportunity

Assuming that you have clarified your objectives, settled upon a proposed policy, and identified the appropriate public policymaking venue, the next step is to make contact with those individuals who have the jurisdiction and capability of making change. If you have done your homework by carefully researching and analyzing the issue, the most essential part of your advocacy will be in place: the determination of a problem and selection of a policy proposal to address it. You are ready to present that case to those who can do something about your issue.

The effort at this point requires careful preparation on your part so as to assure the greatest potential for success. That's because time is a precious commodity for policymakers and their staffs. You can help policymakers help you if your time with them helps these "change agents" understand your issue in ways that they would not have done otherwise. Realize that these are busy people and that you may be only one of many constituents. Try to appreciate any meeting from the official's point of view. Besides ordinary courtesy, why should they want to see you? What's in it for them? The nation's founders recognized the value of civic virtue but they also had a healthy respect for the importance of self-interest in public life. So should you.

Below is a "checklist" of six activities designed to help you succeed in connecting your objective with public policymaking authorities. These activities work best at the local level where you have the most direct access to public policymakers; however, many can be adapted for state and national use as well, depending upon the issue.

Timing

Knowing when to take your issue to public policymakers can be as important as the issue itself. The idea here is to make your issue as compelling as possible, thereby increasing the likelihood that policymakers will respond in a positive way. If, for example, you are concerned with providing better storm drains, then a good time to make your case is in the middle of the rainy season when curbs are running over with water. If your issue concerns an expenditure for a civic improvement or new service, it is better to address policymakers before passage of the annual budget rather than after. By picking the right "window," you enhance the relevance of your issue. Otherwise, presentation of the best issue can go for naught.

Advance Warning

Approaching public policymakers should be a direct, "above board" activity. As such, it is best to let them know in advance that you will be coming to address them about your issue. By communicating ahead of your visit, you will give policymakers the opportunity to prepare, allowing them to be more helpful with resolution. Particularly if this is your first effort to persuade officials of the need for change, you may want to be as conciliatory as possible by sending a position paper, a signed petition, or statement of concerns that expresses your feelings on the issue. This will allow them to consult with staff, experts, and opponents, as well as others in the community. The thinking here is to be optimistic, with the assumption of cooperation. If you have made several efforts in the past without success and are returning yet again, you may wish to tell the official that you are informing the local press of your effort to meet with him or her. Suddenly, you may receive an audience and information you have failed to get previously.

Supplies

It may sound mundane, but it is important to have the right supplies in place for your encounter with public policymakers. These necessities may include writing materials, leaflets, petitions, placards, copies of your position papers, or anything else that helps to describe your issue and its importance. If you intend to enlist the help of others at your meeting with public policymakers, you may want to staff an information table, checking with officials in advance, of course, as to the rules on placement and conditions. If you intend to influence with a public protest or demonstration, make sure that you have the necessary permits (usually obtained from the local police department or city clerk's office) in advance of the event; these, too, are supplies. As this may be your only chance to address public policymakers, it is helpful to be as prepared as possible.

Transportation

Often, large numbers of people will have worked together to bring a public policy issue to the attention of decision makers. The presence of large numbers of supporters can be important as a show of unity and purpose. Making sure that your entire group gets to the public policymaking forum (and back to the original meeting place after the meeting) usually requires some coordination. You may wish to use a "telephone tree" or an e-mail blast as a way of telling all of the participants where to assemble and when. You may even have "transportation captains" who have the responsibility for taking designated people to and from the meeting. If you are relying upon public transportation, an advance look at the bus or subway schedule will help people get to and from their destination with a minimum of strain.

Publicity

Taking your issue to the appropriate policymakers is a big part of influencing the process, but that may not be enough for a variety of reasons, ranging from a lack of funds to disinterest on the part of the public official. There is no quick fix to an absence of money, but there are ways to reverse the disinterest of public policymakers in your issue. One way to increase attention is by making the press aware of the issue and what you are attempting to do about it. Thus, if you intend to ask city council members to make available a local public facility for homeless people on cold nights, you may wish to inform the press ahead of time by faxing or e-mailing a press release to local newspapers and radio and TV stations. As part of the press release, you might include statistics on how many people are affected, thereby showing the press that you have done your "homework" on the issue. It is also helpful to include a list of leaders or other well-known people who support your proposal. To bring life to the issue, you may decide to have some homeless people testify at the city council meeting. Should members of the press show up and take interest, their presence and reporting will serve as a microphone by bringing your issue to the attention of thousands of others. In the process, these efforts will increase the attention of public policymakers.[28]

Follow-up

After presenting your "case" to the policymakers, it is important to leave nothing to chance. Several follow-up activities are wise to consider. For example, a letter thanking those public policymakers who heard you is a good way of keeping the door open for further dialogue. As part of your ongoing communication, you might request the city council or mayor to keep you apprised of future policymaking decisions, should any take place. It is also helpful to monitor future actions or decisions by sending representatives to city council meetings or getting official copies of city council minutes, a public record of all council deliberations. Such vigilance will not only keep you informed; it will remind policymakers of their accountability.

You may want to keep the records of your activities in a portfolio or file; that way, you will be able to keep track of how public policymakers, members of the press, and other interests respond to your issue. You may also choose to share your files with public policymakers or the press in the future, depending upon what happens. If nothing is done, you also may wish to make this action (or inaction) an election issue in the future by raising it with candidates for office. Alternatively, you may wish to take your issue to another office or public policymaking level. However, if policymakers respond to your concerns in a favorable way, you may also wish to thank them in an equally public forum. The expression of such gratitude may increase your access opportunities the next time you need to see them.

Returning to our homeless shelter example for a moment, if local authorities decide to do nothing about your effort, you may regroup and approach them in the future with new allies or policy proposals. Then again, if you feel as if you have reached an impasse, you may take your information (and their responses) to a state legislator or federal official, who may be able to do something at his or her level. But if your local public policymakers find common ground with you on your issue, you may wish to acknowledge them so that they—and you—can move on to other things. The point is that public policymaking is not a "one time only" event; it is a fluid, ongoing process that requires constant attention.

Public Policymaking as Complex Activities

Public policymaking rarely succeeds on the first try. The fact is that, regardless of the level of government, public policymakers are sometimes overwhelmed by a crowded agenda. They also tend to be comfortable with the *status quo* because change often invites uncertainty.

Most issues are complicated, with people often taking different sides, constituting yet another factor that discourages resolution. Equally important is that constraints—whether in terms of time, money, interest, or some combination of the three—assure that not all needs will be met for everyone. That is because a policy that pleases one group may well displease another. Even if an issue is popular and deemed worthy of attention by policymakers, all kinds of obstacles can thwart resolution. No wonder the public policy environment is so confusing and uncertain to those who do not understand it, and no wonder so many initially "obvious" issues are resolved with compromises.

If your cause is rejected by those capable of doing something about it, you may be able to propose action at another level of government; that is one of the benefits of federalism. Furthermore, if you do not get the resolution you desire, you may be able to resurrect it in the form of a local or state ballot proposition by collecting the number of signatures necessary to get it on the ballot. On the one hand, such effort means the likelihood of a lot more work; on the other hand, the ability to succeed by taking an alternate public policymaking route shows the extent to which the public policy arena is malleable and open to participation.

Case Study: Campaigning for a Watershed Tax District

Benjamin Franklin once observed that "when the well's run dry, we know the worth of water." Through history this critical resource has been the object of public policy in one form or another. Human beings have worried about it, planned for it, and sometimes fought over it. "Water rights" have long been a policy issue in this country, particularly in the nation's arid regions. Environmental research and activism have made policymakers and all of us increasingly aware of the essential and precarious role of this resource in sustaining civilization, as well as those ecosystems on which the life of the planet depends.

Let's assume that water has become an urgent policy issue in your community. The growth of that community and surrounding communities in recent decades has created environmental problems. Industrial, agricultural, and residential development have all damaged the watershed, which supplies most of the drinking water in local communities. Pollution has raised water treatment costs and threatens to increase health care costs as well. Key wetlands in the area have also been put at risk, threatening the well-being of fragile ecosystems and increasing the dangers of flooding.

Over the years faculty and fellow students at your institution have helped document the nature and extent of the problem in a variety of research and community service projects. Now, some members of the community are responding to the alert. A coalition of government agencies (federal, state, and local), water and sewer system managers, civic and environmental groups, businessmen, farmers, ranchers, and homeowners, as well as the leadership of your institution, are promoting an initiative to address the problem. The initiative would offer a variety of programs, including the improved monitoring of water quality, stream and pond cleanups, the planting of trees along eroded banks, and educational awareness efforts. It would also launch an "Adopt Your Watershed Campaign" for the communities involved.

The initiative calls for the creation of a special watershed tax district to help finance these activities, supplemented by federal and state funding. The district proposal is scheduled to go before the voters at the next election in what promises to be a hard-fought campaign, given voters' general reluctance to endorse tax increases. Your class has decided to support the proposal. Campaign organizers have enlisted your class in the research and preparation of a "campaign blueprint," outlining the strategy and key activities that should be followed to marshal support for the proposal in your area.

1. How would you make your case for the tax district's adoption? What would be your main themes? What arguments would you adopt and how would you document and illustrate them? What advocacy devices would you choose?
2. What arguments of the opposition could you anticipate? How would you propose countering these arguments?
3. In addition to those already a part of the watershed coalition, what constituencies and interest groups might you seek to enlist? How would you appeal to them?
4. What policy gatekeepers might you want to contact? Why?
5. How would you engage the local media in your cause? The resources of the Internet?
6. How would you mobilize support among your campus constituencies—faculty, staff, and students? How could these constituencies help in the effort?

Reflection

The decision for people in power to do or not to do something is the most critical moment of the public policymaking process. But as you see from the discussion up to this point, public policymaking often takes place in intense environments with conflicting pressures and demands. As you think about your issue, take a step back from your specific needs to consider how your concern can be resolved in a way that improves your community, whether it is your college, neighborhood, or town. Think, also, about with whom you need to interact in government to be heard and, it is hoped, succeed.

All of this raises questions about the negotiations that may be necessary for you to achieve success. Is it possible that what you want might actually be at odds with the general values of your community? And if that is the case, how do you reconcile your own needs with the needs of others? Is there any opportunity to find common ground and, if so, what price must you pay to achieve it? Finally, what happens if you have to give too much to get what you want? What do you do then, and how do you make the public policymaking process a "win-win" situation? And what if you cannot? Public policymakers have to deal with these headaches several times each day and over and over again with each issue.

Student Projects

Long-term group—Assuming support for your issue, develop a timeline for bringing your issue to the attention of appropriate public policymakers. Try to anticipate as many obstacles as possible ahead of time so that the effort will be more likely to succeed. Double-check that your objective is achievable and that the group is committed to seeing the project through.

Short-term individual—Take on a school public policy issue such as an open campus, assigned student parking spots, freedom of the press for a student newspaper, or cafeteria selections and work to improve that issue. How can you keep your task manageable? Whom should you work with to maximize the opportunities for success?

Discussion Questions

1. Consensus is a concept that was emphasized by the framers of the Constitution. How do you achieve consensus when some of your colleagues do not agree with your ideas? What do you do in the absence of consensus?

2. Think about an issue today that was not anticipated at the time of the Constitution's creation. Given that the issue is "outside" of what was originally included in the Constitution, how should it be managed and at what level of government?

3. Within the American political process, individuals have countless opportunities to communicate their concerns to public policymakers. Bearing in mind an issue of importance to you, what level of government seems best able to address your issue? Why? Who are the principal policy "gatekeepers" for addressing your policy? The likely supporters and opponents? Who are the likely partners with whom to build a coalition?

4. How would you go about "selling" your proposal to gatekeepers and other likely supporters? How would you connect your proposal to their interests?

5. What sort of advocacy techniques seem most suitable for making your case? Statistics? Anecdotes? How would you express your argument in flowcharts and other visual displays? How would you express it in an op-ed article or pamphlet?

Notes

1. For a modern-day appeal for advocacy, see Paul Rogat Loeb, *Soul of a Citizen: Living with Conviction in a Cynical Time* (New York: St. Martin's Griffin, 1999).

2. Paul A. Sabatier and Hank C. Jenkins-Smith present a series of advocacy studies in their edited work, *Policy Change and Learning: An Advocacy Coalition Approach* (Boulder, CO: Waveland, 1993).

3. There is a large bibliography on the arts of political and policy advocacy. Many excellent studies focus upon particular issues and constituencies. One general and handy primer is Nancy Amidei's *So You Want to Make a Difference: Advocacy Is the Key* (Washington, DC: OMB Watch, 1991). See also Jan Berry, *A Citizen's Guide to Grassroots Campaigns* (New Brunswick, NJ: Rutgers University Press, 2000). In *Advocacy in America* (Lanham, MD: University Press of America, 1987), Gladys Hall examines a wide variety of case studies of policy advocacy, including tenant organization and school desegregation in Baltimore, the enactment of child labor laws in Illinois, and the women's ordination movement in the Episcopal Church.

4. *Public Opinion in the 21st Century* (Boston: Houghton Mifflin Company, 2006), p. 261.

5. John W. Kingdon has a lengthy discussion of agenda building in his *Agendas, Alternatives, and Public Policies,* 2nd ed. (Boston: Little, Brown, 1995), pp. 21–70.

6. See James E. Anderson, *Public Policymaking,* 3rd ed. (Boston: Houghton Mifflin Company, 1997), p. 102.

7. In recent years, presidents have used the executive order with increasing frequency as a means of pushing their agendas. In 2002, for example, President

George W. Bush signed a series of executive orders that authorized the National Security Agency to conduct wiretaps without warrants on Americans living in the United States, a policy that quietly reversed a longstanding tradition. See "Bush Lets U.S. Spy on Callers without Courts," *New York Times,* December 16, 2005, pp. A1, A22. For a full discussion of this mechanism and the "checks" surrounding it, see Joseph A. Pika and John Anthony Maltese, *The Politics of the Presidency,* 6th ed. (Washington, DC: CQ Press, 2004).

8. "How Bush Sidesteps Intent of Congress," *San Francisco Chronicle,* May 7, 2006, pp. A1, A12, A13.

9. Burdett A. Loomis and Wendy J. Schiller, *The Contemporary Congress,* 5th ed. (New York: Thomson Wadsworth, 2006).

10. Some political scientists argue that states are the bastions of citizen government and democracy. See Sarah McCally Morehouse and Malcolm Jewell, *State Politics, Parties, & Policy,* 2nd ed. (Lanham, MD: Rowman & Littlefield, 2003). For an excellent analysis of the workings of state legislatures, see Alan Rosenthal, *The Decline of Representative Democracy: Process, Participation, and Power in State Legislatures* (Washington, DC: CQ Press, 1998).

11. For a discussion of these and other areas of state innovation, see Larry N. Gerston, *American Federalism: A Concise Introduction* (Armonk, NY: M.E. Sharpe, 2007).

12. See David Osborne, *Laboratories of Democracy* (Boston: Harvard Business School Press, 1988).

13. See Anthony Downs, *New Visions for Urban America* (Washington, DC: Brookings Institute, 1995). As Michael Lipsky points out, public service employees at the local level—teachers, police, firefighters, lower courts, representatives of welfare departments, and so forth—are public policymakers and collectively represent most of the government American citizens usually encounter. See his *Street-Level Bureaucracy: Dilemmas of the Individual in Public Services* (New York: Russell Sage Foundation, 1997). See also below, chapter 5.

14. Thomas J. Volgy, a political scientist and former mayor, provides unusually candid insight into the process in his *Politics in the Trenches: Citizens, Politicians, and the Fate of Democracy* (Tucson: University of Arizona Press, 2001).

15. For a series of studies on the power of the media in American politics, see Doris A. Graber, ed., *Media Power in Politics,* 5th ed. (Washington, DC: CQ Press, 2006).

16. For insights into how the Novak article spilled into more controversial questions, see "Cheney's Aide Says President Approved Leak," *New York Times,* April 7, 2006, pp. A1, A20 and "First, a Leak; Now, a Jam," *New York Times,* April 8, 2006, pp. A1, A11.

17. See "BO, U R so Gr8," *The Wall Street Journal,* May 26–27, 2007, pp. A1, A5.

18. "Fundraiser Cashes In—Obama Gets Zero," *San Francisco Chronicle,* July 25, 2007, pp. A1, A10.

19. Many interest groups are intimately involved with the policymaking process. For example, the American Association of Retired Persons, the largest interest group in America, has been heavily involved in the shaping of Social Security legislation. For an account of the group's activity, see Paul Light, *Artful Work: The Politics of Social Security Reform* (New York: Random House, 1985).

20. "Gay Clubs Bring School Use Debate Back into Spotlight," *Los Angeles Times,* December 9, 1999, pp. A1, A32.

21. For a discussion of both sides of the issue, see Jeffrey E. Cohen, Richard Fleisher, and Paul Kantor, eds., *American Political Parties: Decline or Resurgence?* (Washington, DC: CQ Press, 2001).

22. For a review of bureaucratic power and responsibilities, see Kenneth J. Meier, *Politics and the Bureaucracy: Policymaking in the Fourth Branch of Government,* 5th ed. (Belmont, CA: Wadsworth, 2006).

23. Each bureaucracy has its own set of powers and limitations. For a comparison of the Environmental Protection Agency and the Federal Trade Commission, for example, see Richard A. Harris and Sidney M. Milkis, *The Politics of Regulatory Change: A Tale of Two Agencies* (New York: Oxford University Press, 1996).

24. See Lipsky, *Street-Level Bureaucracy.*

25. For Rosa Parks's own reflection on her accomplishments, see Rosa Parks with Gregory J. Reed, *Quiet Strength: The Faith, the Hope, and the Heart of a Woman Who Changed a Nation* (Grand Rapids, MI: Zondervan, 1994). In his *Rosa Parks* (New York: Viking, 2000), historian David Brinkley examines this American hero's struggles and accomplishments in the civil rights movement.

26. Many of these success stories have been chronicled by the Higher Education Service Learning Clearing House Project at UCLA, an adjunct of the National Service-Learning Clearinghouse at the University of Minnesota, and by various publications of Campus Compact. See also Tony Robinson, "Service Learning as Justice Advocacy: Can Political Scientists Do Politics?" *PS: Political Science and Politics,* 33 (September 2000): pp. 605–612.

27. Both classes were using the Center of Civic Education's curriculum, *We the People . . . Project Citizen,* which introduces younger students to the monitoring and influencing of public policy through classroom activities and community outreach. See Kenneth W. Tolo, ed., *An Assessment of We the People . . . Project Citizen: Promoting Citizenship in Classrooms and Communities* (Austin: Lyndon B. Johnson School of Public Affairs at the University of Texas, 1998) and Herbert M. Atherton, "We the People . . . Project Citizen," in Sheilah Mann and John J. Patrick, eds., *Education for Civic Engagement in Democracy: Service Learning and Other Promising Practices* (Washington, DC: Educational Resources Information Center, 2000), pp. 93–102.

28. As we have seen, the media have a major role in agenda setting. For a look at how the media can be enlisted in policy advocacy, see Lawrence Wallack et al., *News for a Change: An Advocate's Guide to Working with the Media* (Thousand Oaks, CA: Sage, 1999).

5 IMPLEMENTATION
Carrying Out Decisions and
Making Them Stick

Whatever the level of decision making, the policymaking process can be filled with tension, drama, and uncertainty. Whether it is city officials debating the construction of a new recreation center or Congress deciding what to do about a proposed tax cut, the air often gets pretty heavy just before the decision-making moment. Because disputes are usually over resources or values, policymakers are left with the unenviable task of attempting to resolve those differences. That's why they are in positions of authority. And it is the drama *of* the fight that often draws so much attention.

When determinations are finally made, the various sides may breathe a collective sigh of relief or anguish at least for the moment, if not longer. Certainly those who are more satisfied with the resolution of a public policy issue probably breathe a lot easier than those who are not, but at least decisions allow the public and the policymakers alike to go on to another issue or back to dealing with other problems. Even those who lose out on the decision will take consolation by knowing that they can renew their case at some point in the future, for public policy decisions are rarely permanent.

Yet, lost in this moment of "high stakes political poker" is the policy-fulfilling effort that happens *after* the decision. Therein lies the process of *implementation,* the administrative task of transferring policy commitments into practice.[1] As part of the public policymaking process, implementation is the means by which decisions are converted into application. In other words, it is the effort that carries out what policymakers decide should be done.

Although it usually takes place out of the limelight and away from the official decision-making arena, implementation is a component of the public policymaking process that does not receive a lot of attention. In fact, most of the time we do not even think about implementation, viewing it, instead, as an automatic extension of the policymaking process.[2] Naively, we tend to think that policies are preprogrammed into the implementation mode. The passage of new public policies by city councils to ban smoking from restaurants or deny the use of fireworks on July 4th, for example, often receive wide coverage in the local media. But how often does anyone follow the actual implementation of such measures? Rarely. Equally important, how often are such measures carried out to the full extent of the policy commitment? Sometimes, not as often as you might expect.

In actuality, implementation is an uncertain undertaking. On the surface, the topic is not very exciting because it is much easier for us to focus on the fight over what *should* be done. We just assume that because decisions are made, someone or something will automatically see to it that policies are carried out as policymakers intended. But there is nothing automatic about implementation. In fact, implementation is fraught with challenges and obstacles. The leap from the drawing board to application can be a very long and tedious effort. The significance of the follow-through, as always, is in the details. Remember, new public policies usually represent change. Some people will welcome the change; others will resent it—either because they disagree with the policy or because they resent the obligations it imposes upon them.

We implement as individuals every day. If you have a reading assignment for a class, you implement that task by reading the book—or face uncertainty on future exams if you do not. When you see a physician about an illness, you implement your own policy dedicated to sound physical health. In this sense, there is nothing particularly unique about implementation. With public policy, however, implementation takes on an additional meaning because it is enacted by individuals or organizations who act on behalf of others.

This chapter is dedicated to understanding implementation. As you read it, you will learn the characteristics of implementation and discover why some public policies are carried out as intended, why some are fulfilled to a degree, and why others do not come to pass. You will also learn about how you can keep your hand on the pulse of the implementation process, which will be of particular interest to you if the public policy you have advocated has been accepted, in whole or in part.

In fact, you should not discount your role in this phase of the public policymaking process. In a sense, it is part of your responsibility to carry through with what you have pursued. It's not enough to say: "We've made our point. Let someone else worry about the consequences." Just because some bureaucrat may have the primary responsibility for putting a policy to work does not mean it is time for you to walk away from it. To the contrary, it's more important then ever for you to see whether the policy you may have fought for is implemented as intended. Moreover, if the policy you have advocated is connected with a service-learning activity with which you have been involved, you may have more of a handle than most people on the many details of implementation. To that extent, your expertise and vigilance may come in handy.

The Art of Implementation

Much like the bulky, unseen mass of a huge iceberg, implementation tends to be almost hidden from public view. And similar to the collision between an iceberg and other object, implementation can have a tremendous impact on the more observable parts of the public policymaking process. Such is the potential benefit of implementation and the potential harm from a policy's derailment in the case when implementation goes awry.

Imagine that some talented rock musicians gather to cut a CD, and after several sessions they generate a product that their managers distribute to leading disc jockeys. The DJs, in turn, promote the CD by playing it on their radio stations. That is implementation. Now imagine those same talented musicians cutting the same CD, but being unable to find a producer or distributor to reach listeners, their targeted audience. Or, worse yet, the DJs say that they will play the record but decide not to follow through for any number of reasons. Guess what? The musicians have failed to implement their objective, which was not simply to produce a CD, but actually to capture public interest and sales. In a nutshell, that is how implementation works—and does not work. It is all about the attempt to convert decisions into practice.

When policymakers make decisions about management of the public good or public resources, implementation is the execution of that decision. But this delicate follow-through effort focuses upon more than ensuring that something is done. To the extent that a public policy is implemented, policymakers have credibility because, in the eyes of the public, they "make good" on their intentions.[3] In other words, with implementation as an extension of the decision or action step, policymakers live up to their bond with the citizens. That is where bureaucracies come into the picture.

For a public policy to work, someone or something must have the authority and will to fulfill the commitment of the individuals who have moved it through the policymaking process. This is an important point, for more times than not, those responsible for deciding on a new public policy and those responsible for implementing it are often (indeed, usually) not the same. Responsibilities for the latter usually are placed into the hands of "bureaucrats" and their agencies, or "bureaucracies," which are administrative bodies of individuals charged with implementing public policies.[4] These individuals are also known as "civil servants," people who work in government units or organizations to do the public's work. Letter carriers, teachers, soldiers, and animal-control workers are all examples of civil servants.

Bureaucracies exist with all organizations—public or private. (The word *bureaucracy* literally means "government by administrative officials."[5]) In the public sector, or "government" as we know it, bureaucracies are administrative units that are created by public policymakers to carry out the decisions of these officials. They are usually permanent, or ongoing organizations because the process of carrying out policies tends to be a never-ending effort that requires constant participation from people with the expertise to do it.[6]

Just as with political parties and presidential nomination systems, there is no mention of bureaucracy in the Constitution. No matter how closely you look, you will not find the EPA, a state department of education, or a local public housing authority in this historic document, yet these and countless other bureaucracies are as real and important as any designated public policymaking entity that is discussed in our nation's charter. The right of bureaucracies to function stems from the offices of government that are created *by* the document. Thus, bureaucracies are authorized by legitimate public policy authorities to act on their behalf.

Bureaucracies as Implementation Agents

Bureaucracies exist at all levels of government; they come in various shapes and sizes. In all, there are about 23 million bureaucrats at work in this country, with the vast majority (nearly 20 million) serving at the state and local levels of government.[7] They run the gamut in size, budgets, and power. At one end of the bureaucratic continuum, some federal organizations or agencies, such as the Department of Defense or the Postal Service, have annual budgets in the hundreds of billions of dollars and contain millions of employees. At the other end, local bureaucracies such as a town's school guard crossing patrol unit or parking meter brigade can have a few people, with annual budgets in the thousands of dollars.

Bureaucrats operate under a variety of titles ranging from "administrators" to "clerks." But their titles are less important than their functions. Whatever level of service, the primary job of the bureaucracy is to implement and administer the policies of those who make them. In other words, their function is to turn objectives into reality.

You might ask, why can't people carry out public policies on their own?

Isn't the bureaucracy just a bunch of unnecessary fluff? A waste of precious resources? Let's test that idea. Consider that a state legislature enacts a highway speed limit of sixty-five miles per hour, with individuals asked to voluntarily comply with the new law without the assistance of the state highway patrol. How long do you think that would last? Imagine the roadside carnage that would result if people drove according to their own rules. In this case, we count on the highway patrol or state police, bureaucracies organized by the legislature, to implement the policy; they do so by issuing a citation if they catch you exceeding the speed limit. Or suppose that your city council eliminates its animal control department as a cost-cutting measure, leaving it to individuals to remove any dead carcasses they find on the road. Chances are that while a few people might act in the name of the public good, most would ignore the issue, possibly leading to a health problem for the entire community. Then there's also the issue of public-spirited volunteers not having the expertise associated with the removal of the dead animals—another potential problem. Public safety and health cannot be treated as marginal matters left to the voluntary will of individuals. On these and other matters of public policy, we count on someone in government with the necessary expertise to enforce the rules and carry out necessary functions. That activity comes with implementation.

Requirements for Implementation

For implementation to occur, bureaucracies and their workforce must operate with four important elements at their disposal: translation ability, resources, limited numbers of players, and accountability. These elements allow bureaucrats to carry out their tasks.

Translation Ability

The people who work at an agency or other policymaking unit must be able to understand clearly their assigned tasks to make the public policy work in accord with the instructions of the decision makers. In other words, there must be clear communication between the public policymaking authority and the bureaucracy.[8] How does that take place? Usually by the written word; the policy is transmitted from those who make the decision to those who must carry it out. This formality is the best way of preventing confusion and helps to provide a "paper trail," or record, in case of any dispute later on in the implementation process.

In some ways, bureaucrats are like the contractors who put into place the plans drawn by the architect—in this case, public policymakers. If bureaucrats are unsure of the job they are assigned to do, they must get clarification from the public officials who developed it. For example, if a college student government passes a rule that allows solicitations on campus, the rule must be clear on the types of causes, where, what times, and under what conditions. Only then can campus administrators be expected to enforce the rule.

Clarity about the policy and how it is to be carried out are key translation requirements for doing the job correctly. When there is agreement among policymakers and bureaucrats about the policy and its objectives, implementation becomes a manageable activity for bureaucrats. In addition, the presence of clear standards or rules helps to establish a chain of responsibility, should implementation of a policy fail to occur per its design.

Resources

Bureaucracies do not have their own sources of revenue or power. Thus, whether it is personnel, equipment, or enforcement assignments, bureaucrats must be given the resources to carry out their implementation tasks. As executors of the public policymaking process, bureaucracies need policymakers to make those tools available much in the same way that a farmer relies upon a tractor to plow his field or a software engineer requires a computer to design a program. As such, resources are critical links between public policymakers and bureaucrats.

Ample resources increase the likelihood that the assignment will be carried out per the instructions of the public policymakers; a decision alone is not enough. If the Internal Revenue Service (IRS) is given the task of ensuring that people pay their share of income taxes, then the agency must be given enough funds by public policymakers to hire auditors, purchase computers, and acquire whatever else it needs to get the job done. Without the necessary tools, experts say that the United States fails to collect more than $300 billion annually in unpaid taxes.[9] Likewise, if a local city council enacts an ordinance to provide free needles to drug users in an effort to prevent diseases such as hepatitis and HIV/AIDS, then the council must allocate the necessary resources to carry out the policy; otherwise, it would be a sham.

Without adequate resources, the public policy is almost sure to fail.[10] That is why the creation of a meaningful public policy must include the means of getting it done; otherwise, the effort is symbolic and nothing more. It also leaves many people questioning why the policy has not been carried out as designed, inviting both confusion and alienation.

Limited Numbers of Players

Have you ever heard the phrase "Too many cooks spoil the broth"? That can happen with implementation. Bureaucracies succeed when relatively few agencies are involved in managing the process.[11] When large numbers of agencies become involved with implementation, their collective participation can produce confusion, competition, or both. To increase the probability of successful implementation, it is helpful for public policymakers to design the policy in such a way that responsibility is funneled to a few key people or agencies.

For example, suppose a city council votes to create a new park, and then instructs all "appropriate agencies" to collaborate on the park's development. Imagine who could get involved: the planning department (land use), the police department (keeping order in the park), the road department (traffic patterns near the proposed park), and the parks and recreation department (structures and facilities), to name a few. With so many public agencies, it would be difficult to coordinate development. However, if the same city council sets up one unit—perhaps the parks and recreation department—as the lead agency for the park's development, then implementation would have a smoother path. The parks and recreation department may enlist the help of other agencies for portions of the task, but it will still serve as the agency of record.

When a single agency is assigned implementation responsibility for a public policy, there is a greater likelihood that it will keep tabs on those individuals who are assigned the task of performing the job. Under these circumstances, coordination becomes more manageable, thereby increasing the likelihood of success.[12] Sharing responsibilities opens the opportunity for implementation assignments to fall "between the cracks" as one bureaucracy may believe that a job is being carried out by another.

Accountability

Almost everyone is accountable to someone. In politics, elected public officials are most accountable to the public for one very important reason: these individuals were entrusted to carry out the public will. In most cases, if policymakers disappoint the public, they can be replaced by the voters at the next election; this is the essence of accountability. Even policymakers who are appointed, such as judges, are accountable to the legislators or others who put them in their positions of authority.

Accountability is a little trickier with bureaucracies because bureaucrats are not elected by anyone. Instead, a bureaucrat is usually accountable to the political bodies that create, oversee, and provide funds for his or her agency.[13] For example, suppose that it is discovered that a town's fire department chief has discriminated in the way he has hired firefighters. Upon making such a discovery, the town council might order policy changes. The council could also suspend or even terminate the chief for failing to conduct himself appropriately. The point is that all bureaucrats are accountable to someone.

To demonstrate its worth, a bureaucracy must complete its assignments on time, on budget, and within all of the rules governing its existence.

Most of the time, bureaucratic responsibilities are ongoing activities. Not only was the Occupational Safety and Health Administration (OSHA) set up by Congress in 1971 to develop rules for the workplace; it also conducts routine inspections of workplaces to ensure that the rules are enforced. Likewise, in addition to being authorized by state governments as education bodies, local school districts carry out education policy by creating and enforcing hundreds of rules every year. Bureaucracies demonstrate their accountability by carrying out the tasks they have been given by public policymaking bodies.

As a general rule, bureaucrats must file periodic reports or appear before public policymakers at hearings, or special meetings, to show them that they have performed their assigned tasks. Sometimes sparks fly when policymakers decide that bureaucrats have not carried out their responsibilities as originally defined. In these instances, policymakers may respond in a variety of ways, from expressions of outrage to withholding of funds for future agency activities. On other occasions, policymakers will make site visits to see for themselves how their policies have been carried out. After Hurricane Katrina battered New Orleans and the Gulf of Mexico Coast in 2005, Congress carried out extensive investigations about the failure of the Federal Emergency Management Agency (FEMA) to bring relief to the area. The capstone emerged in the form of a 600 page report that denounced FEMA and the Department of Homeland Security for a series of passive reactions and critical misjudgments before, during, and after the hurricane struck the Gulf region. The report found that FEMA's poor response demonstrated the agency's inability to implement its disaster relief responsibilities.[14] Such reports are dramatic and get great press, but often yield little follow-up in the form of new policies.[15]

Bureaucratic accountability can also be seen at the state and local levels of government. Most states have an independent auditing agency that oversees programs. At the local level, city councils, boards of supervisors, and other governments routinely call for reports from countless agencies to assure accountability. Thus, if a city council decides that the public water utility must add fluoride to the system for its customers (who are also city residents), it may ask the city attorney to ensure that the policy is implemented in the ways stipulated by the council. The city council might also require the city attorney to report periodically on the implementation of the fluoride program. Or, an independent city auditor may investigate the program to see whether it is working as intended and within budget. Such accountability underscores the point that implementation takes place only when the agency or unit with the responsibility to do it actually does it!

Conditions for Discouraging Implementation

We have discussed basic requirements for bureaucratic success such as translation, resources, limited numbers of players, and accountability. Even under these circumstances, it is easy for implementation to go awry. In some respects, our constitutional system of shared powers among independent branches of government might appear to encourage this.[16] You will recall from chapter 1 that such a system may not be the most efficient in terms of public policymaking. It requires deliberation and cooperation between the different centers of authority—in implementation as well as in decision making—and therefore lends itself to those who would seek to frustrate the implementation of policies they do not support. Obstacles to successful implementation, however, are found throughout the public policymaking framework at all levels and all forms of government. The most likely impediments are postdecision bargaining, new priorities, and poor oversight.

Postdecision Bargaining

To "bargain" means that two or more parties hash out their differences to agree on a solution to a problem. This traditional means of negotiation is also part of the public policymaking process where individuals, with different values and constituencies, often bargain to hammer out something acceptable to satisfy the adversaries. Bargaining is part of the American political system. Indeed, our system of checks and balances involving different branches and levels of government almost guarantees bargaining as a prerequisite to agreement. With one branch of government often able to offset another, bargaining becomes a tool for achieving agreement; similar arrangements take place between leaders of different levels of government.

But it is one matter to negotiate en route to a deal and it is another matter to do so afterward. With postdecision bargaining, the policy is renegotiated among bureaucrats during implementation to make the policy easier to deal with.[17] Remember, to implement any policy means change, and change may generate resistance either from those who opposed it outright on policy grounds or from those who may resent any burdens the process of implementation imposes on them. Under these conditions, individuals who did not even take part in its formulation may undermine the policy, thereby unraveling the original agreement and sometimes ruining the credibility of the policymakers as a consequence.

Suppose that a school district board enacts a policy that requires all athletes to keep a 2.0 grade point average (GPA) as a condition for remaining on the team. After the policy is put into place, the star quarterback at one of the local high schools falls below the necessary GPA, leading the coach or members of the athletic department to ask his teachers to postpone any grades until the player can "get his act together." If the teachers comply with the request, they essentially change the rules *after the fact*. In other words, they rearrange the policy after it has been made even though they had no policymaking role.

Postdecision bargaining is serious business. In effect, the administrator or implementing agent undermines the worth of a public policy by substituting his or her own interpretation in place of the original public policy without any authority to do so. And while the administrator may breathe a sigh of relief because he avoids a problem, he creates a much larger problem through his illegitimate (and possibly illegal) actions.

Bureaucracies the world over are famous (some might say infamous) for reinterpreting or otherwise obstructing policies they do not like, often doing so in the name of expediency. Such discretionary decisions may sometimes be justified in the minds of the bureaucrats, but they have the effect of minimizing the rules negotiated by policymakers who are counting on bureaucrats to carry out the job. In the process of replacing law with convenience, postdecision bargaining weakens the political system. In addition, it can create political alienation among people who expect the rules to be carried out per their design.

New Priorities

Sometimes policymakers change priorities after a public policy has been put into action. Of course, people can change their minds about almost anything.

However, for those who have invested the political energy to develop a policy in the first place, this outcome can be a bitter pill to swallow. After all, we now know about the incredible hurdles that discourage the development of any policy. So, sweeping aside such a commitment because of changed priorities can be disruptive to the coalition of interests that succeeded in the earlier effort, especially if reaching agreement was difficult to do. When such shifts in priorities occur, they put the original policy in jeopardy.

Consider the local government whose public policymakers have established an "open space" area so that wildlife and natural habitat may thrive without fear of human interference. Perhaps environmentalists worked painstakingly with education interests, leading scientists, and business organizations to present a proposal enacted by city leaders. In fact, it may be that the mayor and the city council were elected on a "slow growth" agenda. But then things change. A couple of years later, a new assembly plant or manufacturing facility is built nearby, generating the need for thousands of workers who, of course, need places to live that are close to their workplace. This development generates a demand for additional housing, but the only available land is near the "open space" area. If the city allows construction of the factory, the new priority (perhaps economic growth) may well have the effect of overpowering the old priority (perhaps environmental protection). As a result, it would no longer be possible to implement the earlier open space policy along the lines of its original intentions.

There is nothing wrong or inherently mischievous about new priorities. It is just that with the adoption of a new priority, previous policies may become expendable, sometimes creating uncertainty and inconsistency in their wake. The impacts of such changes are not always recognized until they have occurred, leading people to wonder whether their public policymakers have acted in disingenuous ways.[18] As with other obstacles, the new circumstances help contribute to feelings of disappointment for some groups, although they may be welcome developments to others. In extreme cases, they might lead the voters to petition for a recall election or toss out the "turn-coat" incumbents at the next election. Regardless, such dramatic switches hardly auger public confidence in elected officials.

Poor Oversight

Because bureaucracies are essentially the creations of public policymaking authorities, the oversight of their activities falls on to the shoulders of those same officials. However, public policymakers are not always successful in following up on their own decisions. That's because they gain more exposure and recognition from the act of crafting public policies than the tedious exercise of managing them. Nevertheless, successful implementation, the "back side" of the public policymaking process, is critical to securing success of the policy. Whether local traffic laws, state policies on access to public parks, or federal rules, policies fail if they are not carefully managed.

Think about a state legislature that enacts a policy that forbids smoking in restaurants and bars. As part of the new policy, the implementation responsibility for the "no smoking" law is assigned to local law enforcement authorities who may fail to carry out the policy. Why would such a thing occur? Perhaps the police are so busy enforcing other laws that they do not have time or want to deal with the "no smoking" law. Maybe they just do not want the hassle of confronting angry smokers or restaurant owners. After all, how can we compare a "no smoking" law to a rape or murder?

Sometimes, bureaucrats at different levels of government conflict on the implementation elements of the same public policy. When that clash occurs, nasty struggles can occur between leaders over which level has the authority to act and under precisely what conditions. Nowhere has this been more explosive than over the question of global warming and governmental regulations. After years of painful negotiations, California and several other states accused the EPA of dragging its feet on greenhouse gas regulation. Ultimately, the oversight issue was settled by the U.S. Supreme Court.[19]

Given the relationship between public policymakers and bureaucrats, it is the unenviable job of the public policymaking authority to exercise oversight activities. Commonly such efforts take place in the form of a legislative committee hearing, investigation by the state attorney general, or finding by a judge as the outgrowth of a lawsuit, at which time policymakers may be forced to revisit the issue.

If a public policy is not implemented according to its designs, the entire effort leading to enactment could be wasted. That outcome not only undermines the policy but, as with postdecision bargaining, potentially weakens the credibility of those who created it. Yet, it happens.

Bureaucrats as Public Policymakers

So far, we have discussed bureaucracy as an extension, or applications arm, of the public policymaking process. But there are times when policymakers actually give limited decision-making authority to bureaucrats along with responsibility for their implementation. In these circumstances, the bureaucrat wears two hats—one as the policymaking authority and one as the implementing agency. Such situations bring their own unique challenges.

The instances of bureaucrats-turned-policymakers are most common when traditional public policymakers are confronted with complicated or technical matters outside their realm of general knowledge. Under these circumstances, policymakers defer resolution of difficult questions and their details to individuals with deep expertise and special skills.

Technical experts can deal with specific problems in ways that generalists cannot. Consider a situation where a city council passes an ordinance requiring "safe" drinking water. Under such conditions, the council is likely to give responsibility to the appropriate authority, perhaps the water department, for defining "safe" water as a condition for implementing the ordinance. With that in mind, the water department will work with biologists, chemists, and engineers, and perhaps the federal government's EPA to establish criteria, discover sources of pollution and toxicity, and develop methods of assuring safe, drinkable water.

Despite its independence, odds are that the water department will not be left on its own altogether. In all likelihood, the city council will probably require periodic reports of the department's research and intentions, including such issues as costs, maintenance, and other matters relative to the agency's function. The city council members may also hold public hearings so that residents can testify about their experiences with the water supply. Through this review process, the council can still be involved in the agency's activities. That is important, because it is the city council members—not the water department—who are directly accountable to the public.

Handing over policymaking to administrators may be a necessity in this age of technology and specialization, but policymakers can get in trouble if they lose sight of what is going on altogether. Let us continue with the safe drinking water example for a moment longer to see why. Suppose that the water becomes polluted by a chemical that causes nausea or other illness in the community and that the water department, in an effort to avoid embarrassment or prosecution, fails to advise the city council of the problem. Or perhaps the city council neglects to keep close tabs on costs or other controversies associated with the water department's efforts. Whose necks would be on the chopping block then? Probably those of the city council for letting issues get out of hand and away from their control. That is why elected policymakers are reluctant to turn over any more direct policymaking authority than necessary to bureaucrats.

The "street-level" bureaucrats (police, teachers, welfare department officials, etc.) we learned about in previous chapters play a critical role in shaping as well as implementing public policies because of the unusual amount of discretion that comes with their jobs as well as the close proximity to their "constituents." Indeed, these public policymakers interact with us every day. In this respect, Michael Lipsky writes, public policy "is not best understood as made in legislatures or top-floor suites of ranking administrators, because in important ways it is actually made in the crowded offices and daily encounters of street-level workers."[20] The decisions they make, the routines they carry out, and the devices they create to respond to a variety of circumstances effectively *become* the public policies they are charged with carrying out.

But What About . . . ?

There are times when a bureaucrat believes that the decision made by public policymakers is wrong or unethical. Perhaps it is because the administrator feels that the public policy he or she has been asked to implement is illegal or unconstitutional, thereby leaving that individual uncomfortable about carrying out the task at hand. Or perhaps it is because the bureaucrat believes that he or she must respond to the needs of a particular group that is affected by the policy in a way that the council members just do not understand. Either way, the bureaucrat may feel so uncertain about the legality of the policy that he or she may test the matter in court. If the judge rules in favor of the policymakers, then the bureaucrat will be in an uncomfortable position. At a minimum, he or she may lose the confidence of the elected officials; they even may force the bureaucrat to resign. If the judge confirms the bureaucrat's suspicions, then the public policymakers may suffer great embarrassment. Whatever the outcome, it is high-stakes politics.

The issue becomes particularly murky when a government administrator or employee opposes a policy because of his or her political values or philosophy. If it is a matter of judgment, then the individual is usually wise to resign or ask for a transfer to another agency rather than go head-to-head with a superior or public policymakers about the wisdom of a decision. Here it is important to distinguish between something illegal and something undesirable.

Alternatively, the bureaucrat might take the problem to the press or another public policy authority as a way of capturing the attention of groups or individuals who may sway the public policy process enough to get policymakers to reconsider the issue. Bureaucrats who tell their story in such a way are known as *whistle-blowers;* they "blow the whistle," or publicly complain, about the actions of their bosses or architects of the policy as a way of drawing attention to a misdeed that would not be discovered otherwise. They do so by telling their story to someone who can mobilize public opinion (perhaps the press) or someone who can do something about the source of the problem (public policymakers). Should there be merit to the charge, chances are that the policymakers responsible may suffer some form of rebuke or future rejection at the polls; if the issue is serious enough, criminal charges might actually result. Conversely, if the bureaucrat turns out to be wrong or is unable to prove the claim, then he or she may be out of a job.[21]

When a bureaucrat confronts policymakers about an issue, he or she is crossing the thin line between administration and politics. That's because under most circumstances, it is not up to bureaucrats to decide whether the policy is good or bad; it is their responsibility to do what they have been told to do, assuming that the policymakers have acted within the law. Nevertheless, such distinctions are not always clear, leaving the administrative employee in a sea of uncertainty over what to do.

Keeping Your Hand in the Implementation Mix

With all the talk about rules and procedures, you might think that there is not much of an opportunity for private citizens to be involved with implementation, even when they have been actively involved with the advocacy and adoption of a policy. You couldn't be further from the truth. The fact is that citizens can play a vital role in the implementation process. This role occurs not so much from the standpoint of actual implementation but observing, recording, and even speaking out about the relationships and assigned responsibilities that take place between public policymakers and bureaucrats. Of particular importance is whether the policies are clear and the extent to which the intentions of the policymakers correspond with the implementation efforts of the bureaucrats. If a government bureaucracy has been wholly or even partially successful in the adoption of a new policy, you will want to be able to monitor (and even expedite) its implementation. What follows are some specific suggestions for tracking that implementation—for your policy or, indeed, any new public policy in whose fate you may be interested.

Determining Whether the Policy Is Clear

Bureaucrats are not the only individuals who have access to the decisions of public policymakers; in most circumstances, you do too. To find out whether the public policy is clear, you can communicate with two sets of authorities—those who have created the policy and those who have been assigned to make it work. You will probably want to stay close to both of these groups as long as you are interested in the outcome of the policy that you are following. How can you do these things? Some examples follow.

Suppose that a new policy has been enacted by the state legislature on textbook selection and you want to know the issues and circumstances leading to that policy. Chances are that you will first learn about it through a story in the newspaper or on television; then again, maybe you will find out from a friend or someone at work, through an interest group newsletter or by going online. In almost every case, you are probably not going to get the full story or the entire sequence of events. To get the details, you will want to contact your legislator or the clerk of the legislator's chamber with the request for the entire text as well as any companion bills that guide implementation. You might also want to contact the education reporter of your local newspaper to get his or her sense of the background relating to the new policy. At the same time, you will need to get in touch with your school district superintendent (or designated district official) to ask the same set of questions that you give to the legislator. You can do each of these contacts by phone, letter, e-mail, or in person.

When you connect with the appropriate people, pay close attention to how each policy actor (someone close to or actually involved in the decision making) describes the policy objectives, its desired outcomes, and the process for achieving them. Once you understand the issues and decisions, monitor the way that the messages are related to those in charge of putting the policy into action. You can do this by asking for copies of the administrative directives that have been written to carry out the new policy. In almost every case, these are public documents that you are entitled to see. By undertaking these steps, you will be able to track the emergence and implementation of the new textbook policy. You will also be able to tell the extent to which the policy has been implemented as intended by those who made it.

The same activity can be done at the local level as well. Suppose that the city council and mayor have agreed upon the need for the city to purchase an area with some old homes near a public park, with the expressed intent of leveling those homes to expand the park. Frequently, cities are allowed to do such things under the power of *eminent domain,* an authority that gives local governments the right to take private land for public use, providing that owners are compensated for their loss.

To continue, let's suppose that the city leaders instruct the city attorney or department of real estate to work out the details of the land transfer. Would it not be interesting to know whether the homeowners are being given a "fair" price? How about the basis of determining that price? Would it not be important to know whether the city had other choices? Would it not be just as interesting to learn whether other city residents are comfortable with this expenditure of public funds? The answers to these questions tell us much not only about the policy commitment, but the conditions under which it may be implemented. In this instance, you would want to contact the city clerk and the city attorney or department of real estate to learn their interpretations of this policy. It would be important to get the reactions of elected officials as well. You might be surprised to discover the interpretations of each policymaking unit.

For a public policy to succeed, all participating parties must be "on the same page." The public policymakers and bureaucrats may not all agree about the wisdom of the policy, but they need to agree on what it means and how they are going to carry it out. If different agencies do not share the same vision, then implementation will be difficult, if not impossible. One easy way to determine clarity is to see whether the agencies involved share the same sense of what needs to be done. It can be a fascinating—and eye-opening—experience.

Comparing Intentions with Outcomes

How do you know when a public policy has been carried out? In many cases, it is a matter of constant review of the ongoing efforts undertaken by bureaucrats. In other cases, it's simply a matter of comparing "before" and "after." Before refers to public policy that is about to be implemented; after refers to the public policy once it has been put into place. Ultimately, a policy is implemented when the outcome—the actual result of what is done—corresponds with the intention. Simply put, successful implementation occurs when before and after appear as mirror images of one another.

That having been said, it is important to note that implementation rarely occurs exactly as intended. Insufficient funds, a change of key administrators, new directions, poor oversight, and bargaining can interfere individually or in combination with the implementation process. Rarely do these or other obstacles shoot down a public policy altogether, although often they may affect the extent to which a policy is implemented. Thus, more times than not, we see *implementation by degree,* or the carrying out of a public policy to some extent.

By tracking the described public policy with the actions of bureaucrats, you can determine to what extent the policy is carried out. Here are a few simple rules to follow:

- Make sure that the policy in question is official and that it has been recorded with the proper government authority such as the city attorney, the county clerk, or secretary of state. The more something is "written in stone," the easier it is to be sure of its intentions. You can do this by checking with the appropriate government depository or records department after the new policy is announced.
- Find out whether there is an assigned bureaucracy (or bureaucracies) to carry out the public policy and the specific circumstances and responsibilities of the bureaucracy's work, including if and when members of the bureaucracy are supposed to report to public policymakers.
- Monitor the progress of the policy by reviewing the official implementation reports issued by bureaucrats to policymakers. Along the way, check to see what follow-up, if any, has been undertaken by the media.
- Check out such records as campaign contribution statements or press conferences held by government leaders, interest groups, or powerful individuals who try to change the effect of the public policy as administrators are putting it into place. Your vigilance can go far in keeping everyone "honest," or at least true to the stated objectives of the policy.
- Hold the public policymakers accountable if the bureaucrats fail to administer the policy as designed. Even though local, state, or federal government administrators usually carry out the policies, responsibility for the policy begins and ends with those chosen to decide it. The last thing a public policymaker wants to see is a large group of angry or disappointed people sitting in the foyer of city hall, the legislature, or wherever the policy is made. Citizens like you can have tremendous impact in keeping policymakers "on task." Again, if the policy in question is the product of your efforts and/or is closely connected with community activities in which you have taken part, you will be especially qualified to monitor that policy's implementation.

In the public policymaking process, the camera lights tend to shine on the close legislative votes, executive orders or proclamations, and judicial decisions. Attention is drawn to these venues because they are visible centers of political conflict and the sources of decisions that will affect us down the

CASE STUDY: IMPLEMENTING A NEW POLICY ON RACIAL PROFILING   131

road. But it is after the lights are off and the reporters have left the "photo op" that the mettle of the policy and those who made it are tested.

Case Study: Implementing a New Policy on Racial Profiling

A major civil rights issue in recent years concerns racial profiling, the law enforcement practice of targeting someone for investigation on the basis of that person's race, national origin, or ethnicity. Such stereotyping has long been a grievance of minority groups believing they have been unfairly victimized. The grievance has sometimes been claimed by other groups, including teenagers and young adults, who are often targeted in drug and alcohol investigations. Concerns about racial profiling have increased in recent years as part of the effort to manage illegal immigration. In response to the allegations of poor or unfair treatment, there have been attempts at all levels of government to end law enforcement practices based on discriminatory stereotyping.

Let's assume police officials in your community have followed suit. In response to pressure from federal and state agencies, as well as from civil rights groups, your police commissioner initiated a new policy seeking to end such practices. The policy mandates new guidelines for investigative procedures and a series of training courses for all law enforcement personnel. Implementation of the policy has drawn mixed reviews, with the commissioner's office and the Patrolmen's Benevolent Association (police officers' union) insisting that the new policy is being successfully implemented, and the local chapter of the American Civil Liberties Union and an alliance of minority group organizations insisting that it is not.

To resolve this debate and determine what is really going on, all parties concerned have asked faculty at your institution to undertake a study of the new policy and its implementation. Your instructor is one of the faculty involved and has decided to engage your class in some of the basic research for this project. For a class assignment you have been asked to summarize your preliminary thoughts on the following questions:

1. What would be the first thing you would want to find out in this investigation? What would you first want to look at? How would you determine if the police commissioner's mandate was issued in good faith?

2. How would you define a "successful" implementation of the new policy? What would be your criteria?

3. What sorts of data would you want to look at? Whom would you want to interview? What resources would you want to consider?

4. How would organizational and administrative issues be relevant to this study? What sort of "paper trail" do you think you would have to follow? How would you address the issue of accountability?

5. What does this case study suggest about the role of "street-level bureaucrats" in public policymaking?

6. What might you learn from similar policy initiatives elsewhere? How would such information help your study?

7. Implementation of new policies on volatile issues such as this must deal with differing perceptions of the same set of facts. How would you try to get at the "truth" that might be masked by subjective perceptions and feelings?

8. How should the study distinguish between discriminatory stereotyping and legitimate profiling that law enforcement officers sometimes need to employ in the course of their investigations?

Reflection

Now that you know the power of implementation, take some time to assess the value of this concept upon the public policymaking process. You can do this through group discussions or individually by comparing the design of a policy with the way it has turned out. What criteria would you use to determine whether a public policy has been implemented as intended? How would you feel if a policy you had worked for was scuttled "after the fact?" Conversely, can you imagine a circumstance where society would be better served by someone who undermined the implementation of a policy?

Fundamentally, another set of questions revolves around the relationship between public policymakers and the constitutional framework in which they are supposed to operate. How fair or right is it for someone to place his or her own actions above the rules that have been established for all of us, even if we may agree with the outcome? That is, what good are the rules for society if they can be easily bent or distorted by authorities who choose their own courses of action in spite of those rules? The moral to the story is this: It is a lot more difficult to make a public policy work than it is to create the policy in the first place!

Student Projects

Long-term group—Settle upon a recent public policy enacted at a local level and keep tabs on the follow-through, or implementation, by the assigned bureaucracy. Do this by attending future meetings of the policymaking body. Make notes of what was done to assure implementation. Are there efforts to change the policy after the fact, and if so, by whom? If the public policy was not carried out according to plan, try to determine what kept it from being put into place. What can you do to ensure that the public policy is carried out as intended?

Short-term individual—Focus on a local bureaucracy. Compare what the agency or administrative unit is supposed to do with what it actually does. What factors help the bureaucracy succeed according to its design? What factors undermine its efforts? Based upon your research, are there sufficient controls over the bureaucracy?

Discussion Questions

1. How do you know when you have actually met the objectives of something you intended to do? What kinds of criteria do you use to determine whether you have succeeded?
2. Assuming that you are attempting to carry out a policy, to what extent does your success depend upon the cooperation of others? How can you secure the collaboration of people you need in order to assure success? What impediments might keep you from succeeding?
3. As a participant in the political process, what agencies or policymakers can you call upon to ensure that public policy is carried out along the lines of its original design?
4. Are some public policies easier to monitor than others? What factors come into play?
5. Regarding the constitutional framework, what checks did the framers provide to assure implementation? Given the increased complexity of our society, to what extent do you believe that those checks exist in the twenty-first century?
6. Has your experience with implementation of your public policy altered your view of the various policy alternatives you once considered (chapter 3)? If so, how? Knowing then what you know now, would you have selected a different alternative?

Notes

1. In his seminal work on the subject, Eugene Bardach views implementation as "a form of politics in which the very existence of an already defined policy mandate, legally and legitimately authorized in some prior political process, affects the strategy and tactics of the struggle." In other words, the process is anything but automatic. See *The Implementation Game* (Cambridge, MA: MIT Press, 1979), p. 37.

2. B. Guy Peters, *American Public Policy: Promise and Performance,* 6th ed. (Washington, DC: CQ Press, 2004), p. 105.

3. Malcolm L. Goggin, Ann O'M. Bowman, James P. Lester, and Lawrence J. O'Toole Jr., *Implementation Theory and Practice* (New York: HarperCollins, 1990), pp. 37–38.

4. See Kenneth J. Meier and John Bohte, *Politics and the Bureaucracy: Policymaking in the Fourth Branch of Government,* 5th ed. (Pacific Grove, CA: Wadsworth, 2006).

5. "Bureaucracy" derives from the French word "bureau," originally a special type of desk that was favored by French officials because it had drawers for holding papers. Bureau itself comes from another French word, "burel," a reddish-brown coarse woolen cloth that covered the tops of such desks. Eventually, bureau came to refer to the offices as well as the desks of such public officials. The phrase "red tape," which is commonly associated with bureaucracy and bureaucracies, takes its meaning from the tape in which decrees, regulations, and other documents produced by such offices were bound.

6. Most social scientists consider Max Weber to be the father of the concept of bureaucracy. See his "Bureaucracy" in *From Max Weber: Essays in Sociology,* trans. H. H. Gerth and C. Wright Mills (New York: Oxford University Press, 1962), pp. 196–244. For a more modern treatment of the subject, see Anthony Downs, *Inside Bureaucracy* (Prospect Heights, IL: Waveland, originally published in 1966 and reissued in 1994).

7. Ann O'M. Bowman and Richard C. Kearney, *State and Local Government,* 7th ed. (Boston: Houghton Mifflin, 2008), p. 199.

8. Robert T. Nakamura and Frank Smallwood refer to this capability as a "compliance mechanism." See their book *The Politics of Implementation* (New York: St. Martin's, 1980), pp. 59–60.

9. Several accounts have focused on billions of dollars in lost federal revenue because of a lack of IRS resources to collect the money. See "Uncollected Taxes Reach \$290 Billion," *The Wall Street Journal Online,* February 15, 2006, and "Union Leader Advocates More Resources for IRS, Better Use," *Government Executive,* April 9, 2007, an online publication of *Government Executive Magazine.*

10. Sometimes bureaucracies do not change with the circumstances of their work. Consider the federal Food and Drug Administration (FDA), which is charged with protecting the quality of the nation's food supply as one of its responsibilities. With the discovery of bioengineering techniques to produce genetically engineered animals as food sources, scientists have been awaiting a whole new set of rules from the FDA for more than fifteen years. Yet, without such rules, scientists don't know what is permissible and investors are leery of providing assistance—an uncomfortable

situation in a world where food is becoming scarce and expensive. See "Without U.S. Rules, Biotech Food Lacks Investors," *New York Times,* July 30, 2007, pp. A1, A14.

11. Grover Starling describes a set of "design criteria" to help a bureaucracy succeed in fulfilling its mission. See his *Managing the Public Sector,* 6th ed. (Fort Worth: Harcourt College Publishers, 2006), pp. 305–307.

12. Sometimes, government reorganization can go a long way toward promoting continuity of objectives through the implementation phase. Congress and President George W. Bush attempted to promote antiterrorism efforts through creation of the Department of Homeland Security, a new cabinet department that brought together several federal units that had been operating in a variety of unconnected arrangements. See "Signing Homeland Security Bill, Bush Appoints Ridge as Secretary," *New York Times,* November 26, 2002, pp. A1, A17.

13. The more independent a bureaucracy is, the more difficult it is to hold it accountable for any actions. See Michael D. Reagan, *Regulation: The Politics of Policy* (Boston: Little, Brown, 1987), pp. 55–66.

14. "Katrina Report Spreads Blame," *Washington Post,* February 12, 2006, p. A1.

15. Oversight activity by Congress often sounds better in theory than it is in practice, according to Roger H. Davidson and Walter J. Olesak. See their *Congress & Its Members,* 10th ed. (Washington, DC: CQ Press, 2006), pp. 359–361.

16. For a discussion of the vertical and horizontal matrices of power, see Larry N. Gerston, *American Federalism: A Concise Introduction* (Armonk, NY: M.E. Sharpe, 2007).

17. Theodore J. Lowi deals with this issue extensively in *The End of Liberalism,* 2nd ed. (New York: W.W. Norton, 1989).

18. The shortage of electricity in the West, for example, has led some state governments to forgo clean air in the effort to obtain more electricity generated by smog-polluting plants. This is a trade-off that has generated little discussion. See Gary Polakovic, "Price for More Megawatts Is More Smog," *Los Angeles Times,* June 14, 2001, p. A-1.

19. The case, *Massachusetts v. Environmental Protection Agency* (05–1120), was decided in 2007 by a vote of 5–4. For information leading up to the decision, see "EPA Won't Regulate 'Greenhouse Gases,'" *Los Angeles Times,* August 29, 2003, p. A19 and "California Plots Greenhouse-Gas Strategy," *The Wall Street Journal,* November 17, 2006, p. A4.

20. Michael Lipsky, *Street-Level Bureaucracy* (New York: Russell Sage Foundation, 1983), p. xxi.

21. For an honest look at the trials and tribulations of whistle-blowers, see C. Fred Alford's *Whistleblowers: Broken Lives and Organizational Power* (Ithaca, NY: Cornell University Press, 2001).

6 EVALUATION
Does the Policy Make Sense?

As we pointed out in the previous chapter, much of the interest in the public policymaking process centers on the dynamic energy that goes *into* the decisions. Once the policies are made, interest often drops off in favor of focusing on other problems in need of resolution, and discussion begins anew. Yet we know from our examination of implementation that what happens to a policy *after* the fact can be as or more critical than the development of the policy itself. In fact, it is only during the implementation phase that we learn whether the policy was carried out as the public policymakers designed. Still, there is one more step to completing the public policymaking cycle—the process of *evaluation*.

Evaluation follows implementation. By comparing promises with performance, we are able to determine the extent to which a public policy has matched expectations.[1] And by reviewing the outcome in terms of the overall wisdom or success of the objective, we judge the merit of the public policy.[2] That is what evaluation is all about. Viewed as a "follow-up" experience, evaluation helps us understand the impact of a policy on the various parts of the political, social, or economic systems that it has been designed to address.[3] Evaluation is, in a sense, a report card on how well policy analysts and decision makers have done their job: did they analyze the problem correctly, envision appropriate alternatives, select the most appropriate one, and implement it effectively?

The line between implementation and evaluation is sometimes difficult to grasp.[4] The difference is that with evaluation, we move from whether a public policy was carried out to whether a public policy was carried out the way that we had hoped or anticipated. The distinction may be slight at times, but it is important nonetheless. Properly carried out, evaluation closes the loop on the public policymaking process, confirming a successful response to perceived needs and/or suggesting new needs that require further action.[5] In a sense, evaluation provides the basis for starting the process all over again.

136

Sometimes, we do not evaluate very carefully or thoughtfully because it takes a lot of energy to compare "before" with "after," particularly to the extent that we are affected by any changes. Inertia can be a powerful counterweight to change, as well as any assessments of change. That is because we generally find a comfort level in doing the same thing the same way again and again. In addition, since evaluation tests whether public policies have worked as intended, managers and other bureaucrats sometimes resist the effort because of what might be learned and, more to the point, what they might have to do.[6] Think of the pain someone goes through if, after all the effort to make and carry out a public policy, it doesn't do what people expected. Such knowledge can be disheartening. Given that new policies disrupt comfortable patterns, evaluation becomes an important—if potentially uncomfortable—tool for assessing the public policy effort that threatens to change those patterns.

The evaluation process can be an eye-opening experience for public policymakers as well as individuals. Sometimes, policymakers forget or neglect to assign management of a new policy to the appropriate bureaucracy for implementation. On other occasions, the implementing individuals or unit simply fail to do the assigned job. Even if implementation takes place, those affected by it may not be satisfied with the way in which the new policy meets its objectives. In other cases, evaluation can show that the policy is a poor fit for the objectives established by the public policymakers. Then, there are times when evaluation reveals that the initial issues leading to the policy were inaccurately diagnosed, thus setting the stage for a public policy that will not work. Whether for these or other reasons, evaluation provides the ammunition for future change and policy refinement. It is important to keep these possibilities in mind as you evaluate the public policies around you as well as any that you have helped formulate. It's one thing to know whether a public policy has been carried out; it's quite another to assess whether the public policy as carried out has lived up to expectations, or caused unexpected problems as a result of implementation.

Part of the uniqueness of evaluation is that the experience allows a postimplementation audit of the policy commitment as well as opportunities for change. By examining the consequences of the public policy that has been put in place, we get a handle on whether to continue, amend, or possibly scrap the policy altogether. In this respect, evaluation represents simultaneously the end of the policymaking process and the beginning of the next wave of that process, showing once again the extent to which public policymaking is a continuous activity.

If you have been wholly or partly successful in initiating and implementing a public policy, you will certainly want to take an interest in its outcome. But even if you were not actively involved, you will find the evaluation process and its tools generally useful in monitoring public policy, perhaps especially so where those policies affect directly community projects which you have helped to shape.

Who Evaluates, and Why?

In a sense, we are all evaluators. Throughout the course of our daily routines, we review our own activities from a variety of perspectives such as whether they turned out as we originally hoped; whether they cost more than we first thought; whether they took more time or used more resources than we anticipated; or whether our goals may have changed over time. In other words, evaluation speaks to our level of satisfaction. But evaluation is more than an academic exercise. Through this activity we determine future plans and directions. We may not think of such reviews as "evaluation," but they are.

On an individual level, the evaluation process deals with appraisal. We evaluate because, just like public policymakers, we want to see the best possible results with limited resources, whether it is money, time, or authority. Suppose that you spend much more money than you expected over a period of time and want to understand what "went wrong." That's evaluation. Or maybe you commit to a weekly project such as feeding the homeless or tutoring elementary schoolchildren, only to decide a few weeks into the activity that the program is poorly administered or geared for people who really don't need the agency's services. That is also evaluation. Or perhaps you watch the way a college administration allocates funds for sports, only to decide that the money would be better spent on speakers or community events. Such a judgment, too, is evaluation.

Rather than an instant reaction, true evaluation usually occurs at a point after implementation of the public policy. That's because it is important to see whether the policy will even work to begin with, and we don't know the answer until the policy is given the opportunity to work. That means making sure that the bureaucrats have the necessary tools such as money, time, and political support of the policymakers to carry out their tasks. To evaluate without giving the policy a chance to work is little more than biased prejudgment.

Evaluation in the Public Policymaking Environment

In the public policy environment, evaluation works much the same way as an individual assessment of a personal activity or commitment. There is one major difference, however. The "public" nature of the policy means that individuals in positions of authority respond to decisions that affect a portion, if not all, of society. By undertaking this process, they may well direct public resources to rearrange the ways things happen.

As discussed earlier, we know that the public policymaking process can be full of conflict. We also know that implementation of the decisions emerging from these conflicts may affect people in different ways. Policymakers are aware of this, too. Bearing in mind that they will never satisfy everyone all of the time, they usually want to know if the policy has worked as well as they have hoped. If they see or learn about disappointment, anger, or frustration, these "change agents" may feel the need to rearrange the policy in ways that will leave fewer people upset. This is anything but an academic exercise, for if public policymakers fail to respond to the cry of an angry public, they may lose their jobs at the next election!

Public policymakers are not the only people who evaluate the results of their efforts. On an individual level, we sometimes evaluate public policies, too. We do so not because we can necessarily do anything about them at the moment, but as a way of letting policymakers know what we think about what they have done and how it has or has not worked. How many times have you watched a new policy put into effect, only to say to yourself that it is not doing any good? Or how many times have you observed or read about a new public policy, with the conclusion that it is a dumb or unnecessary thing to do? These reactions are forms of evaluation.

Sometimes, we are intentionally brought into the evaluating process as part of a comprehensive review conducted by others. For example, as students, you are often asked to fill out an evaluation form in a course. That feedback goes to the professor, the department chair, and others who monitor the academic environment. The results may help determine whether the course is taught again, the way that the course is taught, and potentially a professor's tenure or possible salary increase. Similarly, if you take your car in for repair, you may be sent an evaluation form that covers a multitude of issues such as diagnosis, responsiveness, quality, or expectations. As with the feedback on your college courses, in many cases these evaluations will be used as a measurement or guide for future service.

Evaluators

To get the evaluating job done professionally in the public policymaking environment, decision makers usually call upon special agencies or individuals with expertise in the policy area under review. Often these people are professionals such as accountants, economists, statisticians, attorneys, or individuals who have particular insight or skills that provide unique perspective concerning the policy that they are supposed to evaluate. If the review centers on a new academic program, the evaluators may be experienced administrators, master teachers, or subject experts. If the review is about the performance of a state mental health program, the evaluators may be mental health experts, efficiency experts, physicians, law enforcement, hospital administrators, insurance associations, and local support groups. Whatever the program or activity under review, those chosen to evaluate are usually well versed in the area.[7] Further, the more neutral the evaluator, the more likely that his or her assessments will carry weight with those who have called for the review. Therein lies the essence of their credibility as well as the worth of their conclusions and recommendations.

Evaluation takes place at every level of government. Let's consider an example. The charge has been made in many communities in recent years that local police detain many more African-Americans or Latinos than Caucasians in high-crime areas as part of an effort to prevent illegal behavior. Such activity might lead to complaints from individuals or community groups about "racial profiling," or the prejudicial singling out of people for interrogation by police because of their race rather than their actions.[8] With these charges, the mayor or city council might ask the police chief or an independent citizens' police review board to evaluate the practices of the police, and to make recommendations for improving the situation. Pure and simple, that is evaluation.

Similarly, suppose that a state governor announces a new preschool day care program that has not been funded by the legislature. Knowing that all programs cost money, legislative leaders may wonder whether the governor is prematurely (and illegally) earmarking the expenditure of state funds, or relying upon money that comes from the federal government or other sources. To better understand the possibilities of such developments, the legislature may designate a state auditor or other appropriate public official to review and submit a report on the spending activity of the chief executive. The result of that activity might lead to possible action steps ranging from a press conference to a lawsuit. This, too, is evaluation.

On those occasions when professionals are called upon to evaluate, fundamental to the experience are the competency and integrity of the evaluator. Those who are assigned the evaluating task must be thought of as capable in their areas of work because they have been entrusted to determine the worth or success of a public program. For their part, evaluators need to put their own biases aside as much as possible when they review a program or policy. Expertise and objectivity give credibility to the conclusions and recommendations of evaluators.

Evaluation as a Tool of Civic Engagement

Evaluation is critical to your involvement in a community service activity, whether in the form of an individual commitment, class service-learning project, or other venture. Evaluation can be done on an interim basis in the middle of a project; it can also be done in a postimplementation context at the end of the experience.[9]

On an interim basis, you evaluate your efforts at numerous junctures to see how things are going. The technical term for this process is **benchmarking;** it simply means that you are evaluating the program as well as your own progress and success (or failure) at imaginary intersections along the way of your journey. Interim assessments can be valuable, for they may help you see the need to make individual adjustments, react to new assignments, or find better ways of coping with policies or individuals you simply do not like. These internal reviews help us to stay on task and see the job through.

Suppose that you decide to take part in a voter registration project as a means of getting more people involved in the political process. Perhaps your goal is to double the number of registered voters in a particular precinct or neighborhood. If you are assigned to work in an area with disproportionate numbers of people under the age of eighteen, over time the effort may be discouraging as well as unproductive. Armed with this knowledge, you might go to the project director and ask for or suggest a different area to pursue your registration effort. Through this evaluation and input, you can become more effective—thus satisfied—in your service. That is the power of evaluation.

Depending upon the time that the evaluation occurs, the conclusions may be quite different. *Summary* assessments (evaluations undertaken at the end of the process) offer a different perspective from *interim* assessments. Having completed the task gives you a special opportunity to look back on the entire experience in terms of community betterment as well as individual success. Perhaps participation in a project yields unanticipated rewards; perhaps it leads to unanticipated problems. Such lessons may well guide you to consider other activities in the future as well as the merit of the public policy in which you have taken part. On a deeper level, they help you to understand the value of your role as a participant in the public policy arena.

Suppose that you have completed a citizenship training course in which you worked with others to prepare immigrants for the U.S. citizenship examination. In such a program, your responsibilities may well include interaction with Immigration and Customs Enforcement (ICE) officials, employment services, tutors, and others in the political and local economy. Assume, for the sake of argument, that at the end of this hypothetical project only a small portion of the would-be citizens pass the test. What might have gone wrong? Why would the results have turned out as they did? Was the test flawed? Were the teachers poorly trained? Did the "students" have sufficient opportunity to digest the material? The benefit of evaluation at this point might allow you to identify the weak areas of the training program, enabling others to fare better in the future.

Evaluation: Not as Easy as It Looks

At one level, evaluation seems simple enough: it's a matter of comparing outcomes with desired objectives. It takes us back to the policy analysis we looked at in chapter 3. There you learned about the importance of defining objectives or desired outcomes clearly and about selecting appropriate criteria for deciding among alternative policies. If you have handled these nuts and bolts of policy analysis and selection well, you have also provided a sound basis for policy evaluation—for determining whether or not the implemented policy is working.

But is the job really as easy as all that? Not quite. No solution to a problem is ever perfect. As you learned in the last chapter, we can never fully anticipate all of the pitfalls and complications that are likely to be encountered by a policy when it is put into action. However systematically we may have defined our objectives and our selection criteria, often we cannot account for all of the variables that come into play in explaining why something happens or does not happen.

For one thing, our criteria are not always reliable. We live in a world measured ever more by statistics, but statistics are not necessarily valid or relevant. The nineteenth-century British statesman Benjamin Disraeli is supposed to have said that "there are three kinds of lies: lies, damned lies, and statistics."[10] The "facts," in other words, are not always what they seem to be.

Even when the facts are neatly organized for scrutiny, we must be careful in the conclusions we draw from them. Logicians talk about the false inference of post hoc ergo propter hoc (a Latin phrase that means "after this therefore because of this"). An elected public official, for example, may claim that crime in his constituency has gone down because of a particular policy he was responsible for enacting. His claim involves two different questions of evaluation. There may or may not have been a change in the rate of crime and it may or may not have been the result of a particular policy. If there was, in fact, a sizable reduction in crime, it may have been the result of other factors unrelated to the new policy. Separating causal relationships from merely coincidental relationships can sometimes be very difficult but it is essential if evaluation is to succeed.[11]

And there is also the danger of wishful thinking, a danger you need to be especially mindful of when evaluating a policy you believe in or with which you may be closely associated. It can be very difficult for those who have created and strongly advocated a policy to be completely dispassionate, or removed, in evaluating its effectiveness. We may want our policy to succeed so much that we emphasize the evidence in support of our desires while discounting evidence that suggests otherwise. Elected officials sometimes express themselves about their favorite or loathed public policies in such a manner. Faced with the same set of circumstances, those in office "point with pride" while their opponents seeking office "view with alarm." It's sometimes amazing how political leaders in competition choose or emphasize different facts within the same data set. To this extent, you will need to be careful in evaluating your predetermined favorites. The jump from committed advocate to dispassionate judge can be a long one.

Comparing Outcomes with Intentions: Two Approaches

Whether conducted by a public agency or an individual, evaluation tells us much about the performance of the public policymaking experience. Specifically, it shows whether goals have been met and the consequences of the activity related to the achievement of those goals. None of this is to suggest that evaluation is always a neutral or passive experience, despite the expertise of evaluators. That's because beyond the clinical observation of what actually occurs, evaluation also emphasizes our interpretations of what was supposed to take place and whether it was a worthwhile enterprise.

Evaluation entails two components: quantitative measurement and qualitative judgment. Each evaluation component contributes to the answer of a simple question: Has the policy succeeded? Each evaluation component is important in its own right, although sometimes one is more useful than the other. Regardless, evaluation is not simply a matter of an assigned individual or government agency responding to a "checklist"; in fact, the task is filled with uncertainties and contradictions. Nevertheless, quantitative and qualitative evaluation efforts give us a sense of whether the public policy has performed well.

Quantitative Measurement

Quantitative measurement has a "bean counting" focus that scrutinizes the process itself rather than the value of the outcome.[12] The evaluator who uses this approach is likely to stick to "the facts" in terms of measuring the extent to which a public policy has been executed or carried out. There is no matter of judgment here, only the relatively narrow questions of design and compliance, which focus upon whether the policy has been put together correctly and whether implementation has yielded the stated expectations. Thus, with quantitative measurement, evaluators will match the policy objectives with policy outcomes, determine the extent to which the policy has been put into place, attempt to determine the cause of any failure, and make recommendations for corrective action.

Policy Design

Every public policy is launched with a design, which is simply a schematic framework, or political road map, for seeing it through. The design exists to give the implementing authorities direction on such elements as a budget, activities, timeline, procedures, and anything else necessary for assuring success of the public policy. Quantitative evaluation measures outcomes in terms of the intentions outlined in the framework. In other words, has the policy done what it was supposed to do?[13]

Consider a state public policy that requires elementary and secondary teachers to be well-versed in teaching methods as a condition of employment. Now suppose that only some of the local universities include those classes in their curriculum, while others do not. Obviously there is a lack of linkage between the policy objective and its implementation. Analysis of the policy design may tell us why. Perhaps the legislature has neglected to provide the necessary funds for instruction; perhaps there has been poor communication between the state university executives and local university administrators and faculty; maybe there is another explanation, such as school districts failing to check transcripts for this particular preparation. Regardless, the flawed design of a public policy will prevent any substantive evaluation beyond the conclusion that the policy has not even been put to work.

If there is appropriate linkage for application of a public policy, then evaluators will be able to determine the extent to which it has performed as expected. Until then, however, poor design and implementation will prevent anything but a superficial scrutiny. Simply put, you cannot determine the worth of a policy without seeing it in place.

Compliance

An easy way to determine whether a policy succeeds is by measuring the extent to which the implementing agency has done its job in accordance with the instructions or directives. Such quantitative assessments yield a preliminary answer to the simple question, "Has the job been done?"

Suppose that a school district enacts a policy that requires students to achieve a score of 70 percent on a proficiency exam as a requirement for graduation. Anyone failing to reach such a score would be held back until the next year. The task now falls upon the bureaucracy—perhaps the high school principal, dean of students, or examination evaluation team—to carry out that policy.

Concerned about compliance, a bureaucrat or team of bureaucrats would review the examinations to see whether any students fell short of the graduation requirement. Assuming complete or near complete compliance of the policy, the bureaucrat would report successful implementation. However, if a sizable percentage of the students failed to meet the requirement, then the bureaucrat would need to report implementation failure and recommend ways to respond to that failure. Note that all assessments would be based upon a predetermined measurement level (70 percent) and on the numbers of students who passed or failed to meet the objective.

Quantitative measurement depends upon a clear statement and understanding of all the variables relating to a policy. In the example above, the possible variables would include the design of the exam, clear statements of expectations, student performances on the examination, and sanctions for those who fail to meet the expectations. Assuming such clarity, it then becomes a simple matter of determining whether the graduation requirement is enforced and, if not, why not.

Even with such specificity, there can be times when quantitative evaluation gets mushy or imprecise.[14] As we have noted, capturing all of the variables and sorting out causal relationships from the merely coincidental may not be easy. For example, if the schools suffer from a citywide power blackout lasting several days or if sizable numbers of teachers fail to report to work because of the flu, is it possible that there will be causes other than student behavior for the results? If the school personnel teach students from a set of materials not compatible with the proficiency examination, are students operating at a disadvantage? Suddenly, a question once thought to be "cut and dried" (either they meet the expectation or they do not) may have a blunt edge!

Here is another example. Consider a state public policy that prohibits assisted suicide. Suppose the law defines "assisted" as the effort by an individual to provide devices or chemicals that would help terminate another person's life. So far, so good. Given these terms, you could evaluate the success of the law by keeping track of "suicides" that take place under the conditions described as "assisted suicide." But suppose that the law says nothing about a physician who provides verbal or written information to the individual who seeks to take his or her own life. Or suppose that individual has checked out books on assisted suicide from the local library. What happens then? Has an individual broken the law when he or she gives simple advice? Can a librarian be blamed because he or she told an individual where to locate books about the termination of life? Suddenly, even quantitative measurement can be in jeopardy because the definition of the public policy may not be sufficiently precise.

Assuming a well-written public policy, quantitative evaluation can tell us much about whether the policy has succeeded according to its design. But if implementation is open to interpretation because of ambiguously defined objectives, unanticipated issues, or poorly constructed definitions of measurement, then it may be difficult to evaluate the success of the policy.

Qualitative Judgment

Whereas quantitative measurement deals with determining whether something has been implemented according to plan, qualitative judgment responds to the wisdom of the policy itself. Here we move from the questions of possibilities and probabilities to the concerns of ideals, principles, and values. With this form of assessment, the fundamental question centers upon the worth of the policy that has been put into place. In other words, does it make sense? And to whom? This issue, however, raises its own set of complications.[15]

Imagine your public policy on racial profiling has been motivated by concerns about social justice in your community—a worthy goal that might be the basis for evaluating many public policy initiatives. But how does one measure "social justice" or determine whether a particular policy has been successful in attaining it? Inspiring as they can be in addressing and advocating a public issue, such subjective criteria must be translated into discernible goals so as to serve the interests of evaluation.

The "worth" of a particular policy may be determined in several respects. For example, does the public policy have unintended consequences? Does the policy create new problems, even if it addresses the original issue? Is there bias in the way that an evaluator approaches assessment of the policy? Even if the policy is working as intended, is it still a good idea now that it has been put into place? These are some of the key concerns related to qualitative measurement.

Unintended Consequences

Under ideal conditions, public policies are drawn along relatively narrow lines to respond as closely as possible to the issue that has been defined by or for the policymakers. There is a good reason for this approach: inasmuch as new policies usually alter the status quo, the changes most likely to encounter the least resistance are those that are modest in design and clearly directed. Still, even a carefully designed and executed policy may have unintended consequences that create another issue as serious or more serious than the original problem.[16]

Suppose that a university student government enacts an anti-censorship policy that requires the student newspaper to accept all ads regardless of their source or content. The purpose of the policy would be to promote the campus as a center of free speech and free press, cornerstones of the First Amendment. With that policy in place, an individual or organization could submit a newspaper ad that encourages gay-bashing, anti-Semitism, segregation, or other hate-crime behaviors that are either unpalatable to most people or perhaps unconstitutional as defined by the courts. As a result of such inflammatory language, some students or community members might feel provoked or become violent with one another about the issue. Under these circumstances, the policy may be successful in the narrow context of its original intentions but a cause of concern nonetheless, with the unintended consequences serving as the spawning grounds for a new public policy issue—campus unrest.

New Problems

Sometimes a public policy may be carefully designed and implemented in the context of the issue that public policymakers intend to address. Furthermore, evaluation may determine that the policy has thoroughly met its objectives, suggesting successful implementation and closure on the issue. But in solving one problem, the policy may expose another issue that previously escaped notice. This new insight happens not so much as a result of short-sightedness but because of the lack of information prior to creation of the policy that has been put into place.

For example, consider a shopping mall that is used as a "hangout" for local teenagers. Perhaps the pedestrian traffic of these adolescents is so extensive that shop owners demand the city council enact an ordinance that requires mall-visiting teenagers to have an adult with them after 7:00 P.M. As a result of this policy, teenage presence at the shopping mall drops precipitously, fulfilling the hopes of the merchants. Now suppose that in the wake of this ordinance, teenage crime in the city increases dramatically. It may well be that this new "problem" is worse than the original. It may also suggest that the shopping mall policy never addressed the real issue, which is unsupervised youngsters with too much free time or without a neighborhood recreation center of their own. With this new question on the table, city leaders may be forced to deal with matters far more important than shopping mall traffic.

Bias

Because evaluators are attempting to assess the worth of a policy, their conclusions are very important to policymakers, administrators, and, sometimes, segments of the public. Quite a bit may ride on what these individuals decide; thus, the expectation is that evaluators will do everything possible to keep their own subjective feelings far from the policy that they are asked to assess.

Assuming that evaluators work for public agencies or institutions, they generally attempt to set aside their values as much as possible in an effort to be impartial. Nevertheless, it is sometimes very difficult for the public policy evaluator to step outside of his or her own value setting. As long as people are involved in the evaluating process, this "human" side will inevitably be part of the mix. As we have noted, for you this may be the most difficult challenge of all in policy evaluation, if it concerns a policy with whose implementation you have been involved.

On some occasions, bias may creep into an evaluator's efforts without his or her conscious awareness. Suppose a bureaucrat at the FDA is asked to evaluate the merits of a new oral contraception pill. If that individual has strong pro-life or pro-choice feelings, it is possible that his or her evaluation may be unknowingly tainted, yielding a report with skewed findings. Or imagine a university student council that has to evaluate a proposed allocation for a foreign student exchange program in a country loathed by some of the council members. Such a value system may keep these leaders from evaluating the program without bias. These examples underscore the frailties of qualitative measurement; it is anything but "perfect science."

Although almost everyone has a bias regarding one issue or another, bias does not necessarily render evaluation useless. If there is self-awareness of prejudice, the evaluator may ask to be removed from the assignment. Alternatively, if public policymakers perceive a bias on the part of the evaluator, they may request another evaluation as a form of insurance. Still, it is possible that bias will sneak into the evaluating process regardless of every safeguard imaginable. What does this mean? Only that the public policymaking process begins and ends with human values. It is just something to keep in mind if you undertake the evaluation task.

Changing Values

Modern society is not stagnant. Whether because of technology, invention, war, or other factors, society changes over time, often in unpredictable ways, and with those changes come changes in our expectations of public policy. As you learned in chapter 1, in some ways we expect more and in other ways we expect less of government than previous generations did. We have come to expect government to help provide economic security and to protect the water we drink and the food we eat. We do not anticipate (as our ancestors did) that government will want to regulate the clothes we wear or the activities in our bedrooms. As once-treasured principles or doctrines evolve, we sometimes rethink public policies that carry out those ideas. This type of evaluation can be both painful and lengthy, particularly if the policy in question has been popular over time.

Many controversial public policies—large and small—have been reevaluated because of changing values. For almost a century the United States was a "slave republic," but slavery eventually disappeared, as much because of a change in our society's values as the result of the triumph of the industrial North over an agrarian South in the Civil War. And racial attitudes have continued to evolve. In 1896 the U.S. Supreme Court ruled in *Plessy v. Ferguson* that racial segregation was fully consistent with the nation's constitutional principles and political ideals. Scarcely more than half a century later, the Supreme Court (in *Brown v. Board of Education of Topeka*, 1954) changed its mind and ruled that segregation violated those norms. Changing values (as well as changed social, economic, and cultural circumstances) can sometimes prompt dramatic reversals in public policy. And more recently still, in 2007, the U.S. Supreme Court declared that schools could not use race as a sole criterion when undertaking the process of voluntary school desegregation (*Parents Involved in Community Schools v. Seattle, 2007*).

Similar reconsiderations have occurred on the question of abortion. True enough, the U.S. Supreme Court declared that a woman had full control of her body during the first trimester of pregnancy in the famous *Roe v. Wade* (1972) case. Since then, however, Congress and the states have revisited the issue with numerous laws affecting the conditions and timing of abortions, including mandatory counseling and parental notification.[17] New developments concerning the use of stem cells from aborted fetuses have added even more controversy to the abortion issue as well as laws and court rulings on late-term or "partial birth" abortions.[18] That is the dynamism of the public policymaking process.

Changing values vary in the ways and to the extent that they challenge existing commitments. For example, a city council's decision to rezone a particular land parcel from agricultural to commercial use after evaluating the performance of a ten-year economic growth plan may be important to those closely involved with the old and new policies, but not likely to affect the larger political environment such as a state or the nation. In other words, this evaluation would impact relatively few people concerned with a relatively narrow issue.

Contrast the rezoning issue with the decision of a state legislature that, after evaluating the accuracy of DNA tests, decides to allow them as elements in the judicial appeals process in capital punishment cases. Such a decision is likely to have a profound impact upon the lives of both defendants and of the victim's family members. But on a more fundamental basis, it has the potential of altering historically defined constitutional issues relating to the rights of the accused, thereby impacting all members of society. In this instance, the changing value may be significant to a much larger population and on much more significant grounds.

One Form of Evaluation Every Policymaker Wishes to Avoid

Perhaps the surest sign a particular policy may have failed or be in trouble is finding itself under legal challenge in the courts. The dockets of our state and federal courts are filled with cases of public policies that may have run afoul of the law. Maybe the policy conflicts with other laws or regulations that supersede it. Worse still, it might find itself challenged on constitutional grounds (i.e., in violation of the state or U.S. Constitution). However well intended in its design, however successful in achieving its desired objectives, a policy will fail if it violates such legal norms. This can be the policymaker's worst nightmare. There is no more definitive (or negative) an evaluation of a public policy than the U.S. Supreme Court declaring it null and void on constitutional grounds. Even if the policy survives such a challenge in the courts, litigation may delay or alter its implementation and will likely consume time, money, and other resources in its defense.

As you learned in chapter 1, this liability in our public policymaking has been a peculiar characteristic of American governance over the last two centuries. Until recently, at least, public policymaking in most of the world's constitutional democracies has been in large measure free from such constitutional scrutiny. But, as Tocqueville observed, in the United States most public issues sooner or later become legal issues.[19] No policy, however well crafted, can be made immune to such scrutiny. The policymaker cannot fully anticipate the effects and consequences of a policy initiative—or what a court of law might say about it. There is much truth in Chief Justice Charles Evans Hughes's observation: that the Constitution is what judges say it is.[20] An understanding of the law (or at least knowing where to obtain sound legal advice) is essential if the policymaker is to reduce the likelihood of a negative report card in the courts.

Some Final Tips

So how might you go about evaluating the implementation of your policy (or any policy in your community in which you may be interested)? Once you have clarified the policy's objectives and the criteria for determining its success, the process will likely take you back to the grounds of your initial research (chapter 3): obtaining and reviewing relevant data. If the policy is new (as it is likely to be if you have had a hand in it), there may be little data yet available, but find out what you can from the responsible agencies and beneficiaries of that policy. Some of the old information you uncovered in your initial research may also be useful in providing a frame of reference or comparison. One question you are likely to encounter is this: the policy was successful or unsuccessful compared to what? Similar or different policies addressing the same problem elsewhere may be useful as comparisons in answering this question.

If little relevant data are available, you may decide to generate your own through a variety of survey evaluation instruments. For example, you may wish to survey a group of people about an issue before and after a policy to deal with it has been put in place. The comparisons might be interesting, particularly to the extent that implementation of the new policy changes opinions. If you do not know enough about survey design (how to write questions and how to decide whom to ask are two common problems), your instructor may be able to help—or at least to guide you to appropriate material in the library.

Likewise, you may wish to examine attitudes on a qualitative basis by asking open-ended questions to small gatherings of what are sometimes called "focus groups." Imagine a look at the issue you examined in the previous chapter, racial profiling, through two different focus groups—one white and the other nonwhite. Because of different sets of experiences and values, each group would probably give you radically different responses to the same questions! Such are the benefits of gathering your own data for evaluation.

Conclusions

Evaluation offers the opportunity to assess outcomes of the public policy-making process and reshape the direction of that process; it is the mechanism that compares promise with performance, as well as the linkage between the present and the future. Although measurement characteristics (quantitative assessment) may imply a clear-cut benefit of some forms of evaluation, the process is often dependent upon values and issues (qualitative assessment) that underlie the policy under review. In addition, the results of the evaluation experience may be affected by the values of those individuals and agencies assigned the evaluation task.

These nuances do not negate the value of evaluation. However, knowing the nuances and conditions related to the process affords us a better understanding of the political environment in which evaluation is arranged and the complicated context in which it occurs. Nevertheless, evaluation helps public policymakers understand the extent to which their policies have succeeded or failed, as well as the emergence of issues they never expected.

Case Study: Charter Schools

Education has a long and rich history in this country. The nation's founders believed that widespread education was essential to their experiment in republican self-government. Horace Mann, the leading educational reformer of the early nineteenth century, took much the same view, declaring that "schoolhouses are the republican line of fortifications." By the end of the Civil War, all states adopted some form of public education, with schools usually organized in local districts.

Given this long-standing investment, it is not surprising that education has always been a lively (and often controversial) public policy issue. Very few public policy matters so closely intertwine the actions of government with our everyday lives. Discontent in recent years has prompted calls for greater accountability, parental choice, experimentation, and community involvement in education. Among the reforms suggested and being tried are tuition credits, educational vouchers, and *charter schools*.

Charter schools (public schools that operate independently of many state and local district rules) became popular during the 1990s. Designed and operated by parents, educators, and community leaders, such schools are public institutions that function largely outside of the traditional school bureaucracy and regulations (some federal guidelines and constitutional guarantees excepted). They are established by a contract or "charter" with either a state agency or local school board. In return for this freedom, charter schools are held accountable to the objectives stated in their charters, most notably improving student performance.

Let's assume that a few years ago, frustrated by the many problems and obstacles of a large, underfunded school district, the department of education at your institution joined a consortium of parents and community leaders to establish a charter school. With greater autonomy, the sponsors believed, such a school would respond more effectively to the educational needs of local youngsters and would allow for curriculum experimentation. Your institution's involvement with this venture brings with it years of experience and familiarity with the educational needs and opportunities of the area. Faculty, staff, and students have long been active in the community's schools, as parents, consultants, and volunteers. Your fellow students have volunteered over the years as reading tutors, organizers of recreational activities, and in other capacities. Student volunteerism has been a major component of the new charter school.

The time has now arrived for the charter school's sponsors to begin to document the success of their venture. In one sense, evaluation is the easiest and most clear-cut part of charter school initiatives. Charter schools are "bottom-line" operations. As noted, they are granted their license to operate with a large measure of independence in return for producing results, usually in the form of improved performance by students attending such a school. A charter school's right to continue operating is dependent upon producing such results. Evaluation in this case, therefore, is clear, specific, and sharply focused.

But is it really that simple? As with all evaluations, asking the right questions is at least as important as getting the right answers.

1. How would you go about evaluating such an effort? What values or measuring criteria would you use? What benchmarking data? How would you determine whether the program was a success or failure?

2. How would you determine whether or not this venture had brought about improved performance in students? How would you isolate the school's influence from other possible factors?

3. Assuming the programs of the school have resulted in better performance, how would you ascertain *why* they had such a result?

4. Though freed from most administrative red tape of their school district, even charter schools must comply with some state and federal regulations, including constitutional guarantees of nondiscrimination and fair treatment. How would you go about determining such compliance?

5. As you have learned, evaluators use both quantitative and qualitative methods of analysis. How could both approaches be used here? What potential variables come to mind? What comparative data?

6. In what ways might a strong familiarity with the school and its programs be an advantage for the evaluator? In what ways might this be a handicap?

7. A good evaluation should examine its subject from multiple perspectives. What perspectives should be examined in this study? What different constituencies should be surveyed? What questions would you want to ask to determine the inherent worth of the policy being implemented?

Reflection

It's easy to conceive of evaluation as an almost sterile process where a technician reviews a list of performance criteria. That's often the case in situations where evaluation depends upon measurement. Giving away school lunches as a way to reduce hunger is a measurable enterprise—weight charts before and after the program can be used to measure the extent to which the program has succeeded. Another measuring stick might consider student performance on standardized tests before and after the new policy.

But you now know that in most circumstances, evaluation is just as important from the standpoint of values as it is in terms of "data points." In the case of a free school lunch program for the hungry, some people might well ask whether such a program even belongs in the schools to begin with. Such concerns underscore some critical questions such as, do the values of the public policymakers mesh with the general values of society, and if not, what are the long-term consequences of major differences? Do the values of the policymakers who create the policy mesh with those of the evaluators? Can the process succeed if the various parties have irreconcilable differences?

Think about a recent experience in which you knowingly (or perhaps unknowingly at the time) evaluated a program or policy. To what extent were your findings measurable? To what extent did your conclusions depend upon your own values? How did your values relate to those individuals who made the public policy? Can we include both measurement and values in the evaluation process, or are there times when they are incompatible? Knowing the answers to these questions only helps in your efforts to assess all that goes on around you.

Student Projects

Long-term group—Discuss among yourselves a school policy that remained the same over the year and another one that seemed to change. What criteria would you use for evaluation? Why has the first policy remained intact? What conditions, pressures, or new facts led the second one to change?

Short-term individual—Trace a "policy" developed in your family regarding a rule or expected behavior. Was it carried out as intended? If so, under what conditions or terms? If not, what kept the policy from its implementation? What evaluation criteria would you use to reach your conclusions?

Discussion Questions

1. It is relatively easy to quantify or measure change. But are numbers enough to decide the merit of a public policy? What other factors might be involved? Why should people bother to evaluate a public policy, anyway?

2. Imagine that you have been asked to evaluate a public policy (perhaps the policy on which you have been working). How would you go about designing an evaluation plan to determine whether the policy is meeting its specified objectives?

3. How can you minimize the impact of personal value judgments and bias in your evaluation? Is it possible for someone to evaluate a policy free of such subjective influences?

4. Assume that your policy initiative has been prompted by a concern for social justice in your community. How would you go about determining whether such an overriding objective has been met? Could the evaluation be complicated by differing opinions of what constitutes social justice? If so, how? And how do you deal with such a problem?

5. Can you identify a public policy in your locality or state that was challenged in a court of law? What were the legal and constitutional issues involved? What happened to the case?

Notes

1. Joseph S. Wholey, Mark A. Abramson, and Christopher Bellavita write that evaluation is critical to determining whether programs live up to their expectations. See "Managing for High Performance: Roles for Evaluators," in their edited volume *Performance and Credibility* (Lexington, MA: Lexington, 1986), p. 2.

2. Guy Beneviste, *Bureaucracy* (San Francisco: Boyd and Fraser, 1977), pp. 42–43.

3. For an example of the unintended effects of implementation that is detected through evaluation, see Mark E. Rushevsky, *Public Policy in the United States* (Pacific Grove, CA: Brooks/Cole, 1990), pp. 16–17.

4. Frank Fischer, *Evaluating Public Policy* (Chicago: Nelson-Hall, 1995), p. 44.

5. Public policymaking is fraught with numerous examples that reveal policy outcomes, or results, quite different from expectations. One such case has existed with deregulation of the telecommunications industry. See "Rising Phone Bills Are Likely Result of Deregulation," *New York Times,* March 30, 1997, pp. 1, 12, and "Cheaper Phone Bills Still On Hold," *San Francisco Chronicle,* February 8, 1999, pp. C-1, C-5.

6. Arnold Love makes this point in "Implementation Evaluation," a chapter in Joseph S. Wholey, Harry P. Hatry, and Kathryn E. Newcomer, eds., *Handbook of*

Practical Evaluation, 2nd ed. (San Francisco: Jossey-Bass, 2004). See pp. 95–96.

7. Joseph Stewart Jr., David M. Gedge, and James P. Lester divide evaluators into two categories: *internal* evaluators, people who are part of a program, and *external* evaluators, people who operate from positions outside the program. See *Public Policy: An Evolutionary Approach,* 3rd ed. (Boston: Thomson Wadsworth, 2008), pp. 133–135.

8. An example of such a study was undertaken by the San Jose, California, Police Department in 2007. The study of more than 34,000 arrests found that blacks and Latinos were considerably more likely than whites to be arrested by force. See "Blacks, Latinos More Likely to Be Arrested by Force," *San Jose Mercury News,* March 21, 2007, pp. 1A, 17A.

9. Part of the evaluation process may take place through the service-learning concept of reflection, where a student periodically reviews his or her experiences. On the importance of reflection in the pedagogy of service learning, see David Kolb, *Experiential Learning: Experiences As the Source of Learning and Development* (Englewood Cliffs, NJ: Prentice-Hall, 1984); Jane C. Kendall, ed., *Combining Service and Learning: A Resource Book for Community and Public Service* (Raleigh, NC: National Society for Experiential Education, 1990); Robert L. Sigmon, *Linking Service with Learning* (Washington, DC: Council of Independent Colleges, 1994); Gail Albert, ed., *Service Learning Reader: Reflections and Perspectives on Service* (Raleigh, NC: National Society for Experiential Education, 1994); and Richard M. Battistoni, *Public Schooling and the Education of Democratic Citizens* (Jackson: University Press of Mississippi, 1985), p. 39.

10. A remark attributed to Disraeli by Mark Twain in his *Autobiography.*

11. Students of evaluation sometimes refer to this dilemma as the problem of determining causal relationships. See Peter H. Rossi, Howard E. Freeman, and Mark W. Lipsey, *Evaluation: A Systematic Approach,* 6th ed. (Thousand Oaks, CA: Sage, 1999), pp. 241–244.

12. For a thorough discussion of quantitative methodologies, see Lawrence B. Mohr, *Impact Analysis for Program Evaluation* (Pacific Grove, CA: Brooks/Cole, 1988).

13. For approaches to quantitative analysis, see Peter J. Haas and J. Fred Springer, *Applied Policy Research* (New York: Garland, 1998). With respect to survey design, see Floyd J. Fowler Jr., *Improving Survey Questions: Design and Evaluation* (Thousand Oaks, CA: Sage, 1995); Arlene Fink and Jacqueline Kosecoff, *How to Conduct Surveys: A Step-by-Step Guide* (Thousand Oaks, CA: Sage Publications, 1985); and Louis M. Rea et al., *Designing and Conducting Survey Research: A Comprehensive Guide* (San Francisco: Jossey-Bass, 1997).

14. In his discussion of environmental policies, Walter A. Rosenbaum complains that bureaucratic discretion can interfere with strict compliance. Such discretion is typically given to the bureaucracy by traditional policymaking authorities such as the legislature and/or executive branch. See his *Environmental Politics and Policy,* 6th ed. (Washington, DC: CQ Press, 2005), pp. 79–80.

15. Qualitative evaluation is discussed in Louise White, *Political Analysis: Technique and Practice,* 3rd ed. (Belmont, CA: Wadsworth, 1994), pp. 211–229.

16. Gene mapping is an excellent case in point. Supported by the National Institutes of Health (which, in turn, is funded by Congress), gene mapping holds the promise of disease eradication. Yet some bioethicists have concluded that the new

capability has raised serious questions in the areas of medical privacy, employment, and reproduction. See "Decoding Raises a Double-Edged Sword on Ethics," *Los Angeles Times,* June 27, 2000, pp. A-1, A-12.

17. See "Mandatory Delays and Biased Information Requirements, Center for Reproductive Rights," December 9, 2005, www.crlp.org/pub_fac_manddelay1.html.

18. "Stem Cell Dissent Roils States," *Los Angeles Times,* August 1, 2007, p. A12.

19. Alexis de Tocqueville, *Democracy in America,* 2 vols. (New York: Vintage, 1945), pp. i, 290.

20. "We are under a Constitution, but the Constitution is what the judges say it is, and the judiciary is the safeguard of our liberty and of our property under the Constitution," from a speech at Elmira, New York, May 3, 1907, quoted in Merlo John Pusey, *Charles Evans Hughes* (New York: Macmillan, 1951), p. 204. Judges, however, use this power over public policy at their own risk. After the U.S. Supreme Court struck down key legislation of the New Deal, an exasperated President Franklin D. Roosevelt introduced a plan to enlarge the Court to make it more amenable to the policies of his administration. Roosevelt's "court-packing" scheme was soundly rejected, but the justices got the message. The threat, together with some timely retirements, produced a change of attitude on the nation's highest bench, characterized ever since as the "switch in time that saved nine."

7

PARTICIPATION, POLITICS, AND POLICYMAKING
Putting It Together

Almost everything and everyone in life connects to something or someone else. The sun is a component of our galaxy, children are members of families, and public policymaking is part of the political system. More times than not, our connections are multiple and therefore quite complex, making relationships difficult to understand in their totality. The sun, while belonging to the galaxy, is host to numerous planets and moons, yet a relatively insignificant element of the universe. Children connect not only to their families but to schools, extended families, and informal friendship networks.

Public policymaking is no different. As we have seen throughout this book, the public policymaking process responds to community needs something like the stock exchange responds to competing financial conditions and issues. Instead of buyers and sellers, there are conflicting demands for actions ranging from maintenance of the status quo to outright change. Upon occasion, changed directions result from those demands.[1] The public policymaking process has both vertical and horizontal dimensions. By that we mean that this complicated political exchange network functions between levels of government as well as within individual levels of government, suggesting the equivalent of an imaginary, three-dimensional tic-tac-toe game.[2]

Whereas the earlier chapters introduced you to the political process, this concluding chapter reviews some of the key elements of what you may have learned and examines your reactions after venturing into this complicated world. Thus, we devote most of these final pages to you—or rather, to the questions you might want to consider in reflecting upon your experience yourself—and to offering some final thoughts for the future.

Some of What You May Have Learned

The Constitution established a framework of complex relationships, part of which concerns the direct connection between individuals and their government. Depending upon your own civic identity and views about citizenship, that connection can be passive or active.[3] The *passive* approach allows public policies to flow in a caretaker fashion, with individuals doing little more than perpetuating already defined terms of authority, governance, and participation. Under this approach, citizens usually defer to leaders, choosing to be casual, if not disinterested, observers of the political process.

The *active* perspective assumes that individuals insert themselves into the public policymaking process when they feel the need to take part, thereby attempting to have a direct impact on the issues that are defined, discussed, and, it is hoped, resolved. With this outlook, public participation is critical to defining and redefining the contents of the public policymaking environment. In the case of the public policymaking process, civic engagement through analysis and advocacy of issues allows you to hone the skills of citizenship. In other words, you have the opportunity not only to define the problem but be part of the solution.[4]

With public policymaking as the participation vehicle, you become intimately involved with a variety of issues and tools relating to governance, including:

- Conflict between the rights of individuals and the needs of society
- Rights and liberties for all individuals regardless of their political station, social status, or economic position
- The diversity of values, interests, and perspectives that are involved with most issues
- Issues that harm some elements of society while helping others, many of which are wrapped in the concept of majority rule and minority rights
- Disputes between leaders at different levels of public policymaking authority
- Competing priorities in political environments with limited resources
- The experience of cooperating with others in an effort to achieve a mutually sought objective
- The struggle for and distribution of power
- Resolution as a way of achieving closure concerning controversial political issues
- The triumph of reaching a goal and the disappointment of failure
- The process of putting policies to work
- The evaluation of a policy in terms of whether it turned out as intended
- Reflection on participation in the political process

Through participation in service-learning experiences, you and your peers have become part of the public policymaking process. Fundamentally, you have had an opportunity to learn as a by-product of your participation—an acquisition of insight-through-experience that you cannot get in the same way by reading books or watching others carry out activities. By learning how to monitor and influence public policymaking, you have enhanced your capacities as a citizen.

Still, the question arises: Is it a good idea to jump into the public policy-making mix? What is the value of becoming politically active as a potential change agent? Only you can answer these questions, but clearly there are "costs" and "benefits" either way. Through participation, you can have a role in the political process, although you may pay a price in terms of the political, social, and psychological energy you expend along the way. Should you decide not to participate, you certainly save the energy (and perhaps aggravation!), yet you surrender any claim to promote the policies and values that may be important to you. Therein lies the trade-off.

The Most Important Evaluation of All

In the last chapter we talked about evaluation, but we left out what for you will be the most important evaluation of all: how the process has affected you personally. What have you learned from the experience? About politics and public policy? About political engagement? About citizenship? And about yourself? Assuming that you grabbed on to an issue or policy objective, your involvement may have been much more of a learning adventure than you had ever anticipated. Who knows, it may have been rewarding, and even been fun! In any case, this is a good time to take stock of what the experience has meant to you and, perhaps, how it has changed you. Reflection is about remembering and about trying to draw some meaning from what you remember.[5]

You have had opportunities, of course, to reflect along the path of this academic and philosophical exercise. In fact, to a great extent, the very nature of the problem-solving process we have pursued in previous chapters has made reflection unavoidable. This book has also attempted to prompt self-examination in each chapter with suggested exercises, questions, and a case study. Perhaps you have kept a journal along the way, written reports for your class, or shared in class discussions.

As important as such interim reflection can be, there is at least as much value, however, in looking back once the entire experience is over. Even if you have been only partially successful—or even unsuccessful—in reaching certain objectives, there will be some sorting out to do from the rich diversity of experiences you may have encountered, mixing classroom and community, theory and practice, the familiar with the altogether new. If the experience has not unsettled you at least a little, it will have fallen short of its objectives.

What follows is an inventory of sorts—suggested queries you and your classmates may wish to consider in taking stock of what your venture into the world of public policymaking and civic engagement has meant. Some questions will undoubtedly be more relevant than others—depending on the nature of your project and your involvement with it. Other questions will no doubt occur to you and to your instructor.

Questions About Yourself

First, let us begin (naturally enough) with you on *you:* reviewing how the experience has affected and changed you personally.

- How has your involvement affected your self-identity, your sense of who *you* are? Do you feel differently about yourself from how you did at the outset of this experience? If so, how?
- What did you get from this experience? What did you give? Was it worth the energy you expended?
- Did you discover any hidden strengths or weaknesses? If so, what were they? What was the most satisfying part of the experience? The most discouraging or unsettling?
- Has the experience improved your self-confidence? If so, how and why?
- Has the experience altered your values and priorities, and if so, how and why?
- Has it changed your views about your education in terms of its objectives? If so, how and why?
- Do you feel more connected to the political process than before you learned about approaches to participation?
- Has the experience affected your career goals in any way? How?

Questions About You as a Citizen

Next, let us consider how the experience has developed and changed your sense of you as a citizen and your understanding of citizenship. You will recall that in chapter 1 and other parts of the book we discussed the many alternative views involved with this subject. In the course of the text you have learned (and, it is hoped, had a chance to develop) the many different qualities of an effective citizen.

- How important is your "civic identity" to your overall identity as a person? Is it more important now than before? If so, how?
- Which of the various models of citizenship discussed in chapter 1 best describe you? Explain your selection. Do you have your own model? If so, describe it.
- Were you prepared to "go the distance" in pursuing a public policy issue, or did you just need to have your say?
- Effective citizenship requires the necessary knowledge, thinking skills, participatory (advocacy) skills, and dispositions (attitudes and values). How would you rate your effectiveness as a citizen according to these attributes? What are your strengths? Your weaknesses?
- For you, what is the single most important quality of citizenship? Why?
- To what extent do you feel that you made a difference?

Questions About You and the Community

This has been a book about public policymaking and civic engagement. It therefore intertwines with your sense of yourself as you discover the world around you and your ability to observe, analyze, and influence that world, specifically in its public arena.

- How has this experience changed your understanding of the community in which you live? What new connections has it made between you and that community?
- Did the experience bring you into contact with individuals and groups whose circumstances were very different from your own? If so, what did you learn from that contact?
- How has the experience affected your views of your fellow classmates? What did you learn from working with them on this project?
- In what ways, if any, has the experience altered your understanding of what the relationship between your college or university and the surrounding community is (or should be)? How?
- Has the experience changed your views of public officials and what they do? If so, how?

- What connections were you able to make between community service and public policymaking? In what ways has this experience broadened your understanding of those community issues that interest you? Has it enriched your views about community service? If so, how?
- Has this experience led you to new opportunities for community service? If so, what are they?
- What do you think about participation of people like you in the public policy process? Is it valuable? Are there any costs? Does it make someone a "better" person or is it the political equivalent of "too many cooks in the kitchen"?
- How has your work with fellow students, community leaders, and others affected your views about democracy and democratic decision making? In other words, what do you think of the "system" now, compared to the beginning of the semester or quarter?

And Some Last Questions

College is perhaps the last time most of us have many opportunities to experiment freely, to try things that are altogether new and unfamiliar, without the risk of serious consequences. With that in mind,

- What was the greatest risk you took in this experience? How did it work out? How do you feel about it now?
- Has your involvement in such risk taking changed you as a person? If so, in what ways?
- How has your involvement affected your understanding of the public policymaking process?
- In the years to come, what do you believe will be the most memorable moment of this experience? Try to think of an anecdote, event, or favorite moment that may well summarize the experience for you in future years. Describe it.

Some Final Thoughts (from the Soapbox)

Your project in civic engagement and public policymaking may have exceeded your wildest dreams, perhaps even led you to discover capacities within yourself you never knew you had. Better lightbulbs can be made, they do sell, and they can make the world a better place. Given your capabilities to affect the system, never underestimate your capacity to make a difference, both individually and in collaboration with others; conversely, never underestimate the consequences of opting out.

We hope that the questions suggested above will encourage you to explore the meaning of whatever satisfactions and self-discoveries you may have had. Before closing, however, we should deal with the possibility that your efforts may have in one way or another fallen short of what you expected and may have generated some feelings of disappointment or frustration.

Handling Disappointment and Frustration

Perhaps your attempt to bring about change in your community failed to be adopted or even fell on deaf ears. That sort of "failure" happens to policy proposals more often than not. You will remember from your reading of chapter 1 how difficult it is for issues to become part of the public agenda. Governments are called upon to do many more things than time and limited resources will allow. The status quo is a powerful element in politics. Human nature leaves people often more comfortable with the known than the unknown that accompanies change.

As mentioned in chapter 2, policymaking is very much a matter of good timing (along with scope, intensity, timing, and a concern for resources). This, in fact, is a key variable in that three-dimensional tic-tac-toe game we have described. Yesterday's rejected proposal may achieve success tomorrow because the timing suddenly becomes right. For you this may be an especially difficult reality to accept: your class project cannot wait until "tomorrow" when you may well be moving on to other things.

You may have experienced some frustration with individuals in authority and with how the "system" works. Then again, perhaps after reading this book and having an opportunity to work with the public policymaking process, you will have a more realistic understanding of our system of government, with all its virtues and its vices. Like you, perhaps, the individuals who founded this country had a profound distrust of power. They sought to design a government that would enable those in power to meet their responsibilities but at the same time reduce the likelihood of their abusing it. The solution our founders devised has its faults. Our system of government may sometimes seem a messy and terribly inefficient way of getting things done. For the most part, however, it has worked well over the course of more than two centuries in providing for careful deliberation of public policymaking and increasing the likelihood that all voices that deserve to have a say are heard. It has also worked to the advantage of compromise and consensus.

As we noted at the beginning of this book, there is evidence to suggest that many Americans (especially younger Americans) are alienated by what they see as the selfishness and hypocrisy that dominate public life today.[6] The relative importance of self-interest and public-mindedness (or "civic virtue" as the nation's founders called it) in public life is certainly an issue that deserves consideration. You will recall that we examined this topic in chapter 1 in our discussion of different models of citizenship. The founders wrestled with the question and even disagreed among themselves about the relative importance of such different motivations. Among the shrewdest of them—the writers of the *Federalist* essays—argued that the Constitution created by the framers was so designed as to take maximum advantage of both selfishness and altruism. They realized that "self-interest" and "civic virtue" often amounted to the same thing: As often as not public officials seek to accomplish great things and to build honorable reputations because it is in their self-interest to do so. It is important to their self-esteem.[7]

Understanding the Opportunities and Limits of the System

If your project has brought you into contact with public officials, you may well now have a better understanding of what they do and of the many different influences that affect their actions and decisions. As with all human beings in positions of authority, their actions are prompted by a variety of values and motives ranging from an interest in promoting their personal careers to a desire to leave their community better than they found it. Keep in mind that whatever the mix of their motives might be, public leaders are by nature opportunistic, ever eager to receive and make use of good ideas.

None of this is to suggest that the system is perfect. Our history is tattered with all kinds of examples of discrimination, abuse, and indifference. From racial discrimination to the convictions of innocent individuals, the public policymaking process has let people down and, upon occasion, not lived up to the principles articulated in the U.S. Constitution. That said, no system is perfect. What makes the American political system intriguing, however, is the opportunity to right those things that are wrong. Sometimes it takes a while, such as when more than four decades after the fact, the U.S. Congress issued an official apology to the 110,000 Japanese-Americans who were forcibly removed from their homes and "interned" during World War II, or when the U.S. Supreme Court finally struck down discrimination. But these and other instances show the extent to which the public policymaking process is relatively porous and open to influence.

Skepticism, Yes; Cynicism, No

Beware of *cynicism*. Cynicism may sometimes entertain, but it rarely enables meaningful or thoughtful change. In fact, cynicism can be a very self-defeating indulgence, reducing our capacity to influence and operate effectively in the world around us. Guard yourself against the cynical, for more often than not, it becomes an easy way out of thinking, mulling, and participating.

Skepticism is another matter altogether. Skepticism encourages an inquiring mind, coupled with an unwillingness to accept things at face value. Together, these are important, indeed essential, attributes of effective citizenship. Remember that the nation's founders were skeptics. The greatest among them were prone to challenge authority, and they loved to question and debate ideas. (In all likelihood, they would be surprised and even disappointed with the uncritical reverence in which they have been held by most Americans throughout our history.)

To be sure, the alternatives to cynicism can sometimes seem "labor-intensive," requiring us to steel ourselves with the challenging virtues of patience, persistence, and even courage. It may not be easy, but such tenacity has its own special reward. Susan B. Anthony struggled all her adult life on behalf of women's right to vote and never lived to see the passage of the Nineteenth Amendment. The champions of civil rights for African-Americans braved many frustrations, defeats, and dangers to their personal safety before seeing any of their objectives realized. These and other examples show that public policy objectives are sometimes not attained for long periods of time. Even if such objectives are never fully realized, the process of struggling for them is essential to the practice of democracy.

If your efforts have fallen short of what you had hoped they would accomplish, you might take heart from the words of the poet and essayist T.S. Eliot: "We fight for lost causes because we know that our defeat and dismay may be the preface to our successors' victory."[8] And it is Theodore Roosevelt who reminds us that it is far better "to dare mighty things, to win glorious triumphs, even though checkered by failure, than to take rank with those poor spirits who neither enjoy much nor suffer much, because they live in the gray twilight that knows not victory nor defeat."[9]

Why Civic Obligation?

We have not talked much about "obligation" or "responsibility" in the course of this book.[10] Rights and opportunities have received more attention. (We hope that you now have a better idea of your rights and opportunities as citizens than when you started.) What needs to be said about your obligations? We are inclined to leave the exercise of obligations—like that of rights— to the choice of individual citizens. If, when, how, and why you choose to exercise your rights and responsibilities as a citizen are ultimately your business. Your legal obligations of citizenship are very few. *Moral* obligations of citizenship are another matter altogether.

Not everyone, in fact, accepts obligation as part of citizenship. Some critics argue that the concept leads to compulsory participation, therefore working at cross-purposes with the value of freedom.[11] It is an interesting dilemma. How "free" are our freedoms if no one is there to protect them? Yet, if we are compelled to participate, how can such activity equate with freedom, which implies choice as part of its definition? Therein lies the rub. There is no easy answer to this dilemma, but perhaps one way to try to resolve it is to be found in Tocqueville's concept of *enlightened self-interest*. Good citizenship, Tocqueville argued, expresses an appreciation of the connections between our personal concerns and those of the larger community of which we are a part.[12]

Ethical awareness and a sense of the obligations and responsibilities we owe others are certainly a part of this enlightened self-interest in the largest sense. They reflect a crucial part of who we are as mature human beings living in a community with others. Indeed, they provide much of the inspiration for wanting to get involved. But civic engagement can also be justified on basic pragmatic grounds. Just like physical exercise tones the body, political exercise tones our sense of participation and involvement. "Political democracy," Walt Whitman said, "supplies a training school for making first class men. It is life's gymnasium." And no one can do the exercises for us.[13]

If we leave to those in power the task of guaranteeing our rights, what makes us believe that they will automatically or fairly promote such benefits? Where is it written that people are automatically kind and good? The answer, of course, is that there is nothing automatic about freedom, liberty, and any of the other fundamental concepts we have inherited as our legacy. These rights are best protected when they are used or practiced on a regular basis. Indeed, democracy is anything but a spectator sport; rather, it requires public participation to thrive.

Obligation is not only an element of citizenship but an imperative for protecting the integrity of the political process. Most of us acknowledge in some degree that the personal enjoyment of our rights carries with it the obligation to respect the enjoyment of those same rights by others. We probably do not appreciate as much as we should the ways in which the enjoyment of rights in our private pursuits carries with it an implied obligation to participate in public affairs. For most Americans the most cherished part of the U.S. Constitution is the First Amendment, guaranteeing freedom of speech, religion, and association. We rightly regard such freedoms as precious to us as citizens in our private lives.

As originally envisioned by the framers of the Bill of Rights, however, these freedoms also had an important public dimension. The architects of the First Amendment considered its freedoms essential to good governance and public policymaking. Freedom of expression, in fact, was secured primarily to allow citizens to monitor and influence their government effectively. In its origins, freedom of association had much the same purpose. It derives from the right to freedom of assembly, a vital condition for citizens to properly deliberate and influence their government through petitioning and in other ways. Courts ever since have regarded this freedom as among the most essential to the working of democracy.[14]

Even those provisions guaranteeing freedom of religion had a public policy purpose in mind: to free public affairs from religious strife and dogma, to prevent alike the tyranny of one official religion and the sectarian conflict of a small number of faiths contending for supremacy. The architects of the Bill of Rights realized that the best (if somewhat paradoxical) way to remove such private matters from the public forum was to promote as wide a diversity of faiths as possible.[15]

The more we take an active part in the well-being of the political process, the more we practice democracy. That is our obligation as members of the body politic otherwise known as society. So, by taking your issue and your proposals for making a change to the state legislature, city council, or even the governing authorities of your university or college, your participation in the political process helps to keep that process working as the framers designed it.

By introducing you to the nature of public policymaking and to the tools for monitoring and influencing it, this book, we hope, will have increased your capacity to make a difference in the world whenever you choose to do so, to become involved in the ever-changing process of self-government from beginning to end, only to be part of the beginning again.

Notes

1. Charles O. Jones has one of the clearest explanations of the relationship between public policymaking and the political system. See *An Introduction to the Study of Public Policy*, 3rd ed. (Monterey, CA: Brooks/Cole, 1984).

2. For an analytical description of policymaking relationships and actors, see Michael E. Kraft and Scott R. Furlong, *Public Policy: Politics, Analysis, and Alternatives* (Washington, DC: CQ Press, 2004), pp. 32–65.

3. Sidney Verba, Kay Lehman Schlozman, and Henry E. Brady provide an extensive analysis of the attitudes and roles of citizens in the American political process. See their *Voice and Equality: Civic Voluntarism in American Politics* (Cambridge, MA: Harvard University Press, 1995). See also endnote 26 of chapter 1 in the present volume.

4. For another "hands-on" approach to advocacy, see Katherine Isaac, *Practicing Democracy* (New York: St. Martin's, 1997). Also see Paul A. Sabatier and Hank C. Jenkins-Smith, *Policy Change and Learning: An Advocacy Coalition Approach* (Boulder, CO: Westview Press, 2001).

5. On reflection as a pedagogical component of service learning, see chapter 6, endnote 9, of the present volume.

6. The attitudes of "Generation X" and "Generation Y" (as the younger generations of American citizens have been called) toward civic engagement have been the subject of considerable examination and some controversy in recent years. For a variety of different perspectives on this complex subject, see Alexander W. Astin, "The Changing American College Student: Thirty-year Trends, 1966–1996," *Review of Higher Education* 21, no. 2 (1998): 115–135; Deborah J. Hirsch, "Politics Through Action: Student Service and Activism in the '90s," *Change: The Magazine of Higher Learning* 25, no. 4 (1993): 32–36; Geoffrey T. Holtz, *Welcome to the Jungle: The Why Behind "Generation X"* (New York: St. Martin's, 1995); Arthur Levine and Jeanette S. Cureton, "Student Politics: The New Localism," *Review of Higher Education* 21, no. 2 (1998): 137–150; Ernest T. Pascarella and Patrick T. Terenzini, "Studying College Students in the 21st Century: Meeting New Challenges," *Review of Higher Education* 21, no. 2 (1998): 51–165; Robert A. Rhoads, "In the Service of Citizenship: A Study of Student Involvement in Community Service," *Journal of Higher Education* 69, no. 3 (1998): 277–297; James Scannell and Kathleen Simpson, *Shaping College Experience Outside the Classroom* (Rochester, NY: Boydell and Brewer, 1996); Richard D. Thau and Jay S. Heflin, eds., *Generations Apart: Xers Vs Boomers Vs the Elderly* (Amherst, NY: Prometheus), 1997. Robert D. Putnam speaks to this in his book *Bowling Alone* (New York: Simon and Schuster, 2000), pp. 137–147.

7. See Douglass Adair, *Fame and the Founding Fathers: Essays,* ed. Trevor Colbourn (Indianapolis, IN: Liberty Fund, 1998). The connection between self-interest and public reputation is a point examined by Alexander Hamilton in several of his *Federalist* essays. See, for example, *Federalist No. 76*.

8. T.S. Eliot, *Selected Essays.* New edition (New York: Harcourt, Brace and World, 1932, 1964), p. 399.

9. Theodore Roosevelt, *The Strenuous Life: Essays and Addresses* (New York: Century, 1903), p. 4.

10. For a discussion on obligation as a political imperative, see Joseph Tussman, *Obligation and the Body Politic* (New York: Oxford University Press, 1960).

11. See, for example, Milton and Rose Friedman, *Free to Choose* (New York: Harcourt Brace Jovanovich, 1979).

12. See Toqueville's discussion of "How the Americans Combat Individualism by the Principle of Self-Interest Rightly Understood," *Democracy in America,* p. ii, chapter viii.

13. Walt Whitman, *Democratic Vistas* (New York: Liberal Arts Press, 1949), p. 25.

14. For an interesting discussion of the connections between the Bill of Rights and civic engagement, see Akhil Amar, *The Bill of Rights: Its Creation and Reconstruction* (New Haven, CT: Yale University Press, 1998).

15. A point well argued by James Madison in *Federalist No. 51* as applying both to political factions and religious sects.

APPENDIX A: GLOSSARY

accountability—the two-way linkage of responsibility between public policymakers and the public, wherein each element must consider the values of the other.

advocacy—the art of speaking for or otherwise supporting something; from the Latin *ad* and *vocare,* meaning "to call to."

agenda builders—individuals or organizations that have the capability to capture the attention of public policymakers.

anti-Federalists—individuals who were opposed to the ratification of the Constitution because they believed it gave too much power to the federal government and did not afford sufficient protections for civil and political rights.

benchmarking—a term used to describe interim evaluations of public policies at various stages of development.

bureaucracy—a unit of government that carries out the decisions made by public policymakers; from the French word *bureau,* which referred originally to a type of desk favored by public officials.

chartered rights—rights articulated in a charter or other formal document (e.g., the Magna Carta, U.S. Bill of Rights, United Nations Universal Declaration of Human Rights).

charter schools—public schools that are granted a license or "charter" to operate in large measure independently of the established bureaucracy and regulations of the school jurisdiction in which they exist, in return for which they are held accountable for producing specific results, typically improved student performance.

checks and balances—the sharing and balancing of power among the different branches of government so that no one branch can dominate the others. (See *separation of powers.*)

citizenship—the status of being a citizen or member of a given society, usually recognized as such by law and accorded certain rights and responsibilities associated with that status. Citizenship is distinguished from the status of others living in the same society (e.g., resident aliens), who may enjoy some but not all of those rights and responsibilities. (See the *rights-bearing model of citizenship, communitarian model of citizenship,* and *citizenship as public work.*)

citizenship as public work—a model of citizenship in which citizens are regarded as "practical agents" who work together in public ways and spaces to solve problems they collectively face. This model makes close connection between citizenship and proactive, pragmatic problem solving in the public arena. (See also *rights-bearing model of citizenship* and *communitarian model of citizenship.*)

civic identity—how each individual sees himself as a citizen and defines his relationship to the state or nation of which he is a part. (See *rights-bearing model of citizenship, communitarian model of citizenship,* and *citizenship as public work.*)

civic virtue—the dedication of citizens to the common good, even at the expense of their individual self-interests; public spiritedness. (See *classical republicanism.*)

civil disobedience—a form of civic protest that involves deliberately breaking a law or decree to demonstrate its injustice. One who practices civil disobedience usually does so openly and with a willingness to accept the legal consequences of his or her action.

civil society—the autonomous, self-organized portion of a free society that is outside formal political and legal institutions.

classical republicanism—a body of political principles associated by the nation's founders with the political ideals of ancient Greece and Rome; specifically, the theory that the best kind of government is one that favors the good of the community over the interests of individual citizens or groups of citizens. (See *civic virtue.*)

communitarian model of citizenship—a model of citizenship grounded in membership in a community defined by common values and a common concern for the welfare of all. A "responsibilities-bearing" model of citizenship as compared with the individualistic "rights-bearing" model. It emphasizes the obligations and responsibilities owed by citizens to the community of which they are a part. (See *rights-bearing model of citizenship* and *citizenship as public work.*)

constitution—variously used over time to describe the essential nature, character, or "spirit" of a form of government; certain laws of special importance; or the sum total of basic laws, institutions, and conventions that define a form of government. Now most commonly taken to mean the set of fundamental rules by which a political entity is governed. Within the

American tradition, a written frame of government and higher law that can only be changed by extraordinary measures (i.e., the amending process).

constitutionalism—the political principle that government is obligated to operate in a manner consistent with purposes and limits provided by its constitution.

cynicism—an attitude of mind that encourages one to deny and to ridicule the sincerity or goodness of human motives and actions, or to constantly find fault with them.

due process clause—usually a reference to part of Section 1 of the Fourteenth Amendment, forbidding states in the Union from depriving any person of life, liberty, or property without "due process of law." Sometimes referred to as the "incorporation clause" of the U.S. Constitution, the due process clause has provided a mechanism by which most of the rights secured in the U.S. Bill of Rights against the national government have been secured against state and local governments as well. Protection of due process against the actions of the federal government is secured in the Fifth Amendment. (See *due process of law*.)

due process of law—a key principle of constitutionalism denying the arbitrary deprivation of a person's life, liberty, or property by the state. Government, in other words, may take action against its citizens only in accordance with procedures and rules that are established, fair, and consistently applied. The Fourth through Eighth Amendments of the U.S. Bill of Rights contain essential guarantees of due process of law. (See *due process clause*.)

eminent domain—the power of a government to take private property for public use. This power is granted to the federal government in the "takings clause" of the Fifth Amendment of the U.S. Constitution, which also provides, however, for just compensation of the owners of the property taken.

empowerment—the quality of being enabled; specifically, the capacity of citizens to exert influence effectively in the political society to which they belong—that is, possessing the necessary knowledge, skills, and dispositions for doing so.

equal protection clause—part of Section 1 of the Fourteenth Amendment, forbidding states in the Union from denying to any person within their jurisdiction the "equal protection of the laws." This clause has enshrined the principle of equality in public policymaking at the state and local levels.

equal protection of the law—a constitutional guarantee that means that no person or class of person may be denied the same protection of the law enjoyed by other persons or classes of persons in the same circumstances. In other words, government can make distinctions at law between individuals or groups only when there is a legitimate reason for doing so (e.g., laws that set a minimum age for holding a driver's license). (See *equal protection clause.*)

establishment clause—that part of the First Amendment declaring that "Congress shall make no law respecting an establishment of religion."

federalism—a principle most commonly used to describe a form of government combining centralized and decentralized features—for example, a national or federal government on the one hand and a multiplicity of regional or local governments on the other. Federal systems of government are therefore distinguished from unitary (centralized) forms and from confederal (decentralized) forms of government.

Federalists—individuals who favored ratification of the U.S. Constitution and who in general believed in a stronger and more centralized national government than that provided for by the Articles of Confederation.

implementation—the act of transferring decisions into practice and making the policy a reality.

implementation by degree—partially carrying out a public policy, leaving portions unrealized.

initiatives—proposed public policies that are placed on the ballot as a result of sponsors obtaining a required number of signatures; used in about half of the states. Initiatives are distinguished from *referenda,* a term now commonly used to describe policy proposals referred to the voters by a traditional public policymaking authority, usually a state legislature. *Plebiscite* is a general term used to describe any popular mandate, including initiatives, referenda, and elections to office.

interest groups—organizations of individuals with similar needs or values that attempt to influence the public policymaking process.

judicial review—the power of a court of law to review and determine the constitutionality of a law, regulation, decree, or other government initiative.

justiciable—the quality of being subject to the jurisdiction of a court of law.

natural rights philosophy—a philosophy of government that holds that all human beings are possessed of certain universal rights that are part of the law of nature, whose protection it is the primary obligation of all governments to secure and protect; most commonly associated with John Locke and other liberal theorists of the late seventeenth and eighteenth centuries.

policy—from the Latin word *politia,* referring broadly to matters of citizenship and government; originally, a form of government; later, the general task of governing (and more specifically, wise government); today, more commonly defined as specific measures of government.

polity—the body of people that provides the legitimacy for social, political, legal, and constitutional arrangements.

popular sovereignty—the concept that ultimate authority in a state resides in the collective will of its people, who have the right to establish, alter, or abolish governments of that state. Popular sovereignty is a cardinal tenet of democracy. (See *sovereignty.*)

public agenda—the collection of issues awaiting resolution by public policymakers; changes over time.

public policymaking—the combination of basic decisions, commitments, and actions made by those who hold or affect government positions or authority.

representative government—a system wherein a few are democratically selected to govern for the many.

republic—from the Latin *res publicus* (the people's *thing* or *affairs*), a word that has come to have many definitions and distinctions. Classically, a form of government in which the administration of affairs is directly or indirectly open to all its citizens. For James Madison, an indirect or representative democracy. Commonly used today to describe any form of government that is not a monarchy. The U.S. Constitution provides for a republican form of government at the federal level and in the "guarantee clause" of Article IV secures republican government at the state level as well.

rights-bearing model of citizenship—a model of citizenship and civic identity grounded in individualism and self-interest and focusing on the exercise of individual rights. Government's primary obligation is to protect the rights of individual citizens. The duties or responsibilities of the citizen, in turn, are narrowly defined by his or her obligations under the law (e.g., pay one's taxes, serve on juries when called, etc.). Sometimes referred to as the "liberal" view of citizenship.

self-government—in general, the quality of being autonomous, not liable to the control or interference of others; a characteristic of republican and democratic forms of government ("government of the people, by the people, for the people").

self-interest—an exclusive regard for one's own advantage, as contrasted with selflessness, altruism, public-spiritedness. (See *rights-bearing model of citizenship.*)

separation of powers—a fundamental organizational principle of American constitutionalism that divides power among different branches and levels of government. The principle is now more commonly characterized as providing for a system of shared powers among independent branches of government, with each branch assigned a distinct policymaking responsibility and with cooperation among branches necessary to make law. The principle is also applied in the division of power between national and state levels of government. (See *checks and balances* and *federalism*.)

skepticism—an attitude of mind that encourages one to doubt and question, to refuse to accept things at face value.

social contract—the agreement among all the people in a society to give up part of their freedom to a government in return for the protection of their natural rights by that government.

social indicators—a collection of values and assessment tools that are used to evaluate the success of a public policy after implementation.

sovereignty—the ultimate power in a state. (See *popular sovereignty*.)

special districts—small governments created to carry out specific tasks; typically found at the local government level.

supremacy clause—Article VI, Section 2 of the U.S. Constitution, which states that the Constitution, as well as laws passed by the federal government and international treaties concluded by the same, shall be "the supreme law of the land," binding on all state governments.

triggering mechanisms—indicators (scope, intensity, duration, resources) that collectively determine whether a problem is a public policy issue.

whistle-blower—an individual who challenges the legality of the public policies carried out by the public agency in which he or she works by sharing undisclosed and damaging information with public authorities and/or the press.

APPENDIX B: PROJECT CITIZEN—
A BRIEF INTRODUCTION

Public Policy and Representative Democracy: Connecting the Dots

Most of our day-to-day activities are private undertakings that lie well outside of the sphere of government institutions and officials. People work, recreate, socialize, and conduct themselves for extensive periods without any government interaction. However, when issues affect the public good or well-being, government officials sometimes make decisions in the form of public policies, committing public resources to carry out those objectives. These activities take place at all levels of government, ranging from the declaration of war by the U.S. Congress to the establishment of a speed limit or zoning law by a local community to the decision of a class instructor to use essay exams. All of these commitments are public policies for various constituencies, groups affected by those policies.

At its root, a public policy is an authoritative action step by someone in power. Depending upon the form of government, those in positions to rule may or may not be accountable for their actions. In a representative democracy, most of the officeholders who have responsibility for making public policies are elected on a periodic basis, although judges and bureaucrats are not. That most of these policymakers serve at the pleasure of the electorate helps to make them accountable to those who place them in office. Depending upon the office, periodically the people have the opportunity through elections to keep policymakers in office or replace them with others. Even those who are appointed are not immune from public assessments, whether they be in the forms of public meetings, letters to the editor, blogs, or massive protests, to name a few of many opportunities.

Representative democracy functions best when people are interested in and aware of key issues that affect their lives and the lives of others around them. Under this form of governance, people interact on a regular basis with public policymakers as concerns require them to do so. Yet, there is nothing automatic about this relationship. To the extent that the public withdraws from participation in the political process, public policymakers may enact policies in a vacuum without accountability or approval. The more that this takes place, the greater the possibility that such actions may differ from the values, needs, and hopes of the public. Thus, public involvement is critical to the maintenance of representative democracy.

Wither Civic Engagement?

But there is a growing problem. Over the past few decades, political participation in the United States has dropped precipitously. Casual observers often have identified shrinking voter turnouts as a primary indicator of less citizen involvement. However, the widespread absence of political engagement is considerably more serious than reduced numbers of voters. The indifference includes

- the lack of meaningful exchanges about political concepts and ideas such as equality, tolerance, civil rights, public obligations, to name a few;
- the appropriate roles for and boundaries of government in our lives;
- widespread unawareness of democratic values;
- a lack of commitment to greater community; and
- a general retreat from individual investment in the political system.

Combined, these indicators point to reduced public involvement in the political process, and that growing distance has caused concern among those who see the benefits of connection between the governed and the governors.

What has brought about this rupture in the connection between the people and government? Scholars differ on the root causes of civic disengagement. Some point to the movement away from newspaper reading, others focus on less group interaction, some point to the growth of mobility, and still others focus upon a shift in K–12 classroom instruction from dialogue and debate to the memorization of facts in preparation for standardized tests. Whatever the causes, the outcome has resulted in a large portion of the polity removed from the political process. The unfortunate result combines a downward spiral and self-fulfilling prophecy into a potentially harmful pattern: the less people know, the less people care, and the less people care, the less people know.

The lack of linkage between citizens and participation threatens our democracy, which depends upon an involved citizenry. In the movie *Field of Dreams,* there is a line where the dreamer, an Iowa corn farmer, discusses with an inner-voice the potential fan interest in a baseball stadium constructed in the middle of his cornfield: "If you build it, they will come," the inner-voice predicts, suggesting that people will become involved if they are presented the opportunity. This also applies to civic engagement. If we help people see how they can participate and the benefits of their participation, then they will become more involved.

Enter Project Citizen

Project Citizen provides an interactive participation vehicle for engaging students in the political process and, as a by-product, bringing people closer to the public policymaking arena. Originally developed by the Center for Civic Education as a program for middle school students in 1996 (www.civiced.org), Project Citizen can be adapted to all student populations, from elementary school to the university setting. This participatory tool is predicated upon the idea that "hands-on" involvement facilitates knowledge about and interest in the political process. Project Citizen has the potential for transforming the passive bystander into an active, engaged member of the polity.

With Project Citizen, students identify a public problem or issue in need of attention from the public policymakers who have responsibility for dealing with it. Students research the nature and extent of the issue, potential solutions to the issue, and consequences of responding to the issue. In the process, they learn what levels of government are appropriate for responding to different concerns. For example, the presidency is not the appropriate public policymaking authority for addressing a cracked sidewalk in front of the school; likewise, the local city council does not have responsibility for managing issues such as stem cell research or global warming. Understanding who can do what is a crucial element to participating in Project Citizen.

As an outgrowth of their research, students then recommend a public policy to address the issue by taking their "case" to the appropriate public policymaker(s). By participating in Project Citizen, these individuals assume an active, meaningful role in representative democracy.

With Project Citizen, the public policymaking process may be engaged at any level of government, ranging from national government to university administration. For the purposes of this exercise, however, it's easier for student activity to focus upon issues that may be resolved at the state or local levels. "Local" includes government authorities at the county, city, regional, and university levels. By staying local, students have the greatest opportunities for direct contact with appropriate public policymakers.

Service Learning versus Community Service

Project Citizen is a form of *service learning;* as such, it focuses upon people coming to terms with the public policymaking process by identifying public problems and taking their concerns to those in public policy positions. It is NOT about discovering a problem and solving it through direct citizen action; this type of activity is best described as *community service.* The difference lies in the approach to problem solving: whereas community service focuses on people dealing with issues directly, service learning includes a component where upon identifying a problem, people take their concerns to the officials in power to correct the problem. This distinction is important because while we would like to think that we can fix a number of problems around us, we can't solve thorny issues that extract vast resources—that's where public policymakers can be helpful.

Consider a beach strewn with garbage. Presenting the issue to the relevant public policymaker(s) with the request for garbage cans and fines for those who are caught dropping garbage on the beach would be an effort to make public policy. Here there is an effort to govern and perhaps change behavior through new rules. On the other hand, the gathering of a scout troop or church group one Saturday each month to pick up garbage on the beach would constitute community service. In this instance, participants do not seek to change the political process or influence the actions of public policymakers responsible for dealing with conditions at the beach; rather, they seek to improve their community. Both service learning and community service are valuable tools for citizen participation. That said, one attempts to influence policymakers, whereas the other emphasizes individuals operating on more of an ad hoc basis.

Project Citizen in Steps

Following are the steps that should be used for Project Citizen at the university level.[1] These steps should serve as the basis of the outline for group project and the final product, which appears in the form of a term paper. Note that this is defined as a "group" project. If the class is broken down into groups of four to six participants, the numbers will be sufficient enough for various tasks to be assigned without being overly burdensome for any member. If the numbers in each group are fewer than four, then the responsibilities may be too great to complete within the allotted time period; on the other hand, if the numbers are more than six, then the students may not have enough to do.

In the outline below, there are four steps of collective student involvement. It is recommended that student groups collectively write up their findings and analyses as they complete each step. The fifth step, reflection, is particularly valuable for soliciting student reaction to the Project Citizen experience and determining whether there is any new awareness of the political process. It may be valuable for each student to share his or her thoughts individually in a short paper.

Before proceeding, it is important to deal with a few potential hazards. First, sometimes students have difficulty distinguishing public issues from private issues. They must always remember that public issues include public resources that are managed by public authorities; these are critical elements to the making of public policy. Second, it is best if students determine the issue, not the professor. Student selection helps to secure "buy-in," a sense of ownership that reinforces commitment to the effort; if the professor provides the issue, then the students are more likely to view the project as just another assignment. Third, sometimes students want to take on issues that will be very difficult to research and influence, particularly within the timeframe of a quarter or semester. For these and other reasons, it is recommended that students receive the approval of the class professor before proceeding with the first phases of Project Citizen. It is further recommended that the professor meet with the student groups at several junctures during the semester or quarter—particularly as the students near completion of each step. These regularly scheduled meetings help to keep the projects on course.

Keeping a Journal

Part of the benefit of Project Citizen lies with the growth of student engagement during the process. Writing a daily journal about the project helps the student to appreciate the "baby steps" that become part of the path to a powerful journey. The journal should contain the student's feelings about the effort. Challenges from project partners, difficulties in getting information, and surprises about preliminary assumptions are just a few of the observations that should be included in the journal. The journal is important for another reason as well: Should the professor assign a "reflection" paper, a post–Project Citizen review of the experience, the journal will provide considerable information for that effort.

Step 1: Identify the Public Policy Issue

- Specifically, what is the problem or issue in need of change?
- What evidence exists that there is a problem?

- Is it a "public" problem?
- What has caused the problem?
- What policies, if any, are currently in place regarding the problem?

Here are some examples of potential local issues:

polluted streams
discarded computers/monitors/cell phones
police brutality
cigarette butts dumped on the roads
cracked sidewalks
intersections where people run stop signs or red lights
inadequate student housing near the University
student cheating
student cafeterias that serve food of questionable nutritional value

In each case, students must see the problem as something adverscly affecting sizable portions of the community.

Step 2: Gather Information

- What history is there, if any, of public policymakers dealing with the issue? At what levels of government?
- How can the issue be quantified?
- What is the intensity of public opinion on this issue?
- Who can you speak to about the issue?
- What observations can you make about the issue?
- Can you find data on your problem at other places?
- How long has the issue existed?
- To what extent are people bothered by the issue? What evidence shows that people are bothered enough to seek meaningful change?

Suggested activities:

Connect the issue with the appropriate public policymakers who might be able to deal with it.

Shadow a public policymaker who has decision-making capabilities for your issue.

Find ways to measure the problem so that others can understand the extent to which it exists, perhaps a brief survey of those potentially affected by the issue.

Interview a member of the press who has written stories on the issue.

Step 3: Possible Public Policy Solutions

- How have similar policymaking bodies elsewhere addressed this issue? Or has it been ignored?
- What are the possible considerations for public policymakers?
- Public benefits
  - Qualitative?
  - Quantitative?
- Public costs
  - Dollars?
  - Lives?
  - Values?
- Could this problem be managed by more than one public policymaking entity?
- If so, which do you believe is most appropriate, and why?
- If so, what, if any, problems do you foresee?
- What are the costs/benefits of continuing with the *status quo?*

Step 4: Proposed Public Policy

- To which public policymakers will you propose your public policy, and why?
- Why have you chosen your proposed public policy instead of the other options?
- What other groups might join with you to promote your proposed public policy? What are the costs/benefits of such alliances?
- What might keep this proposed policy from being adopted, and why?
- What changes might you make in your proposal to enhance its chances of adoption?

Step 5: Reflection—What Has Project Citizen Taught You About

- The political process?
- The responsiveness (or lack thereof) of those who make public policies?

- Working in a group?
- Your own political values?
- Your role as a citizen?
- The costs and benefits of civic engagement?
- Would you recommend Project Citizen? Why? Why not?

Project Citizen and Public Policy: Measuring Success

The value of Project Citizen lies in the student becoming immersed in the public policymaking process. By going through the steps of issue identification, research, and policy recommendations, the student can undertake a meaningful role in attempting to make change. By evaluating what comes of the public policymaking process with respect to a particular issue, the student better understands why some issues are managed and some are not. Such activities serve to bridge the gap between theory and action.

Beware of Unreasonable Expectations

Still, there is an important cautionary to consider: Too often students confuse political involvement with results. Of course, we want to see our values and issues prevail, but we all can't win all the time. The value of Project Citizen lies much more in participation than public policy outcomes. Of significance is that the student sees how he or she can be a *part* of the process rather than a *spectator* of the process, and how participation provides a sense of fulfillment. Thus, whether public policymakers adopt a proposal is secondary to the student mining, understanding, and presenting the issues—in other words, taking an active part in the political process.

It's About Civic Engagement

Knowing the opportunities for involvement, what to do, who to approach, and how to do it are critical elements for bringing people into the political process. But there is a personal element as well. Appreciating the importance of involvement makes the student a better citizen. And understanding the consequences of inaction helps the student to see the benefits of participation as well as the costs of not doing so. Think about the moment in *Field of Dreams* when it was decided to build the baseball field in terms of representative democracy: If students see how to participate and the benefits of their involvement, they will be more likely to do so. And our representative democracy will be better for it.

Note

1. The Center for Civic Education has materials organized for elementary, middle, and high school students. All of these include a portfolio that captures the process. At the university level, I recommend replacing the portfolio with group papers.

APPENDIX C: RECOMMENDED READINGS

Gail Albert, ed., *Service Learning Reader: Reflections and Perspectives on Service* (Raleigh, NC: National Society for Experiential Education, 1994).

Gabriel A. Almond and Sidney Verba, *The Civic Culture* (Boston: Little, Brown, 1966).

Nancy Amidei, *So You Want to Make a Difference: Advocacy Is the Key* (Washington, DC: OMB Watch, 1991).

James E. Anderson, *Public Policymaking*, 3rd ed. (Boston: Houghton Mifflin, 1997).

Benjamin R. Barber, *An Aristocracy of Everyone: The Politics of Education and the Future of America* (New York: Oxford University Press, 1992).

James David Barber, *The Book of Democracy* (Englewood Cliffs, NJ: Prentice Hall, 1995).

Eugene Bardach, *The Implementation Game* (Cambridge, MA: MIT Press, 1979).

Richard M. Battistoni and William E. Hudson, eds., *Experiencing Citizenship: Concepts and Models for Service-Learning in Political Science* (Washington, DC: American Association of Higher Education, 1997).

Robert N. Bellah, Richard Madsen, William M. Sullivan, Ann Swidler, and Steven M. Tipton, *Habits of the Heart: Individualism and Commitment in American Life* (New York: Harper and Row, 1985).

Thomas A. Birkland, *After Disaster: Agenda Setting, Public Policy and Focusing Events* (Washington, DC: Georgetown University Press, 1997).

William T. Bluhm and Robert A. Heineman, *Ethics and Public Policy: Method and Cases* (Upper Saddle River, NJ: Pearson Education, 2007).

Richard D. Brown, *The Strength of a People: The Idea of an Informed Citizen in America, 1650–1870* (Chapel Hill: University of North Carolina Press, 1996).

Robert A. Dahl, *Pluralist Democracy in the United States* (Chicago: Rand McNally, 1966).

Thomas R. Dye, *Understanding Public Policy,* 12th ed. (Upper Saddle River, NJ: Pearson Education, 2008).

Thomas Ehrlich, ed., *Civic Responsibility and Higher Education* (Phoenix, AZ: Oryx, 2000).

Nina Eliasoph, *Avoiding Politics: How Americans Produce Apathy in Everyday Life* (Cambridge: Cambridge University Press, 1998).

Amitai Etzioni, *The Spirit of Community: Rights, Responsibilities and the Communitarian Agenda* (New York: Crown, 1993).

Max Farrand, ed., *The Records of the Federal Convention of 1787,* 4 vols. (New Haven, CT: Yale University Press, 1966).

The Federalist Papers: Alexander Hamilton, James Madison, John Jay, ed. Clinton Rossiter and Charles R. Resler (New York: Mentor Books, 1999).

Arlene Fink and Jacqueline Kosecoff, *How to Conduct Surveys: A Step-by-Step Guide* (Thousand Oaks, CA: Sage, 1985).

Louis Fisher, *The Politics of Shared Power* (Washington, DC: CQ Press, 1993).

Floyd J. Fowler Jr., *Improving Survey Questions: Design and Evaluation* (Thousand Oaks, CA: Sage, 1995).

Elizabeth R. Gerber, Arthur Lupia, Mathew D. McCubbins, and D. Roderick Kiewiet, *Stealing the Initiative: How State Government Responds to Direct Democracy* (Upper Saddle River, NJ: Prentice-Hall, 2001).

Larry N. Gerston, *American Federalism: A Concise Introduction* (Armonk, NY: M.E. Sharpe, 2007).

Larry N. Gerston, *Public Policymaking: Process and Principles* (Armonk, NY: M.E. Sharpe, 1997).

Larry N. Gerston and Terry Christensen, *California Politics and Government: A Practical Approach,* 9th ed. (Belmont, CA: Thompson Wadsworth, 2007).

Malcolm L. Goggin, Ann O'M. Bowman, James P. Lester, and Lawrence J. O'Toole Jr., *Implementation Theory and Practice* (New York: HarperCollins, 1990).

Robert A. Goldwin, *From Parchment to Power: How James Madison Used the Bill of Rights to Save the Constitution* (Washington, DC: AEA Press, 1997).

Raymond Gordon, *Basic Interviewing Skills* (Itasca, IL: F.E. Peacock, 1992).

Rick Gordon et al., eds., *Problem Based Service Learning: A Fieldguide for Making a Difference in Higher Education* (Keene, NH: Antioch New England Graduate School, 2000).

Richard Hofstadter, *The American Political Tradition* (New York: Knopf, 1948).

William E. Hudson, *American Democracy in Peril,* 5th ed. (Washington, DC: CQ Press, 2006).

Katherine Isaac, *Practicing Democracy: A Guide to Student Action* (New York: St. Martin's, 1997).

Issues for Debate in American Public Policy, 2nd ed. (Washington, DC: Congressional Quarterly, 2000).

Barbara Jacoby and Associates, *Service-Learning in Higher Education: Concepts and Practices* (San Francisco: Jossey-Bass, 1996).

Charles O. Jones, *An Introduction to the Study of Public Policy,* 3rd ed. (Belmont, CA: Brooks/Cole, 1984).

Michael Kammen, ed., *The Origins of the American Constitution: A Documentary History* (New York: Penguin, 1986).

Jane C. Kendall, ed., *Combining Service and Learning: A Resource Book for Community and Public Service* (Raleigh, NC: National Society for Experiential Education, 1990).

John W. Kingdon, *Agendas, Alternatives, and Public Policies,* 2nd ed. (New York: Longman, 1995).

Everett Carll Ladd, *The Ladd Report* (New York: Free Press, 1999).

Celina C. Lake with Pat Callbeck Harper, *Public Opinion Polling: A Handbook for Public Interest and Citizen Advocacy* (Washington, DC: Island Press, 1987).

Leonard W. Levy and Kenneth L. Karst, eds., *Encyclopedia of the American Constitution,* 2nd ed., 6 vols. (New York: Macmillan Reference USA, 2000).

Michael Lipsky, *Street-Level Bureaucracy: Dilemmas of the Individual in Public Services* (New York: Russell Sage Foundation, 1997).

Paul Rogat Loeb, *Soul of a Citizen: Living with Conviction in a Cynical Time* (New York: St. Martin's, 1999).

Kenneth J. Meier and John Bohte, *Politics and the Bureaucracy: Policy Making in the Fourth Branch of Government,* 5th ed. (Belmont, CA: Thomson Wadsworth, 2007).

Steven L. Nock and Paul W. Kingston, *The Sociology of Public Issues* (Belmont, CA: Wadsworth, 1989).

J.W. Peltason, *Corwin and Peltason's Understanding the Constitution,* 8th ed. (New York: Holt, Rinehart, and Winston, 1979).

Robert D. Putnam, *Bowling Alone: The Collapse and Revival of American Community* (New York: Simon and Schuster, 2000).

Jack Rakove, *Original Meanings: Politics and Ideas in the Making of the Constitution* (New York: Vintage, 1996).

Nathan Rosenberg, *Exploring the Black Box: Technology, Economics and History* (Cambridge: Cambridge University Press, 1994).

Alan Rosenthal, *The Decline of Representative Democracy: Process, Participation, and Power in State Legislatures* (Washington, DC: CQ Press, 1998).

Peter H. Rossi and Leonard E. Freeman, *Evaluation: A Systematic Approach,* 5th ed. (Newbury Park, CA: Sage, 1993).

Paul A. Sabatier, ed., *Theories of the Political Process* (Boulder, CO: Westview, 1999).

Paul A. Sabatier and Hank C. Jenkins-Smith, eds., *Policy Change and Learning: An Advocacy Approach* (Boulder, CO: Westview, 1993).

E.E. Schattschneider, *The Semi-Sovereign People* (New York: Holt, Rinehart, and Winston, 1960).

Richard Scher, Jon L. Mills, and John J. Hotaling, *Voting Rights and Democracy* (Chicago: Nelson-Hall, 1997).

Arnold K. Sherman and Aliza Kolker, *The Social Bases of Politics* (Belmont, CA: Wadsworth, 1989).

Fengan Shi, *The Real Thing: Contemporary Documents in American Government* (New York: St. Martin's, 1997).

Theda Skocpol and Morris P. Fiorina, eds., *Civic Engagement in American Democracy* (Washington, DC: Brookings Institute, 1999).

Alexis de Tocqueville, *Democracy in America,* 2 vols. (New York: Vintage Books, 1945, 1956).

Joseph Tussman, *Obligation and the Body Politic* (New York: Oxford University Press, 1960).

Sidney Verba, Kay Lehman Schlozman, and Henry E. Brady, *Voice and Equality: Civic Voluntarism in American Politics* (Cambridge, MA: Harvard University Press, 1995).

Thomas J. Volgy, *Politics in the Trenches: Citizens, Politicians, and the Fate of Democracy* (Tucson: University of Arizona Press, 2001).

Oliver H. Woshinsky, *Culture and Politics: An Introduction to Mass and Elite Political Behavior* (Englewood Cliffs, NJ: Prentice-Hall, 1995).

APPENDIX D: RECOMMENDED WEB SITES AS RESEARCH SOURCE MATERIALS

Selected Concepts/Issues/ Organizations	Site
U.S. Government Organizations and Resources	
Consumer Product Safety Commission	www.cpsc.gov
C-Span	www.c-span.org
Federal Communications Commission	www.fcc.gov
Federal Election Commission	www.fec.gov
Federal Judicial Center	www.fjc.gov
Federal Judiciary Homepage	www.uscourts.gov
Library of Congress	http://lcweb.loc.gov/ homepage/lchp.html
Thomas Legislative Information	http://thomas.loc.gov
Univ. of Michigan Documents Center: Executive Agency Research	www.lib.umich.edu/govdocs
U.S. Census Bureau	www.census.gov
U.S. Congress	www.congresslink.org
U.S. Supreme Court on the Web	www.usscplus.com
White House	www.whitehouse.gov
States	
Alabama	www.alaweb.asc.edu
Alaska	www.state.ak.us
Arizona	www.state.az.us
Arkansas	www.state.ar.us
California	http://www.state.ca.us/s

Colorado	www.state.co.us
Connecticut	www.state.ct.us
Delaware	www.state.de.us
Florida	www.state.fl.us
Georgia	www.state.ga.us
Hawaii	www.hawaii.gov
Idaho	www.state.id.us
Illinois	www.state.il.us
Indiana	www.state.in.us
Iowa	www.state.ia.us
Kansas	www.accesskansas.org
Kentucky	www.state.ky.us
Louisiana	www.state.la.us
Maine	www.state.me.us
Maryland	www.maryland.gov
Massachusetts	www.magnet.state.ma.us
Michigan	www.migov.state.mi.us
Minnesota	www.state.mn.us
Mississippi	www.state.ms.us
Missouri	www.state.mo.us
Montana	www.mt.gov
Nebraska	www.state.ne.us
Nevada	www.state.nv.us
New Hampshire	www.state.nh.us
New Jersey	www.state.nj.us
New Mexico	www.state.nm.us
New York	www.state.ny.us
North Carolina	www.sips.state.nc.us
North Dakota	www.state.nd.us
Ohio	www.ohio.gov
Oklahoma	www.oklaosf.state.ok.us
Oregon	www.state.or.us
Pennsylvania	www.state.pa.us
Rhode Island	www.athena.state.ri.us/info
South Carolina	www.state.sc.us
South Dakota	www.state.sd.us
Tennessee	www.state.tn.us
Texas	www.texas.gov

Utah	www.state.ut.us
Vermont	www.cit.state.vt.us
Virginia	www.state.va.us
Washington	www.wa.gov
West Virginia	www.state.wv.us
Wisconsin	www.state.wi.us
Wyoming	www.state.wy.us

State and Local Government Organizations

National Association of Counties	www.naco.org
National Association of State Information Resource Executives	www.nasire.org
National Center for State Courts	www.ncsconline.org
National Conference of State Legislatures	www.ncsl.org
National Governors Association	www.nga.org
National League of Cities	www.nlc.org
U.S. Census Bureau: State and County Quick Facts	http://quickfacts.census.gov/qfd/index.html
U.S. Conference of Mayors	www.usmayors.org

Federalism

Center for the Study of Federalism	www.temple.edu/federalism
Council of State Governments	www.csg.org
National Conference of State Legislatures	www.ncsl.org
National Governors Association	www.nga.org
States News	www.statesnews.org
Meyner Center for the Study of State and Local Government	www.lafayette.edu/publius

Civic Education

Ackerman Center for Democratic Citizenship	www.edci.purdue.edu/ackerman
American Political Science Association (service learning)	www.apsanet.org/teach/service
Center for Civic Education	www.civiced.org

Civic Education Project, Yale University	www.cep.org.hu
Civnet	http://civnet.org
Close Up Foundation	http://closeup.org
Constitutional Rights Foundation	www.crf-usa.org
Content of Our Character Project	www.contentofourcharacter.org
Freedoms Foundation at Valley Forge	www.ffvf.org
Indiana Program for Law-Related Education	www.indiana.edu/~ssdc/iplre.html
James Madison Memorial Fellowship Foundation	www.jamesmadison.com
Kellogg Foundation	www.wkkf.org
National Commission on Civic Renewal	www.puaf.umd.edu/Affiliates

Civic Renewal

National Constitution Center	www.constitutioncenter.org
National Institute for Citizen Education in the Law (NICEL)	www.indiana.edu/~ssdc/nicel.html
Street Law, Inc.	www.streetlaw.org
Washington Center for Internships and Academic Seminars	www.twc.edu
Washington Semester	www.washingtonsemester.com

Service Learning

American Association for Higher Education Service-Learning Project	www.aahe.org/service/srv-lrn.htm
American Association of Community Colleges, Service Learning Initiatives	www.aacc.nche.edu/initiatives/horizons
American Council on Education	www.cns.gov
Break Away	www.alternativebreaks.com
Campus Compact	www.compact.org
Campus Outreach Opportunity League	www.cool2serve.org
Center for Democracy and Citizenship: Public Achievement	www.publicachievement.org
Communitarian Network	www.gwu.edu/~ccps
Corporation for National Service	www.cns.gov

DEEP (Democracy Ethics and Educational Principles)	www.democracy.org
Learn & Serve America	www.nationalservice.org/learn/index.html
National Service-Learning Clearinghouse	www.nicsl.coled.umn.edu
National Society for Experiential Education	www.nsee.org
National Youth Leadership Council	www.nylc.org
New England Resource Center for Higher Education (NERCHE)	www.nerche.org
Points of Light Foundation	www.pointsoflight.org
Robin's Guide To College and University Service-Learning Programs	http://csf.colorado.edu/sl/academic.html
Rural Clearinghouse for Lifelong Education and Development (Service Learning in Rural Settings)	www.personal.ksu.edu/~rcled
Service-Learning: The Home of Service-Learning on the WWW	http://csf.colorado.edu/sl
UCLA Service-Learning Clearinghouse Project	www.gseis.ucla.edu/slc

Abortion

National Abortion and Reproductive Rights Action League	www.naral.org
National Organization for Women	www.now.org
National Right to Life	www.nrlc.org
Religious Freedom Coalition	www.rfc.net.org

Environmental Issues

Center for Health, Environment and Justice	www.essential.org/cchw
Earthjustice Legal Defense Fund	www.earthjustice.org
Environmental Council of the States	www.sso.org/ecos
Environmental Protection Agency Watershed Protection	www.epa.gov/OWOW/watershed
Friends of the Earth	www.foe.org
National Wildlife Federation	www.nwf.org/nwf

Poverty, Homelessness, and Welfare Reform

American Bar Association: Commission on Homeless and Poverty	www.abanet.org/homeless/home.html
Department of Health and Human Services: Homelessness	http://aspe.os.dhhs.gov/progsys/homeless
Department of Housing and Urban Development: Homelessness	www.hud.gov/hmless.html
Habitat for Humanity International	www.habitat.org
National Alliance to End Homelessness	www.endhomelessnessnow.org
National Law Center on Homelessness and Poverty	www.nlchp.org
National Resource Center for Homelessness and Mental Illness	
U.S. Department of HHS: Welfare Reform	www.acf.dhhs.gov/news/welfare
Welfare Information Network	www.welfareinfo.org

Geriatrics

The Gerontological Society of America	www.geron.org
National Council on the Aging	www.ncoa.org

Health Care

American Public Human Services Association	www.aphsa.org
Association for Benchmarking Health Care	www.abhc.org
Health Insurance Association of America	www.hiaa.org

Crime, Violence, and Law Enforcement

APBNews.com	www.apbonline.com
International Association of Chiefs of Police	www.theiacp.org
The Justice Research Association	http://cjcentral.com/jra

The National Crime Victim Bar Association	www.ncvc.org
Security on Campus, Inc.	www.campussafety.org
U.S. Department of Justice	. www.usdoj.gov

Urban Planning and Community Development

American Planning Association	www.planning.org
National Association of Towns and Townspeople	www.natat.org
National Civic League	www.ncl.org
National League of Cities	www.nlc.org
National Urban League	www.nul.org
Stone Soup Fresno	www.stonesoup-fresno.org
University of Pennsylvania: Center for Community Partnerships	www.upenn.edu/ccp
U.S. Conference of Mayors	www.usmayors.org

Firearms Regulation

Bureau of Alcohol, Tobacco, and Firearms	www.atf.treas.gov
Citizens Committee for the Right to Keep and Bear Arms	www.ccrkba.org
Handgun Control Inc.	www.handguncontrol.org
National Rifle Association	www.nra.org
Violence Policy Center	www.vpc.org

Education and School Choice

American Federation of Teachers	www.aft.org//index.html
Center for Education Reform	www.edreform.com
Charter School Project	www.charterproject.org
Christian Coalition	www.cc.org
Education Commission of the States	www.ecs.org
Institute for Justice	www.instituteforjustice.org
National Education Association	www.nea.org
Thomas B. Fordham Foundation	www.edexcellence.net

Civil Rights and Civil Liberties

American Civil Liberties Union	www.aclu.org

Amnesty International — www.amnesty.org
Citizens Commission on Civil Rights — www.cccr.org
Lamda Legal Defense Fund — www.lamda.org
National Assn. for the Advancement of Colored People — www.naacp.org
National Coalition Against Censorship — www.ncac.org

Public Interest Organizations

Association of Community Organizations for Reform Now — www.acorn.org/community
Common Cause — www.commoncause.org
Heritage Foundation — www.heritage.org
Roll Call Online — www.rollcall.com

Public Policy Monitoring and Advocacy

ACCRA: Research for Community and Economic Development — www.accra.org
Action Without Borders: Directory of Nonprofit Organizations — www.idealist.org
American Political Science Association: Policy Section — www.fsu.edu/~spap/orgs/apsa.html
Association for Public Policy Analysis and Management — http://qsilver.queensu.ca/~appamwww
Brookings Institution — brookings.edu
Center for Policy Alternatives — www.cfpa.org
Electronic Policy Network — http://epn.org
Hubert H. Humphrey Institute Network — www.hhh.umn.edu/pubpol
National Center for Policy Analysis — www.ncpa.org
National Council of Nonprofit Organizations — www.ncna.org
National Political Index — www.politicalindex.com
National Taxpayers Union — www.ntu.org
SpeakOut.com — www.speakout.com

Religion

Americans United for Separation of Church and State — www.au.org
Eagle Forum — www.eagleforum.org
Focus on the Family — www.family.org

Journalistic Sources

Cable News Network	www.cnn.com
Los Angeles Times	www.latimes.com
Media Research Center	www.mrc.org
National Journal	www.cloakroom.com
New York Times	www.nytimes.com
New York Times Learning Network, grades 6–12	www.nytimes.com/learning
Pew Center for Civic Journalism	www.pewcenter.org

INDEX

ABOUT THE AUTHOR

A professor of political science at San Jose State University for more than three decades, Larry Gerston has written nine books on politics and the public policy process at the national and state levels. In addition to his academic responsibilities, Gerston is the political analyst at NBC11 (serving the San Francisco Bay area). He also writes "Up Front," a monthly column in *San Jose Magazine*. More than one hundred of his op-ed columns have appeared in the *San Jose Mercury News*, the *San Francisco Chronicle*, the *Christian Science Monitor*, the *Los Angeles Times*, and other leading newspapers. A nationally known speaker, Gerston gives several talks each year for the "Project Citizen" program sponsored by the Center for Civic Education.